Reading and Writing Instruction *for*

FOURTH- & FIFTH-GRADE

Classrooms *in a* PLC at Work®

Kathy Tuchman Glass

EDITED BY
Mark Onuscheck
Jeanne Spiller

Solution Tree | Press

a division of
Solution Tree

555 North Morton Street
Bloomington, IN 47404
800.733.6786 (toll free) / 812.336.7700
FAX: 812.336.7790

email: info@SolutionTree.com
SolutionTree.com

Visit **go.SolutionTree.com/literacy** to download the free reproducibles in this book.

Printed in the United States of America

Library of Congress Cataloging-in-Publication Data

Names: Glass, Kathy Tuchman, author.
Title: Reading and writing instruction for fourth- and fifth-grade
    classrooms in a PLC at work / Kathy Tuchman Glass.
Description: Bloomington, IN : Solution Tree Press, 2020. | Series: Every
    teacher is a literacy teacher | Includes bibliographical references and
    index.
Identifiers: LCCN 2020003874 (print) | LCCN 2020003875 (ebook) | ISBN
    9781947604933 (paperback) | ISBN 9781947604940 (ebook)
Subjects: LCSH: Language arts (Elementary) | Reading (Elementary) |
    Composition (Language arts)--Study and teaching (Elementary) |
    Professional learning communities.
Classification: LCC LB1576 .G47493 2020 (print) | LCC LB1576 (ebook) |
    DDC 372.6--dc23
LC record available at https://lccn.loc.gov/2020003874
LC ebook record available at https://lccn.loc.gov/2020003875

Solution Tree
Jeffrey C. Jones, CEO
Edmund M. Ackerman, President

Solution Tree Press
President and Publisher: Douglas M. Rife
Associate Publisher: Sarah Payne-Mills
Art Director: Rian Anderson
Managing Production Editor: Kendra Slayton
Senior Production Editor: Todd Brakke
Content Development Specialist: Amy Rubenstein
Copy Editor: Jessi Finn
Text and Cover Designer: Abigail Bowen
Editorial Assistants: Sarah Ludwig and Elijah Oates

ACKNOWLEDGMENTS

It has been a privilege to write alongside a talented team of educators on the *Every Teacher Is a Literacy Teacher* series. Thank you to Jeanne Spiller for leading the charge and ensuring consistency, direction, and insight. Her impressive talents and contributions within a professional learning community have exponential implications for innumerable students. I also extend a special note of gratitude to Douglas Rife and Claudia Wheatley at Solution Tree for introducing me to Jeanne so that I could work with this dynamic writing team.

Additionally, many thanks to the hardworking staff at Solution Tree Press, including Rian Anderson and his stellar design team. Without them, this book's layout would resemble a litany of mere words on a page void of visual appeal. I'm grateful to Sarah Payne-Mills and her team of experienced editors who ensure truly comprehensible and organized prose for readers to take away what is intended. In particular, I extend a hearty thank-you to Todd Brakke for his exceptional skills and guidance.

For his unending support and role as chief champion of all that I do and find so gratifying, I wholeheartedly thank my husband, Mike.

Solution Tree would like to thank the following reviewers:

Lindi Clancy
Curriculum Instructor
Barrett Elementary School
Birmingham, Alabama

Teri Gough
Fifth-Grade Teacher
Sundance Elementary School
Los Lunas, New Mexico

Dusti Larsen
Fourth-Grade Teacher
Gravette Upper Elementary
Gravette, Arkansas

Sarah Rogers
Fourth-Grade Teacher
Lincoln Elementary School
Merrillan, Wisconsin

Visit **go.SolutionTree.com/literacy** to download the free reproducibles in this book.

TABLE OF CONTENTS

Reproducible pages are in italics.

ABOUT THE SERIES EDITORS

Mark Onuscheck is director of curriculum, instruction, and assessment at Adlai E. Stevenson High School in Lincolnshire, Illinois. He is a former English teacher and director of communication arts. As director of curriculum, instruction, and assessment, Mark works with academic divisions around professional learning, articulation, curricular and instructional revision, evaluation, assessment, social-emotional learning, technologies, and Common Core implementation. He is also an adjunct professor at DePaul University.

Mark was awarded the Quality Matters Star Rating for his work in online teaching. He helps to build curriculum and instructional practices for TimeLine Theatre's arts integration program for Chicago Public Schools. Additionally, he is a National Endowment for the Humanities grant recipient and a member of the Association for Supervision and Curriculum Development, the National Council of Teachers of English, the International Literacy Association, and Learning Forward.

Mark earned a bachelor's degree in English and classical studies from Allegheny College and a master's degree in teaching English from the University of Pittsburgh.

Jeanne Spiller is assistant superintendent for teaching and learning for Kildeer Countryside Community Consolidated School District 96 in Buffalo Grove, Illinois. School District 96 is recognized on AllThingsPLC (www.AllThingsPLC.info) as one of only a small number of school districts where all schools in the district earn the distinction of model professional learning community (PLC). Jeanne's work focuses on standards-aligned instruction and assessment practices. She supports schools and districts across the United States to gain clarity about and implement the four critical questions of PLCs. She is passionate about collaborating with schools to develop systems for teaching and learning that keep the focus on student results and helping teachers determine how to approach instruction so that all students learn at high levels.

Jeanne received a 2014 Illinois Those Who Excel Award for significant contributions to the state's public and nonpublic elementary schools in administration. She is a graduate of the 2008 Learning Forward Academy, where she learned how to plan and implement professional learning that improves educator practice and increases student achievement. She has served as a classroom teacher, team leader, middle school administrator, and director of professional learning.

Jeanne earned a master's degree in educational teaching and leadership from Saint Xavier University, a master's degree in educational administration from Loyola University Chicago, and an educational administrative superintendent endorsement from Northern Illinois University.

To learn more about Jeanne's work, follow @jeeneemarie on Twitter.

To book Mark Onuscheck or Jeanne Spiller for professional development, contact pd@SolutionTree.com.

ABOUT THE AUTHOR

Kathy Tuchman Glass strives to empower teachers to maximize student potential. She is a consultant, trainer, and former classroom teacher with more than twenty-five years of experience in education. Additionally, she is an accomplished author of many books, including *The New Art and Science of Teaching Writing*, coauthored with Robert J. Marzano, and the *(Re)designing Writing Units* series.

Recognized for her expertise in myriad areas concerning curriculum and instruction, Kathy provides dynamic and interactive professional learning to K–12 educators. Her topics include differentiated instruction, standards work around English language arts, literacy, instructional strategies, assessments, and backward planning for unit and lesson design. She is a member of the International Literacy Association, the National Council of Teachers of English, the Association for Supervision and Curriculum Development, and Learning Forward.

Kathy has a bachelor's degree from Indiana University Bloomington and a master's degree in education from San Francisco State University.

To learn more about Kathy's work, visit Glass Educational Consulting (https://kathyglassconsulting.com).

To book Kathy Tuchman Glass for professional development, contact pd@SolutionTree.com.

Every Teacher Is a Literacy Teacher

The words *literacy* and *learning* possess an inseparable connection. In infancy, we learn to produce our first sounds; as toddlers, we sprawl paint across a page to communicate an idea; in elementary school, we learn the power of comprehension to unveil the essence of an author's words; in middle and high school, we learn to evaluate sources with a keen eye and construct arguments to defend our claims; and as adults, we strive to better our abilities to read widely, write clearly, and communicate articulately. In truth, the multiple facets of literacy surround all of us every day of our lives. Therefore, a literacy level that guarantees students will fully function and engage in society must be the reality for *every* student because, undeniably, illiteracy is not an option for any student. As educators, we recognize this reality and cannot afford to allow students to leave our care without guaranteeing they can read, write, and communicate as they move across grade levels.

The expectations for students in fourth and fifth grade increase in intensity from their earlier years in school. For example, in addition to using details from a text to identify what it states explicitly—a requirement in grade 3—students in upper-elementary grades must also use textual evidence to draw inferences and incorporate quotes to develop their writing. Fourth- and fifth-grade standards also dictate that students must be able not just to assert their opinions with reasons, as they did in third grade, but also support their reasoning with facts and details drawn from sources.

Students at these grade levels also encounter reading challenges that make learning new knowledge difficult. For one, texts they read contain new content with previously unfamiliar topics and concepts. Because the material is novel to them, they lack the prior knowledge to make inferences and connections to grasp this information.

Second, plodding through the content presents some obstacles, such as more complicated sentence constructions and unfamiliar multisyllabic words that students did not experience in lower elementary grades. Furthermore, expectations for tasks increase in difficulty from their early elementary years, when students were asked to retell or describe the main idea of a text or to make connections with the advantage of more robust and explicit prompting. In fourth and fifth grade, students graduate to more sophisticated tasks like independently describing characters and explaining how their actions fuel the plot. Given sound instruction, many students can grapple well with these increased demands; others—especially those who struggled with mastering reading before entering fourth grade—are candidates for additional literacy intervention to make the leap and progress in their learning.

Teachers in grades 4 and 5 must acknowledge and address this pivotal shift in expectations through their instruction. The reality is that many students are ill equipped to meet the demands required of them in these grades. According to the National Assessment of Educational Progress (NAEP, 2019), 35 percent of fourth-grade students in the United States' public and nonpublic schools scored at or above the proficient level for reading in 2019. The organization has not published new results for writing for fourth grade, but in 2002, the number was 28 percent (NAEP, 2002), and in a 2011 report on eighth-grade students, it was just 27 percent, indicating the situation has not improved (NAEP, 2011). Students are in dire need of assistance in these critical areas of literacy; without it, they will continue to struggle with complex text and writing tasks, which will impact their potential for long-term success in and out of school.

Given these factors, it's logical to ask, "What does high-quality instruction look like in grades 4 and 5?" Just as important, how can a professional learning community (PLC) help support this kind of instruction to ensure its mission that all students learn? In the rest of this introduction, we explore both these topics as well as the purpose of the *Every Teacher Is a Literacy Teacher* series, the structure of this book, and how this book can support grades 4–5 teacher teams in ensuring students' success as they prepare for the leap into secondary education.

What High-Quality Instruction Looks Like in Grades 4–5

As we've established, in fourth and fifth grade, the complexity of materials and the amount and types of texts students read increase, and the writing tasks become more involved. Students also must be adept at content-area literacy skills so that they can comprehend subject-matter texts, such as those used in science and social studies. In this regard, teachers begin to introduce disciplinary literacy into their teaching repertoire. *Disciplinary literacy* is "an approach [that] emphasizes the specialized knowledge and abilities possessed by those who create, communicate, and use knowledge within each of the disciplines" (Shanahan & Shanahan, 2012, p. 7).

Although research shows the woeful prevalence of illiteracy (Hernandez, 2011), teachers can make an extraordinary impact and make literacy accessible for all students by setting high expectations aligned to standards and making instructional moves that assist students to rise to the rigor of grades 4 and 5. Whether teachers inherit students who lag behind their peers in literacy, all students from fourth grade onward benefit from teachers applying effective instructional reading practices that bolster students' skills and strategies as they work to decipher increasingly complex text across subjects and grades (Goldman, Snow, & Vaughn, 2016).

When providing high-quality literacy instruction, educators should teach reading and writing together and do so with an interdisciplinary mindset. There is an interconnectedness between the two that supports literacy development in students, and it is present not just in English language arts (ELA) but in every academic content area, from how students read and understand a story problem in mathematics to how they write notes about a science lab experiment. In their report *Writing to Read*, Steve Graham and Michael Hebert (2010) affirm the findings of multiple research-backed resources on the interrelated benefits of reading and writing. They maintain that writing has the potential to improve students' reading in three ways.

1. **Reading and writing are both functional activities:** Students combine these skills to accomplish specific goals, such as learning new ideas from a text and describing that learning (Fitzgerald & Shanahan, 2000). For instance, writing about information in a science text should facilitate comprehension and learning, as it provides the reader with a means for recording, connecting, analyzing, personalizing, and manipulating key ideas from the text.

2. **Reading and writing are connected:** Because they draw on common knowledge and cognitive processes (Shanahan, 2006), when students improve their writing skills, they simultaneously improve their reading skills.

3. **Reading and writing are both communication activities:** When writers create text, they gain insights about what they read. This deepens their comprehension (Tierney & Shanahan, 1991).

Although reading and writing are interconnected, the other two strands of literacy—speaking and listening—are important as well. As students engage in discussion, presentation, and performance during literacy instruction, they develop higher levels of understanding. Also intertwined with students' acquisition of literacy skills is their connection to technology. Teachers are wise to recognize the pervasive nature of the technology that they and their students have—quite literally—at their fingertips. As members of a thriving digital world, educators must provide high-quality literacy instruction to support students in utilizing technology. In "Why Personalized Learning Requires Technology and Thinking Humans," founder and CEO of ThinkCERCA Eileen Murphy Buckley (n.d.) writes:

> Let's face it, even the most basic Google search requires productive struggle and persistence. Eventually we will send our students out into the wild, where newspapers of record, college courses, bosses and colleagues, and increasingly, health care providers, bankers, and others will not provide them with accessible texts.

Further, not only do students need to learn how to appropriately find, comprehend, and evaluate digital resources; they must also understand the power and learning that come from their interaction with the information. How are students interpreting information, critically thinking about information, sharing opinions, creating reasons, finding evidence, and deepening their level of understanding? It is the obligation of every teacher to ensure that students function at high literacy levels and learn to appropriately navigate complex digital and printed texts to prepare them for their pursuits in secondary school and beyond.

The Value of the PLC Process in Literacy

As teachers, we must possess a repertoire of instructional strategies to build on the strengths and address the needs of a richly diverse classroom of students who have a range of reading, writing, speaking, and listening capabilities. The reality is that teachers rarely have all the skills, knowledge, and time necessary to meet the wide-ranging demands of literacy on their own. This complex and important process of teaching students literacy becomes more manageable and tangible as educators engage in the process together. Therefore, it truly makes a positive difference for all learners if collaborative teams effectively contribute to teachers making meaningful changes in classroom practices. When we integrate high-quality literacy instruction within the collective efforts representative of a PLC, literacy learning soars to new levels.

Those familiar with PLC culture know that the foundation of a PLC's work is built on three distinct big ideas: (1) a focus on student learning, (2) a collaborative culture and collective responsibility, and (3) a results orientation (DuFour, DuFour, Eaker, Many, & Mattos, 2016). Four critical questions guide educators as they collaborate to provide quality instruction for all learners (DuFour et al., 2016).

1. What is it we want our students to learn?

2. How will we know if each student has learned it?

3. How will we respond when some students don't learn it?

4. How can we extend and enrich the learning for students who have demonstrated proficiency?

The About This Book section (page 7) explains how the chapters and team action steps in this book align with these critical questions.

Within a PLC, teachers are organized into collaborative teams that "work interdependently to achieve common goals for which members are mutually accountable" (DuFour et al., 2016, p. 12). Together, they come to a clear understanding of the essential literacy skills that all students should know and be able to do, and they design assessments that align with the learning outcomes. They collaborate around sound instructional practices, sharing strategies that proved successful, and work as a team to develop differentiated lessons along the way. Further, they openly discuss and analyze student data as a way to make informed instructional decisions to move students' learning forward.

This book provides resources and tools to accomplish these critical tasks so teams can operate effectively and maximize their collective strengths in the service of students. Through these collective efforts, teachers establish a guaranteed and viable curriculum that ensures equal opportunities to learn. Thus, students are guaranteed access to the same content, knowledge, and skills, regardless of their teacher (Marzano, 2003). Put plainly, teachers within a PLC work *together* to ensure that every student, in every classroom, receives what he or she needs to master essential skills and pave the way for a promising future.

With collaboration as one of the three big ideas of a PLC, a concerted effort is no doubt essential. But what happens when you are the sole literacy teacher at your grade level? We often refer to these teachers as *singletons*—the one fourth- or fifth-grade teacher in an elementary school, for example. In these situations, it is important to collaborate with other professionals who can help support and guide you through the work of the PLC process. In many cases, a teacher from the preceding or following grade level can become a great working partner, as he or she has a wealth of knowledge about the skills students have acquired or will need to acquire for the next school year. Grade-level partners who teach other content areas can also be helpful as you work collaboratively to provide a guaranteed and viable curriculum for every student in every classroom across the school. Finally, take advantage of an online, interconnected world and reach out to grade-level teachers in other districts. Use technology to collaborate as you do the work of ensuring a consistent and viable literacy-focused curriculum.

As noted earlier in this section, when teachers collaborate to teach students literacy skills, the learning process becomes more manageable and tangible.

About This Series

This book is part of the *Every Teacher Is a Literacy Teacher* series, which provides guidance on literacy-focused instruction and classroom strategies for grades preK–12. The elementary segment of this series includes separate titles focused on instruction in grades preK–1, grades 2–3, and grades 4–5. While each of these books follows a similar approach and structure, the content and examples these books include address the discrete demands of each grade-level band. All the chapters are dedicated to the steps collaborative teams must take before engaging in instruction to ensure clarity about standards, assessment, learning progressions, mastery expectations, interventions, gradual release of responsibility, use of instructional time, instructional strategies, and diversity and equity. Each chapter also includes specific collaborative team exercises, paving the way for teams to engage in the work that the chapter describes.

The various secondary school books in this series each feature classroom literacy strategies for a subject area in grades 6–12, such as science or ELA. The expert educators writing these secondary-level books approach literacy in varying and innovative ways and examine the role every teacher must play in supporting students' literacy development in all subject areas throughout their grades 6–12 schooling.

Woven throughout each book is the idea that collaboration plays a crucial role in the success of any school dedicated to building effective teams in a PLC culture. When experts collaborate, innovative ideas emerge in ways that support student learning and generate positive results. Further, schools that invest in a PLC culture work in more unified and cohesive ways, prioritizing concerns and working together to innovate positive changes. In this series, we are excited to share ways a PLC can function to radiate change when thoughtful educators dedicate themselves to supporting the literacy development of all students.

About This Book

We constructed this book to assist schools, and, more specifically, collaborative teams within a school, to design standards-aligned instruction, assessment, and intervention that support the literacy development of all students. We've focused it through the lens of PLC culture, with each of the first five chapters centered on how collaborative teams may begin to answer one or more of the four critical questions that drive the first big idea—a focus on learning (DuFour et al., 2016).

Chapter 1 addresses what collaborative teams want students to learn by introducing the pre-unit protocol (PREP). This protocol assists teams in gaining clarity about student learning expectations before beginning a unit of instruction.

Chapters 2–4 address how teams can know what learning has taken place. Chapter 2 reviews the myriad assessment types, including how teams ensure a literacy focus. It features an example unit assessment continuum and ways teachers may use each type of assessment within a unit of instruction. Chapter 3 offers a process for creating an instructional learning progression for each learning standard a team identified using PREP. The learning progression assists teams in the development of learning target–aligned assessments and high-quality instruction. Chapter 4 considers student proficiency, the various rubric types, rubric development, student checklists, and collaborative scoring.

Chapter 5 addresses how teams use data and determine next steps to support students who haven't achieved mastery or to extend learning for those who have. The chapter focuses on the data-inquiry process, scaffolded instruction, and extension opportunities.

In chapters 6–9, we address instructional processes connected to literacy. Topics include using the gradual release of responsibility model (chapter 6), planning high-quality literacy instruction within the literacy block (chapter 7), selecting appropriate instructional strategies to facilitate high-quality literacy instruction (chapter 8), and considering diversity and equity in literacy instruction (chapter 9).

We also include an array of useful resources in this book's appendices. Appendix A consists of a variety of reproducible versions of tools from the book, including the PREP template. Appendix B expands on chapter 1's content related to priority standards by providing an effective process that teams can use to determine them. Appendix C offers extended details on Norman Webb's (1997, 1999) Depth of Knowledge (DOK) levels, which we introduce in chapter 1. Appendix D includes extra information about developing essential understandings and guiding questions when filling out the PREP template. Appendix E provides a list of the figures featured throughout the book. Finally, we have assembled a bonus online appendix at **go.SolutionTree.com/literacy** that collects the different team exercises we include throughout the book.

The place to begin is gaining clarity as a team about what your students should know and be able to do. This is why, in chapter 1, we provide teacher teams with tools to arrive at a collective understanding of the literacy standards and the specific learning outcomes necessary for proficiency in grades 4 and 5. We provide a process to help your team examine and unwrap (also called *unpack*) the standards, and we share strategies for focusing conversations as you dig into the often complicated and ambiguous wording of your literacy standards. The critical work you do in chapter 1 will set the foundation for establishing a rich and robust plan for quality literacy instruction and assessment.

CHAPTER 1

Establish Clarity About Student Learning Expectations

The PLC process asserts that each student is entitled to a guaranteed and viable curriculum (DuFour et al., 2016; Marzano, 2003). *Guaranteed* expressly stipulates that schools grant all students the opportunity to learn a core curriculum to position them for success. To deliver this guaranteed curriculum, schools must ensure the curriculum is *viable*, meaning that schools ensure the necessary time is available as well as protected. With a deficit in students who excel in literacy, and by virtue of literacy contributing to lifelong success, there is a strong case for safeguarding essential literacy skills as guaranteed and viable.

The first question that drives the work of a PLC aligns with this promise by asking, *What is it we want our students to learn?* (DuFour et al., 2016). Put another way, *What do we want students to know and be able to do?* With regard to teaching literacy, this pivotal question means, for example, that before introducing a complex text, launching into a writing activity, or conducting an assessment, teacher teams must interpret language arts standards in the same way and use them to guide a robust and rigorous instruction and assessment plan. If teachers do not work together to analyze literacy standards and reach consensus on what each one means across the strands, they will not afford students access to the same content, knowledge, and skills. In essence, any lack of clarity we have as educators interferes with students' access to a guaranteed and viable curriculum.

Answering this first critical question requires careful consideration of the following components that work together to guide any effective instruction and assessment plan; in this text, we apply them to support students' literacy advancement.

- ▸ Standards

- ▸ Knowledge

- ▸ Skills

- ▸ Depth of knowledge

- ▸ Learning targets

To address these key components, teams of teachers must collaborate to become completely clear about the specific knowledge and skills that all students must know and be able to do by the end of a particular unit. To support this endeavor, we propose teams follow a pre-unit protocol (PREP) that they begin at least a week or more prior to instruction for a unit.

In this chapter, we detail Kathy's work to apply the PREP process with a fourth-grade team in Kildeer Countryside Community Consolidated School District 96, a K–8 district in Buffalo Grove, Illinois. We first provide an overview of the six steps in the PREP process and then continue with a deep explanation of each step.

Pre-Unit Protocol Steps

By following the six PREP steps, teams can focus on the most important standards present in a unit of instruction, particularly those tied to literacy, and unwrap them such that each team member has a collective sense of the critical knowledge and skills that make up a standard.

1. Enter unit standards onto the PREP template.

2. Indicate (or determine) priority standards.

3. Unwrap unit priority standards.

4. Identify knowledge items.

5. Determine skills.

6. Assign levels of rigor for learning targets.

When applying this process, teams can use the explanations and examples articulated in this chapter as tools to learn the significance of each component. Teams inclined to extend this process beyond the six steps can also build essential understandings and guiding questions. *Essential understandings* crystallize and articulate conceptual thinking for teachers to guide curriculum design more deeply, and *guiding questions* set the purpose for students' learning. For thorough definitions and rationales of these latter two components and information on where they reside within curriculum design, read appendix D (page 253).

Because mandated district, state, provincial, and national content-area standards can be complex and often lead to various interpretations among educators, adhering to this process protects student learning by establishing distinct expectations for learners across all grade-level classrooms. Participating in this protocol also sets the groundwork for subsequent collaborative efforts—building common assessments, critiquing the efficacy of existing units, and designing new lessons that guide students toward mastery of each learning standard.

Figure 1.1 (page 13) features a completed PREP template for a two-week dialogue unit to reflect the outcome of this process. Although this sample template shows fourth-grade ELA content standards, with some adjustments, it can apply to a fifth-grade unit, as well. We have used the Common Core State Standards for English language arts in this sample; however, when teams complete the process, they can access national, state, provincial, or school standards that they are obligated to implement. (For a blank reproducible version of this figure for your team to use, see page 234.)

To clarify our use of this dialogue unit example, teachers conduct other units related to narrative so that fourth- or fifth-grade students examine the elements of literature (such as plot, character, setting, point of view, and theme) as well as narrative techniques (for example, foreshadowing, characterization, dialect, or suspense). Within these units, students read appropriately challenging fiction and nonfiction narrative complex texts at the center of instruction. They respond to teacher- and student-generated text-dependent questions and participate in myriad activities and assessments around these selected works. Teachers also guide students through the writing process as they prewrite, draft, revise, and edit to produce (publish) a polished story, which represents the culminating assessment. Dialogue, which is the focus for this PREP process sample, is a technique that meaningfully serves various purposes within a narrative. For example, it can help to develop the plot; reveal characters' thoughts, beliefs, and actions; and serve as an opportunity for making inferences.

In *The New Art and Science of Teaching*, Robert Marzano (2017) emphasizes that teachers need to chunk content when teaching new information. Breaking hefty content into digestible pieces helps students learn since they "can hold only small amounts of information in their working memories" (p. 30). Aside from the effectiveness of this approach for all learners, students in grades 4–5 might especially need each facet of a unit broken down since the increased demands from primary

Unit 2: The Power of Dialogue Within a Narrative | **Time Frame:** Approximately two weeks in October | **Grade: 4**

Unit Standards (Priority standards are in bold and italic typeface.)

Strand: Reading for Literature

- *Refer to details and examples in a text when explaining what the text says explicitly and when drawing inferences from the text. (RL.4.1)*

- Describe in depth a character, setting, or event in a story or drama, drawing on specific details in the text (e.g., a character's thoughts, words, or actions). (RL.4.3)

- Compare and contrast the point of view from which different stories are narrated, including the difference between first- and third-person narrations. (RL.4.6)

Strand: Writing

- Write narratives to develop real or imagined experiences or events using effective technique, descriptive details, and clear event sequences. (W.4.3)

  - Orient the reader by establishing a situation and introducing a narrator and/or characters; organize an event sequence that unfolds naturally. (W.4.3a)

  - *Use dialogue and description to develop experiences and events or show the responses of characters to situations. (W.4.3b)*

  - Use a variety of transitional words and phrases to manage the sequence of events. (W.4.3c)

  - Use concrete words and phrases and sensory details to convey experiences and events precisely. (W.4.3d)

  - Provide a conclusion that follows from the narrated experiences or events. (W.4.3e)

- Produce clear and coherent writing in which the development and organization are appropriate to task, purpose, and audience. (W.4.4)

- With guidance and support from peers and adults, develop and strengthen writing as needed by planning, revising, and editing. (W.4.5)

- With some guidance and support from adults, use technology, including the Internet, to produce and publish writing as well as to interact and collaborate with others; demonstrate sufficient command of keyboarding skills to type a minimum of one page in a single sitting. (W.4.6)

Strand: Language

- *Use correct capitalization. (L.4.2a)*

- *Use commas and quotation marks to mark direct speech and quotations from a text. (L.4.2b)*

- *Choose words and phrases to convey ideas precisely. (L.4.3a)*

- Use context (e.g., definitions, examples, or restatements in text) as a clue to the meaning of a word or phrase. (L.4.4a)
- Explain the meaning of simple similes and metaphors (e.g., as pretty as a picture) in context. (L.5.5a)

Unwrapped Unit Priority Standards	Knowledge Items	Skills (Learning Targets and DOK Levels)
RL.4.1 (A): Refer to details and examples in a text when explaining what the text says explicitly.	Literal and explicit details from a text are directly stated. Terms: *Literal, explicit*	Identify details and examples in a text to explain what it says explicitly. (DOK 1)
RL.4.1 (B): Refer to details and examples in a text when drawing inferences from the text.	Inferences—implied information that is not directly or explicitly stated Terms: *Imply, infer, inference*	Make inferences using details and examples in a text. (DOK 2)
W.4.3b (A): Use dialogue to develop experiences and events or show the responses of characters to situations.	Purpose and function of dialogue Dialogue is meaningful and serves a function—to develop the plot or to show characters' responses to situations.	Write dialogue to develop a plot or to show characters' responses to situations. (DOK 2)
W.4.3b (B): Use description to develop experiences and events or show the responses of characters to situations.	Descriptive details—precise nouns, vivid verbs, and colorful adjectives	Write descriptive detail to develop a plot or show characters' responses to situations. (DOK 2)
L.4.2a: Use correct capitalization. **L.4.2b:** Use commas and quotation marks to mark direct speech and quotations from a text.	Punctuation and capitalization rules for the different types of dialogue or speaker tags	Use proper conventions when writing dialogue. (DOK 1)
L.4.3a: Choose words and phrases to convey ideas precisely.	Types of dialogue (or speaker) tags—beginning, middle, end, or no tag Dialogue tag verbs provide description to indicate how characters speak to one another. Term: *Dialogue tag (speaker tag)*	Use words and phrases to convey ideas in a dialogue tag. (DOK 1)

Source for standards: National Governors Association Center for Best Practices (NGA) & Council of Chief State School Officers (CCSSO), 2010.

Figure 1.1: Pre-unit protocol example for grade 4—Dialogue.

grades are steep. Consider how a team might apply this thinking to the dialogue example in figure 1.1 (page 13). During lessons around this key component, students examine the purpose and function of dialogue and write conversations between characters; they study the writing conventions involved when inserting dialogue into their stories; and they consider alternatives to *said* as a dialogue tag. Students then assimilate these related chunks to incorporate authentic and correctly treated dialogue in stories that they create.

In the following sections, we break down the PREP protocol and explain how the use of each of the six progressive steps helps teams organize and simplify the PREP process and unlock the literacy learning inherent in any curriculum.

Enter Unit Standards Onto the PREP Template

At the start of the process, an essential part of a team's discussions centers on the targeted standards for a unit of study. A *unit* is a subdivision of instruction within a subject matter and, in grades 4–5, might be interdisciplinary; it entails a series of standards-based interconnected lessons that share a common focus. For example, in ELA, teachers might conduct an opinion unit. Within it, students read various works by an author (for example, Patricia Polacco or Chris Van Allsburg), select their favorite, and write an essay asserting their opinion using textual evidence as support. In social studies, a representative topic for a unit might be Native American cultures or a theme such as community workers or conflict and cooperation. In an interdisciplinary unit, students can study the causes and effects of the American Revolution (social studies); conduct research and write an informational report about their findings (ELA); and design various graphs (such as pie or bar graphs) based on the number of soldiers on both sides of the war who died, lived, sustained injuries, and were captured (mathematics). Unit lengths vary from a mini-unit that can span a few days or a week to a comprehensive unit of perhaps eight weeks. Although teacher teams conduct various formative assessments all throughout a unit to determine students' learning, the unit culminates in a summative assessment that measures students' comprehensive understanding of all standards within the unit. (For further information, see the discussion about assessments in chapter 2, page 37.) As specified in figure 1.1, our fourth-grade team anticipated the dialogue unit lasting about two weeks.

To begin the first step, teams identify every standard they will address throughout a unit of instruction. Teams can determine the exact compilation of standards that compose a literacy unit of instruction by accessing teaching resources, like a literature textbook or packaged curriculum, referring to a curriculum-mapping or curriculum-pacing document, or designing their own unit. If the district or school has purchased a reading or writing program or textbook from a publisher, the content standards are typically indicated within the resource, which is organized by units or modules. When using a purchased program, teams should still review the standards to ensure which ones and how many are appropriate. Keep in mind that publishers often list more standards than teachers might address in any given unit.

In another scenario, some schools and districts have designed curriculum maps that outline the standards for a unit or cycle of instruction. If this is the case, teams use these standards. Or, teacher teams sometimes tap their collective professional expertise to design their own units of instruction and determine pertinent standards for the targeted unit. Whichever approach teams take—sometimes blending use of published resources, curriculum maps, and teacher-developed materials—identifying standards represents their initial step so that clarity about what students need to know and do to be proficient by unit's end guides the entire process.

Once teams identify and agree on all the standards for the unit of instruction, teachers enter them in the Unit Standards section of the PREP template. This same process applies for teams addressing literacy standards in subject areas other than ELA. After all, students read complex text to acquire content across disciplines and should write to demonstrate understanding of information. For example, those who teach science or social studies can identify one or more of these four literacy-focused strands—(1) Reading, (2) Writing, (3) Speaking and Listening, and (4) Language—as crucial aspects of learning about ecosystems, natural disasters, exploration, or causes of a war.

It can seem overwhelming to consider teaching all the standards in a limited time due to their sheer number. Therefore, teams may feel compelled to prioritize the standards, choosing only those that are absolutely essential for students to learn. (Note the bold-italic text in the first section of figure 1.1, page 13, which signifies the prioritized standards.) Step 2 of this process will address these concerns. For now, teams enter *all* standards pertaining to a specific unit so they have a clear and comprehensive picture of the overall expected learning outcomes.

EXERCISE

Enter Unit Standards Onto the PREP Template

To prepare for the six-step process, use a blank PREP template (page 234 and downloadable from **go.SolutionTree.com/literacy**) to input the entire set of standards for your targeted unit. As your team reads about each step throughout this chapter, you may stop to participate in the provided exercises and return to this template to record more information. Alternatively, your team can read the entire chapter and then work on all exercises in a fluid fashion. If you are in a situation where you do not have a collaborative team in your building or district (you are a singleton teacher), consider whom you might reach out to as a collaborative partner for this exercise.

Use the following questions to guide this exercise.

★ What unit of instruction will our team work on together to practice the PREP process? When will we teach this unit?

★ How can we work as a collaborative team to identify standards for this first step in the PREP process?

★ What plan can we put in place to address logistical decisions, such as the following: *When and where will we meet? Who will facilitate the meeting? Who will access the template and perhaps convert it to a Google Doc to share with others? Who will enter the information onto the template?*

Indicate (or Determine) Priority Standards

So much to teach and not enough time. This seems to be a universal concern for teachers across all grade levels. With dozens of standards to address, a multitude of essential skills for students to learn, a sea of rich texts to introduce, and an array of lessons to deliver, one question lingers in the minds of educators everywhere: *How do I fit it all in?*

Once teams enter all unit standards onto the PREP template, the critical next step involves indicating which of these standards qualify as priority standards—that is, the standards that are most vital for students to learn (DuFour et al., 2016). Note that some refer to priority standards as *power standards* or *essential standards* (Crawford, 2011); these are all interchangeable terms. Priority standards then become the basis for instruction, assessment, and intervention. If your team has already identified grade-level priority standards for a unit of instruction, simply identify them on the PREP template by marking them in a way that sets them apart from nonpriority standards, such as through highlighting, bolding, under-lining, or using a unique color.

For those unfamiliar with prioritizing standards, this step addresses the real concern of how to fit it all in. Even most veteran teachers would confess that they would be hard-pressed to address every standard and its embedded concepts and skills with ease. They feel challenged to implement the standards with the fidelity and detailed attention required to make a significant impact on students' learning. More than likely, teachers may feel as though they run the distance by covering a lot of ground in reading and writing lessons. However, their instruction often lacks the depth necessary to make real progress in student achievement and ensure learn-ing for all students. For this reason, collaborative teams prioritize content-area stan-dards by carefully selecting those that will become the emphasis for a unit of study.

To perform this task effectively, team members carefully look at each learn-ing standard, combing through the precise language and identifying those stan-dards that most significantly impact students' learning. As a team, they likely agree that all standards within a unit have value and should be taught; however, the priority standards become the primary focus for instruction. Teachers hold stu-dents accountable for learning priority standards as they emphasize them during instruction, design formal assessments around them, and plan interventions to ensure opportunities for all students to reach the expected outcomes. As DuFour et al. (2016) explain:

> The process of prioritizing the standards . . . creates greater clarity about what teachers will teach, which in turn, promotes more efficient planning and sharing of resources. Perhaps the greatest benefit . . . is that it encourages teachers to embrace more in-depth instruction by reducing the pressure to simply cover the material. (p. 117)

Collaborative teams within a PLC adopt a collective understanding of the prior-ity standards most essential for students to master. However, with so many complex standards in a unit, how do teachers determine which standards to prioritize? Also, since ELA standards encompass a multitude of expectations within the strands of Reading, Writing, Speaking, Listening, and Language, how will teams identify literacy-critical aspects of these standards? To make this important decision, teams consider three key factors: (1) endurance, (2) leverage, and (3) readiness (Ainsworth & Viegut, 2015; Bailey, Jakicic, & Spiller, 2014; Reeves, 2002). Additionally, they take into account the knowledge necessary for high-stakes exams. Note, though, that a standard does not necessarily need to meet all these criteria to be deemed a priority. If your team has yet to establish priority standards for a unit, work together to review the following criteria that define the critical factors. (For more guidance, refer to the process for prioritizing standards in appendix B, page 243.)

▸ **Does the standard have *endurance*?** Are the skills and knowledge embedded in the standard critical for students to remember beyond the course or unit in which they are taught? For example, the ability to coherently summarize complex text is a skill that extends beyond a particular unit of instruction. Teachers expect students to be able to summarize key details from their reading from upper elementary through high school; it is useful within some professional careers, too. Therefore, summarizing is an enduring skill worth teaching in grades 4–5.

▸ **Does the standard have *leverage*?** Are the skills and knowledge in the standard applicable across several disciplines? For example, summarizing complex text might be taught in ELA when students experience a literary work, but it is equally valuable when reading content in social studies and science. If the skills embedded in a standard have value in other content areas, the standard has leverage and should become a priority.

▸ **Is the standard needed for student *readiness*?** Does the standard include prerequisite skills and knowledge necessary to prepare students for the next grade? For example, when students learn the structure and elements of an opinion paper, it equips them with the skills they need to tackle the more rigorous work of argumentation writing. Therefore, when prioritizing standards, consider the progression of skills from one grade level to the next, and choose those that build the foundation for future learning.

▸ **Is the standard needed for *high-stakes exams*?** Do students need to know and apply the skills and knowledge of the standard on external exams? For example, in district, state or provincial, college, or vocational exams, students might need to respond to questions or writing prompts geared to the standard. Teachers should consider this when discussing which standards are necessary for student preparedness.

To return to the example in figure 1.1 (page 13), bold-italic typeface indicates priority standards. Our fourth-grade team identified W.4.3b as essential for this particular dialogue unit; therefore, we are using bold-italic typeface to indicate its priority status. In related narrative-related units, we flagged other standards as essential—W.4.3a for establishing the central conflict and narrator, plus organizing a sequence of events; W.4.3c for incorporating transitional words and phrases; and so forth. Since the standard does not dictate the genre within the narrative text type, teachers can ask students to produce either narrative fiction (such as realistic fiction, mystery, or legend) or narrative nonfiction (such as biography, autobiography, memoir, or personal narrative).

Dialogue—a component of narrative—meets the criteria for endurance because it involves critical skills and knowledge that students need to retain in the future in subsequent grades when narrative reading and writing is an expectation. In terms of leverage, students might write narratives incorporating dialogue not only to entertain but also to inform, instruct, or persuade; therefore, these standards can achieve applicability across content areas. For example, students could write a historical fiction piece in social studies to share information and demonstrate an understanding of events and people from the past. Or, students might compose a science fiction story in which they explore and speculate about topics such as environmental issues and natural disasters to instruct others about possible dangerous consequences of human actions or inactions.

As for high-stakes testing, many schools, districts, states, and provinces expect fourth- and fifth-grade students to read and, in some cases, produce narrative writing that includes dialogue as characters speak to one another for various purposes. When inserting dialogue, students must learn to use proper mechanics, so our team considered two complementary language standards, L.4.2a and L.4.2b, as essential.

To craft a well-developed and organized narrative complete with dialogue, students need exposure to published complex text as well as student examples. Our fourth-grade team decided to create learning experiences around specific literary works that help students examine the use and function of dialogue and what it indicates explicitly and inferentially. In doing so, we position students to write their own narratives. These lessons address reading standard RL.4.1, which the team flagged as essential because it augments the writing skills we prioritized. A team may revisit this standard when focusing on other units related to narrative, as well, such as elements of literature, figurative language, and description.

As a reminder, grades 4–5 teachers address all standards during the school year throughout the various units of instruction in which they apply. However, standards not identified as priority move to a supporting role; these standards "support, connect to, or enhance the priority standards. They are taught within the context of the priority standards, but do not receive the same degree of instruction and assessment emphasis as do the priority standards" (Ainsworth, 2013, p. xv). You can learn more about this identification process in appendix B (page 243). For example, teachers surely guide students through the writing process and address this standard: "With guidance and support from peers and adults, develop and strengthen writing as needed by planning, revising, and editing" (W.4.5; NGA & CCSSO, 2010). However, they address it within the priority standard W.4.3, which focuses on producing a well-developed, logically sequenced story complete with narrative techniques. This same notion applies when teachers indicate the writing process standard as supporting in the service of the priority standards for text types—informational, explanatory, and opinion—across content areas. Reading standards, such as determining a theme, comparing and contrasting points of view, and describing characters or events drawing on details from the text, can be subsumed under the reading literature standard (RL.4.1), rendering them supporting as well.

After determining priority standards for the target unit, the team then unwraps these standards to examine the specific knowledge and skills embedded within each one. This helps teams develop assessments and design instruction.

EXERCISE

Indicate (or Determine) Priority Standards

Review the standards you entered onto the PREP template. If your team has already undergone a process for prioritizing them, merely distinguish priority standards from supporting standards by bolding, underlining, or color-coding them. If, however, your team has not yet prioritized standards, use the suggestions from this section along with the process articulated in appendix B to do so. Then, return to the PREP template and mark the priority standards.

Use the following questions to guide this exercise.

★ Which standards will we deem priority or essential?

★ Which priority standards are appropriate for our targeted unit of study?

> ★ Are all team members clear that we will be held accountable for students learning the priority standards? Are priority standards the focus for our teaching, assessment, and intervention?
>
> ★ Which standards serve as supporting standards and, as such, are subsumed under priority standards? Which priority standards subsume them?
>
> ★ Are we clear that we will still address and teach supporting standards but not give them the same time and attention as priority standards?

Unwrap Unit Priority Standards

A common misconception among many teacher teams is that listing unit standards sufficiently represents the basis for all instructional decisions moving forward. One might think, *I've got a list of standards right here, so I'm ready to teach.* However, this is not the case. To fully understand each standard and guarantee a consistent curriculum for grades 4–5 classrooms, teams of teachers must examine each content-area standard and arrive at a collective agreement about its precise meaning and implications for instruction and assessment.

It is the explicit and implicit skills and knowledge embedded within standards from which teams must design a robust instructional and assessment plan. So, teams participate in the process of *unwrapping* (what some refer to as *unpacking*) standards, allowing them to critically examine and parse the words of a standard. By utilizing this strategy, teams can reveal fine-grain learning targets embedded within a standard to guide quality instruction, with an emphasis on literacy, and better support students' efforts to master that targeted standard. In *Simplifying Common Assessment*, Kim Bailey and Chris Jakicic (2017) write:

> The goal of the unwrapping process is twofold: first, to build shared or collective understanding of what the standard asks students to know and do; and second, to identify the smaller increments of learning, or learning targets, that will create a step-by-step path leading to that standard. (p. 21)

To give credence to unwrapping and to provide teachers with an authentic reason for participating in this critical step, teams talk about how they teach to a standard and what evidence of learning they ask students to produce. For example, consider the priority standard RL.4.1—"Refer to details and examples in a text when explaining what the text says explicitly and when drawing inferences from the text" (NGA & CCSSO, 2010)—and the following scenario focusing on drawing inferences.

One teacher on a team provides students with a prepared passage of a complex text that includes underlined words and phrases that have an underlying meaning. In the margin, students write an inference corresponding to the textual evidence the teacher underlined. Another teacher identifies two salient dialogue passages without indicating which might hold deep meaning. Working in pairs, each partner focuses on a different passage and writes a detailed response to this prompt: *How does dialogue uncover characters' beliefs, feelings, or motivations? In your written response, include specific details and examples from the text to support your answer.* Partners share their work to ensure they are drawing correct inferences and citing appropriate textual evidence. They help each other make revisions, then submit their short essays to the teacher.

These two examples illustrate varying degrees of interpretation—one less rigorous in its design and expectation, the other requiring more skills and in-depth application of the standard. By unwrapping standards, teachers on a team avoid translating and teaching a standard in their own potentially highly variable ways. Rather, they ensure that team members apply a consistent approach to teaching and assessing student proficiency.

To unwrap a standard, teams can annotate priority standards, as illustrated in figure 1.2.

- REFER TO details and examples in a text when explaining what the text says explicitly and when drawing inferences from the text. (RL.4.1)
- USE dialogue and description to DEVELOP experiences and events or SHOW the responses of characters to situations. (W.4.3b)

Figure 1.2: Using annotation to unwrap priority standards.

To arrive at these annotated standards, our team answered the following three questions and annotated the standards accordingly.

1. **What priority standard (or standards) are we targeting?** Copy and paste the priority standard or standards onto a blank document or print them out.

2. **What will students need to do to be proficient?** Find and capitalize or circle (or both) pertinent verbs in each standard. The verbs—together with the content and context (step 3)—pinpoint the exact skills students need to achieve proficiency in a standard.

3. **With what content and context will students achieve proficiency?** Find and underline the nouns and phrases that represent the content and concepts to teach within each standard.

Since each standard contains several layers, teachers on a grade-level team may interpret the words differently (as illustrated in the scenario earlier in this section). If teachers misinterpret the intent of a standard, they inadvertently jeopardize a guaranteed curriculum as students across a school and district receive haphazard instruction with varying degrees of rigor. Therefore, during this portion of the PREP process, dedicate time to unwrapping priority standards and achieving collective agreement about them. Doing so requires teachers to closely examine and analyze every verb, noun, and conjunction to fully grasp the complexity and entirety of each ELA standard. This exercise provokes a serious conversation about the specific skills, knowledge, and concepts necessary for effective literacy instruction and assessment that will benefit grades 4–5 students.

Once teams identify significant verbs, they convey the verbs' importance by capitalizing and bolding them (if working electronically) or circling or highlighting them (if using hard copies). As you can see from figure 1.2 (page 22), our fourth-grade team pinpointed *refer* as a key verb. Next, teams must discuss the context of each verb to uncover significant nouns, noun phrases, or other phrases that indicate salient knowledge items necessary for mastery. To illustrate, our team discussed the context of the verb *refer* by asking, "In this standard, what do students refer to exactly?" The team parsed the sentence and determined that the standard expects students to refer to details and examples for two express purposes: (1) to explain what the text states directly (explicitly) and (2) to explain what the text says inferentially (implicitly). Once we agreed, we underlined the noun phrases shown in figure 1.2 and divided the standard in two. To differentiate between them, our team wrote the following targets as complete sentences and added capitalized letters in parentheses beside them.

1. **RL.4.1 (A):** Refer to details and examples in a text when explaining what the text says explicitly.

2. **RL.4.1 (B):** Refer to details and examples in a text when drawing inferences from the text.

Standard W.4.3b seemed a bit trickier to unwrap: "Use dialogue and description to develop experiences and events or show the responses of characters to situations" (NGA & CCSSO, 2010). First, our team located three verbs—(1) *use*, (2) *develop*, and (3) *show*. However, we determined that *use* was the operative word and the other two verbs were tightly linked to it. We marked the verbs but knew *use* was a top priority. Next, we underlined the noun phrases that provide context to answer the question, "What do students use?" It appears that students are to use both dialogue *and* description for an express purpose—*to develop experiences and events*. Then we discussed the conjunction *or* and its placement within this standard to indicate the option of students either developing experiences and events *or* showing the responses of characters to situations. Therefore, we interpreted the standard to mean that dialogue and description are non-negotiable, but students can choose for what purpose they use them. Once again, we divided a standard in two, adding capitalized letters to the bolded targets to distinguish the two embedded skills.

1. **W.4.3b (A):** Use dialogue to develop experiences and events or show the responses of characters to situations.

2. **W.4.3b (B):** Use description to develop experiences and events or show the responses of characters to situations.

As an additional consideration during the unwrapping process, teams should pay attention to these commonly used abbreviations within standards: *e.g.* and *i.e.* When a standard includes *e.g.*, the intent is to provide a list of examples since this Latin abbreviation means "for the sake of example." For instance, this standard gives teachers the option of selecting one or more strategies from a provided list, which isn't finite: *Choose an appropriate organization strategy (e.g., sequence of events, cause–effect, compare–contrast) to convey a message.* If, however, a standard uses *i.e.*, what follows the abbreviation becomes an expectation, as in the following: *Interpret forms of figurative language used in various texts (i.e., simile, metaphor, personification).* Teachers must take the time to scrutinize each standard to capture its intent and work in teams to help decipher and interpret what can sometimes be murky. In *Yes We Can!*, Heather Friziellie, Julie A. Schmidt, and Jeanne Spiller (2016) write:

> Unpacking standards enables every teacher who teaches the standard to develop a deep and consistent understanding of the standard and its component expectations. The outcome is that students will receive instruction that is truly aligned to the expected rigor and complexity of the standard. (p. 46)

After teachers annotate their standards through underlining, circling, bolding, or another method, they keep these standards readily available to use when they identify knowledge items in the following step.

EXERCISE
Unwrap Unit Priority Standards

As a collaborative team, work on unwrapping or unpacking priority standards to gain clarity about learning goals for your unit. To do so, access your work-in-progress PREP template and the explanation for unwrapping standards in this section. Annotate standards according to the protocol steps to uncover smaller, incremental learning goals that exist within each overarching standard.

Use the following questions to guide this exercise.

★ Looking at each priority standard for our targeted unit, what verbs can we capitalize or circle that indicate skills students will need to be proficient?

★ What nouns or phrases can we underline that show the content and concepts to teach in a particular context?

★ Are there conjunctions, such as *and* or *or*, that are important to decipher to help unwrap these standards?

Identify Knowledge Items

After (or even while) teams annotate standards to deconstruct them, they focus collaboratively on identifying what students should *know*—the first part of PLC critical question 1: *What do we want students to learn?* (DuFour et al., 2016). Or, put another way, *What is it we want students to know and be able to do?*

The answer is largely factual information that forms the foundation for addressing standards and leads to understanding deeper concepts for those standards that are more sophisticated.

In this context, *knowledge* comprises facts, dates, people, places, examples, and vocabulary and terms—including concept words—although not all lessons or units necessarily include all of these. Teams can generate a list of these items. When doing so, they use nouns and noun phrases rather than line items that begin with verbs, which would reflect what we want students to *do*—the focus for the second half of the PLC question about skills (see the next section). As an alternative to a list, teachers can represent knowledge in other ways. For example, in a narrative unit, teachers can use a diagram of an inverted checkmark indicating plot elements as shown in figure 1.3. In science, teachers might need students to know the information on a labeled diagram of the respiratory system. In social studies, knowledge can be reflected in a map of the trade routes of early explorers. Eventually, teams will incorporate what they want students to know within curriculum design.

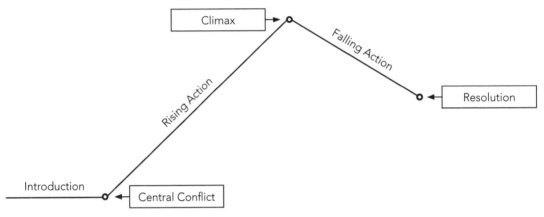

Source: Glass, 2018, p. 133.

Figure 1.3: Basic plot diagram.

To determine knowledge items, regardless of format, teachers refer not just to standards but to multiple resources. Along with tapping colleagues who have expertise in the targeted content of a unit, teachers can access available textbooks plus online and print resources and materials. They do not necessarily need to devise their own list or a graphic organizer. Instead, they might cite a digital resource or a page from a textbook. For example, teachers could cite the dialogue vocabulary terms as a resource for what students should know concerning dialogue tags. (See Concept Attainment, page 206, for an example.) The goal is for team members to collaboratively engage in laser-focused conversations that reveal the explicit and implied knowledge emanating from standards. As a byproduct of these conversations, veteran teachers might consider adding content to embed within instruction, and teachers new to the profession, subject matter, or grade can learn content that is important to teach.

With regard to determining explicit and inferred items, consider an example from the grade 5 standard L.5.2d, "Use underlining, quotation marks, or italics to indicate titles of works" (NGA & CCSSO, 2010). When writing a research report in any content area, students collect and insert evidence (such as facts, quotations, or other information) to develop their topics. In doing so, they identify the titles of sources, which applies to this standard. To compile a list of knowledge items, teams might generate the following entries. Notice that these items are a combination of a fact stated in a sentence, terms students will need to know, and phrases, which all complete the sentence stem *Students will know . . .*

> ▸ Conventions (or mechanics) to indicate titles of works
>
> ▸ Titles of longer works are italicized if typed on an electronic device or underlined if handwritten.
>
> ▸ Titles of shorter works are enclosed in quotes
>
> ▸ Terms: *italics, quotation marks*

Note that the first item merely restates the standard explicitly; the rest of the entries are inferred. To arrive at the latter, teams need to probe their interpretation of this standard. Besides conversing with each other, teams consult outside sources to uncover what is implied in a standard so they have a complete sense of what students will need to know to teach this standard thoroughly.

For the dialogue unit, figure 1.4 illustrates how our fourth-grade team unwrapped the priority standards it chose in its PREP template to identify knowledge items.

Unwrapped Unit Priority Standards	Knowledge Items
RL.4.1 (A): Refer to details and examples in a text when explaining what the text says explicitly.	• Literal and explicit details from a text are directly stated. • Terms: *Literal, explicit*
RL.4.1 (B): Refer to details and examples in a text when drawing inferences from the text.	• Inferences—implied information that is not directly or explicitly stated • Terms: *Imply, infer, inference*
W.4.3b (A): Use dialogue to develop experiences and events or show the responses of characters to situations.	• Purpose and function of dialogue • Dialogue is meaningful and serves a purpose—to develop the plot or to show characters' responses to situations.
W.4.3b (B): Use description to develop experiences and events or show the responses of characters to situations.	• Descriptive details (precise nouns, vivid verbs, and colorful adjectives)

Figure 1.4: Knowledge items for unwrapped unit priority standards—Dialogue. continued ⟶

Unwrapped Unit Priority Standards	Knowledge Items
L.4.2a: Use correct capitalization. **L.4.2b:** Use commas and quotation marks to mark direct speech and quotations from a text.	• Punctuation and capitalization rules for the different types of dialogue or speaker tags
L.4.3a: Choose words and phrases to convey ideas precisely.	• Types of dialogue (or speaker) tags— beginning, middle, end, or no tag • Dialogue tag verbs provide description to indicate how characters speak to one another. • Term: *Dialogue tag (speaker tag)*

In determining the knowledge items for this example, our team considered what students need to know in the reading standard for using details and examples from dialogue to explicitly reveal what a character thinks or does, as well as for drawing inferences from exchanges between characters. Students also need to know the purpose and function of dialogue in general and differentiate meaningful from unnecessary dialogue. When planning learning experiences around these knowledge items, we intend for students to know that dialogue plays a vital role in a story, such as plot development or character responses. Lastly, students must learn about the different ways writers insert dialogue, the conventions associated with properly writing it, and a variety of verbs in dialogue tags as alternatives to *said* or *questioned*.

Next, collaborative teams peruse the annotated, unwrapped standards and the new knowledge items to identify skills.

EXERCISE
Identify Knowledge Items

Work as a collaborative team to identify knowledge items aligned to your unwrapped priority standards. When ready, add the items aligned to each unwrapped standard onto your PREP template. Your team might generate a list, reference a page from a source (for example, a page in a textbook that features a diagram, a list of vocabulary, or the beginning of an engaging story), or create a graphic organizer. Be aware that sometimes a standard is lean and does not include all that it should to design effective instruction. These knowledge items are, therefore, implied.

Use the following questions to guide this exercise.

★ What should students know relative to a priority standard targeted for this lesson?

★ What explicitly stated knowledge items do we expect students to know?

★ What might be implicit in the standard and require us to make inferences?

Determine Skills

At this stage, teams review their annotation of unwrapped priority standards and their knowledge items (a list or graphic representation) to identify skills—what students actually must *do*. Educational consultant and author H. Lynn Erickson (2002) defines *skills* as:

> the specific competencies required for complex process performance. Skills need to be taught directly and practiced in context. For example, some of the skills required for doing the complex performance of research include "accessing information," "identifying main ideas and details," "note taking," and "organizing information." (p. 166)

Therefore, it is incumbent on teachers to plan learning experiences where they explicitly teach skills and directly assess them to ascertain students' levels of proficiency. Equally important is the idea that skills have transfer value so that they apply to new situations. Continuing Erickson's (2002) example, when upper elementary students learn to access information, identify main ideas, and take notes—perhaps for a research report on plate tectonics in a science unit—they will be able to apply these skills in novel ways as they conduct research for other purposes.

The unwrapped, annotated priority standards serve as a guide to determine skills. Standards, like skills, begin with verbs. However, some of the verbs used in content standards are not necessarily observable but rather vaguely measurable mental verbs, such as *understand* and *know*. Instead of these verbs, teams should target using measurable action verbs like *define*, *analyze*, and *compare*. They must study the annotated standards and knowledge items to fashion skills that are sufficient to cover the intent of the standards as well as concrete enough to measure student aptitude. We refer to the skills that teams identify and define as *learning targets*, the incremental and specific skills that students must be able to do to achieve mastery of the entire learning standard. Throughout this book, you'll notice references to standards (overall learning goals) and learning targets (the skills embedded within the standards).

Figure 1.5 shows how our fourth-grade team expanded the unwrapped priority standards and knowledge from figure 1.4 (page 27) to identify the necessary skills.

Unwrapped Unit Priority Standards	Knowledge Items	Skills (Learning Targets)
RL.4.1 (A): Refer to details and examples in a text when explaining what the text says explicitly.	• Literal and explicit details from a text are directly stated. • Terms: *Literal, explicit*	Identify details and examples in a text to explain what it says explicitly.
RL.4.1 (B): Refer to details and examples in a text when drawing inferences from the text.	• Inferences—implied information that is not directly or explicitly stated • Terms: *Imply, infer, inference*	Make inferences using details and examples in a text.
W.4.3b (A): Use dialogue to develop experiences and events or show the responses of characters to situations.	• Purpose and function of dialogue • Dialogue is meaningful and serves a purpose—to develop the plot or to show characters' responses to situations.	Write dialogue to develop a plot or to show characters' responses to situations.
W.4.3b (B): Use description to develop experiences and events or show the responses of characters to situations.	• Descriptive details (precise nouns, vivid verbs, and colorful adjectives)	Write descriptive detail to develop a plot or show characters' responses to situations.

L.4.2a: Use correct capitalization. L.4.2b: Use commas and quotation marks to mark direct speech and quotations from a text.	• Punctuation and capitalization rules for the different types of dialogue or speaker tags	Use proper conventions when writing dialogue.
L.4.3a: Choose words and phrases to convey ideas precisely.	• Types of dialogue (or speaker) tags—beginning, middle, end, or no tag • Dialogue tag verbs provide description to indicate how characters speak to one another. • Term: *Dialogue tag* (*speaker tag*)	Use words and phrases to convey ideas in a dialogue tag.

Figure 1.5: Skills for unwrapped unit priority standards—Dialogue.

Notice that our team replaced the verbs used in the standards when making entries in the Skills column. For example, for the writing standard, we replaced *use* with *write*. We felt that *write* more concretely guides teachers with instruction and assessment than *use*. Our intent is to ask students to write dialogue for stories they generate, which is more rigorous and measurable. In some cases, like L.4.2a and L.4.2b, we maintained the verb *use* because it seemed to indicate that students would incorporate these skills *into* their writing. For L.4.3a, *choose* indicated to us that students select from a predetermined list or source; however, we wanted them not only to choose specific words and phrases but to actually use them in writing and in speaking. Also, before students can write dialogue, they need to be able to recognize it in published works, as reflected in the reading skills in the top two rows of the figure. Teams can apply this kind of thinking across content areas when interpreting standards.

With a collective understanding of what students need to know (knowledge) and be able to do (skills), teams can design instruction that explicitly addresses standards. Therefore, they pay careful attention to the verbs so that the rigor of instruction matches the expectation for students.

After unwrapping priority standards, identifying knowledge items, and determining skills, collaborative teams are primed to consider the level of intended rigor for each learning target. This will help later when teams develop literacy-focused assessments they will issue for students to demonstrate understanding.

EXERCISE
Determine Skills

Using your team's unwrapped, annotated standards and knowledge items, collaborate on determining skills and enter them on your work-in-progress PREP template.

Use the following questions to guide this exercise.

★ What cognitive processes are we asking students to employ?

★ What measurable action verbs aligned to each unwrapped standard can we use to show students can apply what they learn?

★ Do the skills have transfer value, rather than being anchored to specific content?

Assign Levels of Rigor for Learning Targets

At this step, teams return to the unwrapped skills that serve as learning targets to examine their complexity. This scrutiny can lead to powerful team discussions regarding the intended rigor of the learning targets so teachers can match the challenge level in their instruction and assessments. We suggest Norman Webb's (1997, 1999) Depth of Knowledge, a thinking taxonomy, to identify the level of rigor in your learning targets. DOK is a scale of cognitive demand composed of the following four levels. (See appendix C, page 247, for a more extensive explanation of each level.)

1. **Recall:** Level 1 requires rote recall of information, facts, definitions, terms, or simple procedures. The student either knows the answer or does not.

2. **Skills and concepts:** Level 2 requires the engagement of mental processing or decision making beyond recall or reproduction. Items falling into this category often have more than one step, such as organizing and comparing data.

3. **Strategic thinking:** Level 3 requires higher-level thinking than levels 1 and 2 and could include activities or contexts that have more than one possible solution, thereby requiring justification or support for the argument or process.

4. **Extended thinking:** Level 4 requires high cognitive demand in which students are synthesizing ideas across content areas or situations and generalizing that information to solve new problems. Many responses in this category require extensive time because they imply that students complete multiple steps, as in a multivariate investigation and analysis.

Webb's (1997, 1999) DOK asks that teachers look beyond the verb used in the learning target, examine the context in which skills are to be performed, and determine the depth of thinking required. Although the verb choice helps indicate the level of complexity, teachers must consider the full context of the standard since the verb does not always give the complete picture of rigorous expectations. For example, teachers can devise any of the following learning targets using the verb *write*, but each carries a different level of expectation.

- Write dialogue tags to indicate a change in speakers.

- Write dialogue tags using precise action verbs.

- Write dialogue tags to indicate characters' emotions and responses.

Our fourth-grade team engaged in a fruitful discussion when determining the DOK levels for the skills within the narrative unit standard "Refer to details and examples in a text when explaining what the text says explicitly and when drawing inferences from the text" (RL.4.1; NGA & CCSSO, 2010). Consider the following.

- When students identify explicit details and examples from a story's dialogue to explain what characters' words reveal, they participate in a task involving basic comprehension. Hence, this cognitive demand falls under DOK 1.

- The skill necessary to determine what is implicitly stated increases the challenge for students and requires more mental processing. Therefore, making inferences using details and examples from the dialogue is associated with DOK 2.

- When students draw inferences across passages and write an essay explaining their interpretations using textual evidence, they address DOK 3.

With an awareness of their learning targets and associated DOK levels, teams can make intentional and prudent decisions about the types of assessments they give and the intended levels of rigor at which to set them. See chapter 3 (page 59) for discussions about learning progressions and matching assessments to the rigor of skills. Figure 1.6 illustrates how teams add DOK levels to the PREP template, indicating the cognitive demand for each learning target.

Unwrapped Unit Priority Standards	Knowledge Items	Skills (Learning Targets and DOK Levels)
RL.4.1 (A): Refer to details and examples in a text when explaining what the text says explicitly.	• Literal and explicit details from a text are directly stated. • Terms: *Literal, explicit*	Identify details and examples in a text to explain what it says explicitly. **(DOK 1)**
RL.4.1 (B): Refer to details and examples in a text when drawing inferences from the text.	• Inferences—implied information that is not directly or explicitly stated • Terms: *Imply, infer, inference*	Make inferences using details and examples in a text. **(DOK 2)**
W.4.3b (A): Use dialogue to develop experiences and events or show the responses of characters to situations.	• Purpose and function of dialogue • Dialogue is meaningful and serves a purpose—to develop the plot or to show characters' responses to situations.	Write dialogue to develop a plot or to show characters' responses to situations. **(DOK 2)**
W.4.3b (B): Use description to develop experiences and events or show the responses of characters to situations.	• Descriptive details (precise nouns, vivid verbs, and colorful adjectives)	Write descriptive detail to develop a plot or show characters' responses to situations. **(DOK 2)**
L.4.2a: Use correct capitalization. **L.4.2b:** Use commas and quotation marks to mark direct speech and quotations from a text.	• Punctuation and capitalization rules for the different types of dialogue or speaker tags	Use proper conventions when writing dialogue. **(DOK 1)**

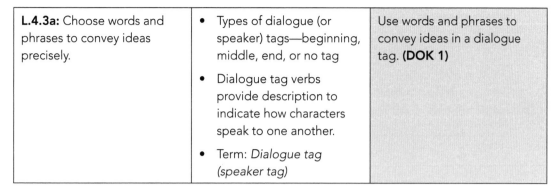

| L.4.3a: Choose words and phrases to convey ideas precisely. | • Types of dialogue (or speaker) tags—beginning, middle, end, or no tag

• Dialogue tag verbs provide description to indicate how characters speak to one another.

• Term: *Dialogue tag (speaker tag)* | Use words and phrases to convey ideas in a dialogue tag. **(DOK 1)** |

Figure 1.6: DOK levels for unwrapped unit priority standards—Dialogue.

When considering learning targets' level of expectations, educators must be careful not to change a target's intended rigor for students with special needs, English learners, or those simply struggling with the content or skills. Teams will need to consider each of these students on a case-by-case basis—particularly for students with severe disabilities who may not be able to function independently as adults—to determine an appropriate instructional plan. You will learn more about responding to students' data for the purposes of intervention in chapter 5 (page 117).

EXERCISE
Assign Levels of Rigor for Learning Targets

Assign and input DOK levels to your team's chosen learning targets onto the work-in-progress PREP template. Refer to appendix C (page 247), as well as the examples in figure 1.6, for support in assigning these levels.

Use the following questions to guide this exercise.

★ Have we considered the full context of the standards rather than relying on the verbs alone, which sometimes gives an incomplete picture of rigor?

★ What is the complexity of each skill embedded within the full standard?

★ Have we keenly reviewed our learning targets to be sure we are not consistently aiming too low or even too high?

Summary

In a PLC, the first critical question is, *What is it we want our students to learn?* (DuFour et al., 2016). This question incorporates several components that begin with and derive from standards that determine what we want students to know and be able to do. All the components, which are embedded in the six-step PREP process articulated in this chapter, have a role and purpose, and together, they drive effective curriculum design. The *knowledge items* represent foundational information that is specific to content material, the *skills* reflect what students are expected to do, and *depth of knowledge* ensures appropriate rigor. As collaborative teams work on the PREP process, they afford their students the high-quality and effective curriculum they so rightly deserve. If your team wishes to extend the process, it may also establish essential understandings and guiding questions. Appendix D (page 253) provides a detailed discussion and direction for addressing these additional components.

In the next chapter, we explore how the PREP work that teams engage in integrates with assessments, which consequently guides instruction. We also discuss the different types and formats of assessment along with the unique characteristics of teaching literacy.

CHAPTER 2

Examine Assessment Options for Literacy

In chapter 1, we took a deep dive into the first critical question of a PLC to establish precisely how teacher teams can use the six-step PREP process to determine what they want students to know and be able to do by the end of a unit. Through this process, teams can secure common learning expectations for every student in every classroom and solidify a foundation from which all subsequent unit planning can evolve. By clarifying the priority standards to be assessed *and* the specific knowledge and skills students must acquire to show proficiency, teachers set the groundwork for the second critical question of a PLC: *How will we know if each student has learned it?* (DuFour et al., 2016).

To provide the tools and guidance necessary to design literacy-focused assessments, this chapter examines assessment types and formats and their usefulness for achieving specific instructional goals. In addition, we highlight the unique features of teaching literacy with assessments in mind. As a natural extension to these topics, the next two chapters focus on developing a learning progression (including making assessment choices and determining common assessments) and designing rubrics.

Assessment Types and Formats

Throughout an instructional cycle, effective teachers administer both common and individual classroom assessments to collect data on student progress that serve to drive learning forward. They design or find assessments, or revise existing ones, that give students multiple opportunities to demonstrate their learning in myriad ways. Whether creating assessments from scratch or planning to administer prepared assessments from a purchased literacy program, teacher teams must ensure that each assessment clearly measures students' understanding of the team's priority learning standards for a unit. Although the convenience of prepackaged assessments often entices teachers, teams need to review and sometimes revamp those assessments to make sure they evaluate precisely the right skills.

In truth, *assessment*—a term used pervasively in education—can cause confusion with its varied terminology of types and formats, such as *formative, summative,* and *performance*; *formal* and *informal*; *obtrusive, unobtrusive,* and *student-generated*; *selected-* and *constructed-response*; and so on. Ultimately, it's about how teachers "assess to gather information about student learning and either use that information *formatively* to advance learning or use it *summatively* to verify that it has occurred" (Schimmer, 2019).

Teachers judiciously choose an appropriate assessment, or even a combination of assessments, based on what will best measure students' proficiency with different learning targets. What follows are explanations of assessment types along with example formats and methods to help elucidate this somewhat murky topic. It includes explorations about the following.

- ▶ Formative and summative assessments
- ▶ Unobtrusive, obtrusive, and student-generated assessments
- ▶ Selected-response, constructed-response, and performance assessments
- ▶ Running records and reading fluency checks

For an in-depth examination of assessment, you may conduct your own search to collect information that will augment the discussion that follows. (We list a variety of useful resources in the Journey of Assessments section, page 50.) Some sources might have slightly different definitions, so make sure you reach a collective agreement on the academic language your team prefers. Always be mindful that assessments must match exactly what you intend to assess so they can inform your teaching and maximize student growth.

Formative and Summative Assessments

Formative assessments are assessments *for* learning (Stiggins, 2005). They check for understanding and allow students the opportunity to practice skills and strategies to eventually master them. In other words, they guide and inform a teacher's instructional plan daily and weekly. According to assessment expert Dylan Wiliam (2018):

An assessment functions formatively to the extent that evidence about student achievement is elicited, interpreted, and used by teachers, learners, or their peers to make decisions about the next steps in instruction that are likely to be better, or better founded, than the decisions they would have made in the absence of that evidence. (p. 48)

Formative assessments, when done well, provide meaningful information about how individual students are progressing throughout an instructional unit. This allows teachers to intervene with students who need a differentiated approach by providing scaffolded support and corrective instruction to those who are almost there, and even extending the learning of already proficient students. Robert J. Marzano (2017) identifies three types of formative assessments to track students' progress: (1) unobtrusive, (2) obtrusive, and (3) student-generated. Obtrusive and even student-generated assessments are more formal methods; in fact, selected-response and constructed-response items, which textbooks and other sources have aplenty, are technically obtrusive. We cover all these types and formats in the upcoming sections.

To check in on student learning, teams also collect data from *summative assessments*—assessments *of* learning (Stiggins, 2005). Traditionally, teachers issue summative assessments at the conclusion of a unit to ascertain what students learned. These assessments serve as the culmination of a comprehensive unit of instruction (or course), like a final writing product. For example, in social studies, students can write an opinion essay to persuade readers to support either the loyalist (Tory) or patriot (Whig) position in the American Revolution. Sometimes teachers consider these assessments evaluative only. Teams typically score summative assessments as evidence of student achievement; also, teachers use them to determine the next instructional steps or even placement in particular classes. However, teams can consider some summative assessments to be formative, as well, based on the way teachers use the assessment data. For example, they can assess mastery of targeted learning objectives at different points within a unit. Carol Ann Tomlinson and Tonya R. Moon (2013) make this point in their book *Assessment and Student Success in a Differentiated Classroom*:

Summative assessment can occur at the end of a unit when all of the learning objectives have been taught, at the end of several lessons that form a subset of meaning in the unit, or even at the end of a single lesson if the lesson objective has been fully met and students have had adequate opportunity to achieve mastery. Using summative assessments at the end of a lesson or set of lessons helps teachers ensure that students have developed the foundation on which subsequent lessons will build. Summative assessment takes its name from its purpose of "summing up" what students have learned at a logical point in time. (p. 92)

Think of the journey through a unit of instruction as a road trip, from an initial starting point to a desired end point. As teachers travel through their instructional unit from point A to point B, formative assessments are the quick pit stops along the way to check in on students' learning, while summative assessments can represent both the longer rest stops (perhaps for lunch) and the final destination. The latter provides evidence of what students have mastered during chunks of instruction plus how far they have traveled at the culmination of a unit of study. Whether teams administer and collect formative or summative assessments, they all reveal who has yet to demonstrate proficiency (and therefore needs additional support to progress toward mastery) as well as who needs extended opportunities to be further challenged. Figure 2.1 illustrates an assessment road trip.

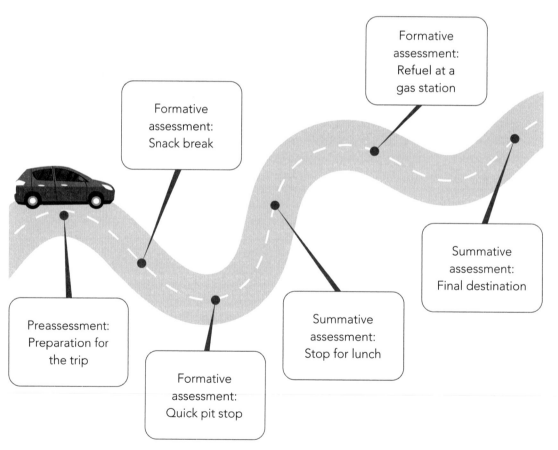

Figure 2.1: Assessment road trip.

Unobtrusive, Obtrusive, and Student-Generated Assessments

Unobtrusive formative assessments occur while students participate in the learning process and tend to be informal in nature. "In contrast to obtrusive assessments, unobtrusive assessments do not interrupt the flow of instruction. In fact, students might not even be aware that they are being assessed during [this kind of] assessment" (Marzano, 2017, p. 24).

During an unobtrusive assessment, teachers watch and listen for specific indicators of student learning, such as the kinds and quality of responses plus the level of engagement. For example, teachers circulate around the room listening in on small-group discussions or observe students as they complete a quick write or a graphic organizer. As needed, teachers approach students to redirect those who are off topic, pose questions to propel students to arrive at a new insight, or clear up any misconceptions. Additionally, teachers intentionally scan the room when delivering content via, for example, a PowerPoint presentation or video excerpt to be sure students actively listen, record key information, or exhibit on-task behavior. If not, they make adjustments on the spot.

Using a checklist or a recordkeeping sheet, teachers might opt to keep track of students' responses and take notes about their contributions, as in the example in figure 2.2 (page 42). As part of their daily classroom instruction, individual teachers informally and unobtrusively assess to check for understanding. However, because conducting a variety of assessments provides teachers with more information to ascertain students' levels of proficiency on priority standards, teachers should also issue more formal assessments to determine how well students can demonstrate a skill.

When teachers assign *obtrusive* assessments, they interrupt classroom instruction and issue a task for students to complete or perform. Students can submit a quiz, an essay, or another artifact that teachers read, provide feedback on, and sometimes score; however, there are a host of other obtrusive methods of assessment at varying degrees of engagement. Remember, though, that any assessment must match the purpose and the complexity of the standards it is measuring. Consider the following examples of obtrusive literacy assessments that are appropriate for grades 4–5 students. Except for the last two list items, the others can apply to material students learn across the disciplines. For example, students can write a summary of a historical event they read about in their social studies textbook or based on a science article.

Data-Recording Tool

Unit: A Story Well Told—The Power of Dialogue Within a Narrative

Concept or skill: Use proper conventions when writing dialogue.

Student	Demonstrates mastery of using proper dialogue conventions; might apply the skill in an advanced way (4.0)	Demonstrates mastery of using proper dialogue conventions (3.0)	Has some understanding of using proper dialogue conventions (2.0)	Demonstrates limited understanding of using dialogue conventions (1.0)
Chloe				Haphazard use of capitalization and punctuation ✓
Kalisi		Remind her to put the commas inside quotation marks consistently ✓		
Jose A.	✓			
Latoya	Sophisticated use of dialogue conventions; uses a variety of techniques & includes extensive dialogue ✓			
Sean		✓		

Figure 2.2: Sample unobtrusive data-recording tool.

Visit go.SolutionTree.com/literacy for a free reproducible version of this figure.

▸ Annotate a student sample of an opinion essay to identify the elements of this genre.

▸ Complete a graphic organizer that captures the main idea and key details of a text.

▸ Write a summary of a complex text.

▸ Create a graphic organizer or comic strip to explain the problem and solution of a text.

▸ Provide an outline for a research paper.

▸ Write an original setting for a story using descriptive details.

▸ Draw a character based on a written or oral description.

Obtrusive assessments can be both formal and informal. The previous examples depict more formal options in that students produce something they submit to teachers for careful review and oral or written feedback (constructed-response assessments). Teachers might also issue quick, informal check-ins that indicate their next instructional steps. For example, they can have students turn in an exit slip (also referred to as an *exit card*) on the way out of class or before a transition period, respond to questions on mini-whiteboards, or signal thumbs-up or thumbs-down to prompts (selected-response assessments). For additional ideas suitable to multiple content areas, see figure 2.3 (page 45); some entries can serve as formative or summative assessments depending on how teachers assign and use them.

When selecting an obtrusive assessment option, choose judiciously to ensure that the item students produce generates responses that will inform teachers whether—and to what degree—students have attained the knowledge and skills indicated in a standard. To achieve this (and avoid merely selecting activities that appear fun and yield little proof of mastery), teachers create a clear standards-based task. They can provide students with options from figure 2.3 to offer choices for showing understanding. For example, teachers might assign this task:

Choose a historical figure from the American Revolution. Write a eulogy, newspaper article, or letter someone would write to him or her. In your writing, use specific details from texts to describe what this individual accomplished, obstacles this person faced, and ways he or she overcame them.

Student-generated assessment—a potentially valuable but underutilized form of assessment—involves students self-selecting ways in which they can demonstrate what they learn. To conduct this type of assessment, teachers lead a brainstorming

A	B	C	D
Academic notebook entries	Bibliography	Cartoons	Descriptive writing (of a setting, character, individual, event, and so on)
Advertisement (newspaper, TV, magazine, or radio script)	Billboard	Case study	Dictionary with pictures
Advice column	Biography	Catalog	Documentary script
All-about book	Blog	Chapter	Drama
Allegory	Book	Character sketch	
Alphabet book	Book cover	Comedy (play or script)	
Anecdote	Brochure	Comic book	
Annotation	Bulletin board	Convention program	
Announcement	Business plan	Creation myth	
Argumentation essay or speech		Critique	
Autobiography			

E	F	G	H
Editorial	Fable	Glossary	Handbook
Essay	Fairy tale	Graphic organizer	Headlines
Eulogy	Fantasy story	Graph with analysis	Historical fiction
Exit slip	Feature story	Greek myth	How-to paper
Explanatory essay or paper (how-to)		Greeting card	
Eyewitness account			

I	J–K	L	M
Informational essay or report	Job descriptions	Lab report	Magazine article or layout
Interview (questions or complete script)	Journal entries (for example, personal or historical accounts)	Labeled diagram	Manual
Invitation (personal or business)		Laws for organization	Memoir
		Legal document	Menu
		Legend	Multimedia project
		Lesson plan	Mural
		Letter (personal or business; résumé cover letter)	Mystery story

		Letter of recommendation Letter to the editor List Literary critique or analysis Lyrics	Myth (creation, Native American, or Greek)
N	**O**	**P**	**Q–R**
Narrative Nature log News story Newsletter Newspaper Notes (Cornell or observational) Novel Novella	Obituary Opinion piece Organization bylaws, or vision or mission statement Outline	Pamphlet Parody Pattern book Personal narrative Petition Poem Political cartoon Portfolio Poster Pourquoi tale PowerPoint, Keynote, or Prezi Press release Program	Questions and answers Reader's theater Recipe Research report or project Résumé Review of a book, movie, experiment, or presentation
S	**T–U**	**V**	**W–Z**
Satire Science fiction Scrapbook (annotated) Short story Song lyrics Speech Storyboard Summary	TED Talk or television script Timeline Travelogue Trickster tale	Venn diagram	Written response

Source: Adapted from Glass & Marzano, 2018, p. 74.

Figure 2.3: Writing assessment options from A to Z.

session in which they ask students to generate a list of options that will show their understanding of a particular topic. Or, teachers can provide students with choices to support them in this endeavor by reminding them of formative assessments they've completed this year or in previous years. As support, teachers can also pull suggestions from figure 2.3 (page 45). The idea to convey to students is that they can demonstrate understanding in a way that they feel resonates with them and provides an opportunity to highlight what they have come to learn. For example, in a lesson focusing on the causes and effects of a historical event, some students might elect to annotate a text by underlining the causes and effects and using the margin to explain what they marked. Others might create or complete a graphic organizer showing the causes and effects of the event. And some might prefer to write a short essay to show awareness of the skill or use technology in some way. This type of formative assessment promotes self-agency and engagement as students determine the best way to provide evidence of their learning.

Selected-Response, Constructed-Response, and Performance Assessments

Sometimes teachers format an assessment by posing multiple-choice, matching, fill-in-the-blank, and true-or-false prompts that ask students to select an answer from a provided list. These *selected-response* assessments allow students to display knowledge of facts, main ideas, and basic skills that involve one correct answer, and they are obtrusive since teachers interrupt instruction to administer them. Students can take these assessments quickly, and teachers score them easily to obtain a broad overview of foundational information students know and don't know. However, with these assessments, students can sometimes guess the answer, and they are not designed for students to demonstrate higher-level understanding (thinking at higher DOK levels). Therefore, teachers may couple selected response with other methods to gain a full impression of students' capabilities.

Students can complete formal selected-response items with pencil and paper or electronically and submit them for teachers to assess. Additionally, teachers can engage students informally by posing a selected-response question and asking students to respond on mini-whiteboards or with hand signals (thumbs or fingers). For thumb signals, teachers present a prompt, and students display thumbs-up to indicate *yes* or *true*, or thumbs-down to indicate *no* or *false*. For finger signals, teachers provide a key to show what each number—one, two, three, or even four fingers—means, and students respond accordingly for each prompt. For both hand and finger signals, students make a fist to signify *I am not sure*.

Figure 2.4 features two variations of selected-response items our fourth-grade team used for dialogue mechanics. As a subsequent assessment option for the first example in the figure, students may revise any incorrect items using proper writing conventions. Since grammar and conventions should not be taught in isolation, these examples originate from a complex text at the center of instruction, *Esperanza Rising* by Pam Muñoz Ryan (2000).

Example 1: Thumbs-Up or Thumbs-Down
Thumbs-up = Correct mechanics   **Thumbs-down** = Incorrect mechanics   **Fist** = I am not sure.
a. "When I get to California, I am going to work for the railroad," said Miguel, looking anxiously toward the horizon.   b. "I'm thirsty. Are they selling juice in the other car?" asked Esperanza.   c. Mama tried not to smile. She whispered back, "It is all right, Esperanza, because now we are peasants, too."   d. "A fire destroyed everything." She and her mother have come to work, like the rest of us said Miguel.   e. Confused, Isabel added, "Esperanza's nice. Her papa died."   f. Well, my father died, too, said Marta before he came to this country, "he fought in the Mexican revolution against people like her father who owned all the land".
Example 2: Finger Signals
One finger = Beginning speaker tag   **Two fingers** = End speaker tag   **Three fingers** = Middle speaker tag   **Fist** = I am not sure.
a. "¿De veras?" asked Isabel.   b. "Yes, it's the truth," said Esperanza, staring at the ceiling that someone had covered with newspaper and cardboard.   c. Then she said, "I am still rich, Isabel. We will only be here until Abuelita is well enough to travel."   d. "Where did all the food come from?" asked Esperanza.   e. "Esperanza," said Mama, "you and Isabel will be watching the babies while the rest of us work."   f. Esperanza took a deep breath and said weakly, "I can learn."

Source for quotes: Ryan, 2000, pp. 74, 77, 97, 105, 107, 115.

Figure 2.4: Selected-response active-participation example for dialogue mechanics.

Broadly speaking, unlike selected-response items—which have students choose a clear-cut answer to an objective prompt—*constructed-response* items require students to respond to open-ended tasks. As the name denotes, this format requires students to construct either a relatively short response or an expanded response without the aid of suggestions or choices like in selected-response items. In this regard, teachers can better gauge students' understanding since their responses are more extensive and not relegated to choosing from among a predetermined list of options. Teachers can make constructed-response items more straightforward for students by asking them to produce just a one- or two-sentence answer. Or, teachers can assign a more involved constructed-response activity by asking students, for example, to make a graphic organizer or an outline; write a summary or descriptive setting, as mentioned earlier under Unobtrusive, Obtrusive, and Student-Generated Assessments (page 41); or write to explain steps in a process.

Constructed-response assessments can span one to even three days of fifty-minute periods. For a more comprehensive task requiring three days, students examine, read, watch, or listen to a stimulus on the first day, such as a text, graphic, short video, or audio clip. The next day, they plan how they will respond by perhaps outlining or brainstorming. On the third day, they craft a response to reveal how well they can apply knowledge and skills in general and how well they can construct meaning and demonstrate understanding from the stimulus. In another scenario, students both plan and write a response on day two. As well, it can all be completed within one day with or without a stimulus. Unlike selected-response items, which teachers can expeditiously score and ascertain a right or wrong answer, students' constructed responses take more time to score, as they are more subjective and require agreement about interpreting the rubric used for scoring purposes. Students who struggle with writing will probably have difficulty accurately revealing what they have learned. We write more about responding to students who struggle in chapter 5 (page 117).

Performance assessments are more complex than the others, span a few days or a week or more, measure multiple learning outcomes, and promote critical thinking. Teachers gather extensive evidence about not only a product or performance that students complete, but also the process used to achieve the finished piece. Like constructed-response items, performance assessments are scored using a rubric. Students find this type of assessment highly engaging, as it allows them to apply knowledge and skills representative of what is happening in the real world. They can work collaboratively but ultimately generate individual products.

According to the Stanford Center for Assessment, Learning, and Equity (SCALE, 2015), a performance assessment requires students to think, produce a product, and demonstrate learning through work authentic to the discipline or real world, and it incorporates four key principles.

1. A performance assessment targets and improves knowledge and higher-order-thinking skills so, ultimately, students can apply what they learn to a novel situation (a hallmark of other assessments, as well). Additionally, it is an assessment *for* and *as* learning.

2. As students work on the assessment, they participate in myriad activities that present inherent learning opportunities. In this regard, they are assessments *for* and *as* learning. Teachers can collect information about the effectiveness of their teaching and can adjust, as needed, while students engage in various tasks.

3. A performance assessment is intrinsically linked to curriculum and instruction, rather than issued as an independent experience at the end of a unit.

4. The process students engage in while producing their products for a performance assessment presents a learning-by-doing situation.

Running Records and Reading Fluency Checks

To investigate the distinct literacy strengths and needs of individual students, in addition to collecting data about standards, teachers can conduct *running records*, an assessment designed by Marie M. Clay (1993). Fountas and Pinnell (2001), in their book *Guiding Readers and Writers, Grades 3–6*, reference running records as a way to observe students' oral reading behavior by learning about their processing strategies. These individually administered assessments monitor a student's reading progress and serve as an ongoing measure of oral-reading capabilities. To conduct a running record, teachers record words students correctly and incorrectly read in real time as students read a text aloud. For each word a student reads accurately, the teacher records a checkmark on a blank form. When students mispronounce words or say other miscues, teachers enter a code that indicates the type of error. Afterward, teachers analyze the marks, look for patterns, and make instructional decisions regarding reading instruction.

With ongoing running records, teachers monitor reading factors that affect comprehension, such as the students' strategy use, rate, accuracy, errors, and ability to self-monitor. From there, "the analysis of running records should have a major impact on the teaching decisions the teacher makes while responding to and helping extend the beginning reader's literacy learning" (Fried, 2013, p. 5). Running records are not always the mainstay in fourth- or fifth-grade classrooms that they are in grades K–3; however, teachers find conducting them valuable for upper elementary students who fail to meet standards and need to increase their rate of development as readers in all content areas.

Also critical to assessment in fourth and fifth grade are frequent checks on reading fluency. In emphasizing the distinct connection between fluency and comprehension, John J. Pikulski and David J. Chard (2005) offer this definition of *fluency*: "Reading fluency refers to efficient, effective word recognition skills that permit a reader to construct the meaning of text. Fluency is also manifested in accurate, rapid, expressive oral reading and is applied during, and makes possible, silent reading comprehension" (p. 510).

To make meaning of the complex curricular materials used throughout instruction and assessment and master rigorous reading standards, fluent reading is essential. Additionally, as students transition to more independent reading, accuracy and automaticity become even more critical. When a student's "cognitive capacity is drained by the processing of decoding words, little or no capacity is available for the attention-demanding process of constructing and responding to the meaning of a text" (Pikulski & Chard, 2005, p. 511). By assessing and monitoring fluency frequently throughout the school year, teachers keep a close eye on students' reading progress and use the formative data to design reading instruction and corrective instruction that bolster essential reading skills with the goal of building fluent and confident readers.

The Journey of Assessments

The field of assessment presents a vast amount of information, much of which this chapter covers. But for a more in-depth treatment, consider reading any of the following additional resources on designing quality-driven assessments. You might participate in a professional book study with team members and conduct a jigsaw activity. After or while reading a particular book, come together to discuss highlights with each other.

  ▸ *Design in Five: Essential Phases to Create Engaging Assessment Practice* by Nicole Dimich Vagle (2015)

▶ *Simplifying Common Assessment: A Guide for Professional Learning Communities at Work* by Kim Bailey and Chris Jakicic (2017)

▶ *Common Formative Assessments 2.0: How Teacher Teams Intentionally Align Standards, Instruction, and Assessment* by Larry Ainsworth and Donald Viegut (2015)

▶ *Designing and Assessing Educational Objectives: Applying the New Taxonomy* by Robert J. Marzano and John S. Kendall (2008)

▶ *Teacher-Made Assessments: How to Connect Curriculum, Instruction, and Student Learning* by Christopher R. Gareis and Leslie W. Grant (2015)

The assessments teachers and teams institute and administer—whether formal or informal, obtrusive or unobtrusive—are only part of the assessment journey. Throughout a unit, teachers repeatedly and continuously assess and collect data to determine how well students grasp specific skills and concepts. This informs their next steps in instruction and the feedback they give to students so that students can progress in their learning against a target. So how can teachers choreograph assessment and instruction?

As a concrete example, consider figure 2.5 (page 52). Notice how this adapted sample from Kildeer Countryside Community Consolidated School District 96, a K–8 district in Buffalo Grove, Illinois, uses the notion of summative assessment to reflect an iterative process. Rather than call the end-of-unit assessment a *summative* assessment, the district elected to use *formative* to indicate that teachers can use the information they glean from the culminating assessment to formatively further students' learning. Through this lens, assessment is a continuum—a recurrent cycle of instructing and assessing. Frequently administering a variety of assessments throughout the life span of a unit, particularly those formative in nature, correlates to student achievement (Marzano, 2006). Therefore, devising and committing to a continuum like the one in figure 2.5 will hold teachers and teams accountable to continuously gauge to what degree students are mastering standards, then act accordingly.

In figure 2.5, the horizontal timeline from the circle on the far left to the one on the far right represents assessments within one cycle or unit of instruction. Each circle reflects a different type of assessment that teachers administer throughout the unit to monitor individual and whole-class student progress both formally and informally. Although the diagram includes four circles, the instructional cycle certainly is not limited to just that number of assessments. Specifically, the second circle indicates several formative classroom assessments—obtrusive, unobtrusive,

PLC critical question 1:
What is it we want our students to learn?

*Team should engage in the pre-unit protocol (PREP) before beginning the unit of instruction.

PLC critical question 2:
How will we know if each student has learned it?

Assessment Continuum and Data Analysis: Repeating Cycle for Units of Instruction

Optional preassessment with data conversation

Data-driven instruction

Formative classroom assessments

Data-driven instruction

During-unit common formative assessments with data conversation

Data-driven instruction

End-of-unit common formative assessment with data conversation

Preassessment
- Administered at least one to two weeks in advance
- Used to determine what students already know to tailor the instructional unit plan and differentiate to meet specific student needs
- May or may not be common

Formative Classroom Assessments
- Administered daily
- Used to make decisions in the moment or day to day (checklists, observations, conferences, and so on)
- May or may not be common

During-Unit Common Formative Assessments
- Administered during the unit of instruction within a defined window
- Used to check in on student progress toward mastery of essential learning outcomes
- Are common at the team or district level

End-of-Unit Common Formative Assessment
- Administered at the end of a unit of instruction within a defined window
- Used to assess students' current level of mastery after a significant amount of instruction
- Is common at the district level

PLC critical question 3:
How will we respond when some students don't learn it?

PLC critical question 4:
How can we extend the learning for students who have demonstrated proficiency?

Source: © 2016 Adapted from Kildeer Countryside Community Consolidated School District 96, Buffalo Grove, Illinois.

Figure 2.5: Example assessment continuum.

and student-generated—such as exit slips, observational data, student conference data, quick writes, journal entries, graphic organizers, or other artifacts of student work. In fact, a true depiction of a particular unit continuum may have six, eight, or even ten (or more!) assessment circles on the timeline. When teachers check in on student learning, they accumulate and examine data to monitor progress and respond in effective ways so they continually promote student growth.

Between the circles on the continuum, the data that teachers collect from each prior assessment drive daily literacy and standards-based instruction. From data, teachers individually and with their teams can identify which students need additional support and which ones are ready to extend their learning. They then proceed to make informed instructional decisions, such as reteaching, introducing new information, scaffolding, increasing the rigor of tasks, or giving students additional opportunities to practice skills. (See chapter 5, page 117, for more information on responding to student data.) This continuous cycle of assessing and instructing ensures that each student receives precisely what he or she needs to progress toward mastery.

Even the end-of-unit assessment is used formatively, since teachers' work to support every student in mastering grade-level standards is never complete. Teacher teams may have taught the unit over the course of several weeks; however, if some students have not demonstrated mastery, teachers and teams must still discuss and find ways to provide differentiated support—hence the truly cyclical nature of an assessment continuum.

Literacy Assessment Considerations

Assessments are a steady and frequent factor in all effective instructional units, and each content area has unique considerations for evaluating students' understanding. A focus on enhancing students' literacy skills can play a role in any assessment. In mathematics, for example, grades 4–5 teachers may gauge students' learning by collecting responses to a word problem. For social studies, teachers can ascertain students' understanding of the main idea and key details of historical events through graphic organizers. In science, teachers can determine how well students follow lab instructions and guides to foster hands-on learning and experimentation. When designing and scoring an assessment, teachers pay attention to various factors, such as lengths and types of texts used as the basis for a response, time parameters, and so forth.

When crafting assessments focused on reading and writing in different content areas, teachers make decisions about the lengths of texts students read for assessment purposes since they can experience both shorter and longer works. Teachers should tailor the qualities of a well-written assessment to the learning standards being measured, which can include complex text of various lengths. Specifically, in states that have adopted the Common Core State Standards:

> shorter, challenging texts that elicit close reading and re-reading are provided regularly at each grade. . . . Novels, plays, and other extended full-length readings are also provided with opportunities for close reading. Students should also be required to read texts of a range of lengths—for a variety of purposes—including several longer texts each year. (Coleman & Pimentel, 2012, p. 4)

This same expectation appears in other state documents, such as Virginia's standards of learning for grades 5–12: "Teachers should introduce students to longer, more complex texts both on grade level and above grade level" (Virginia Department of Education, 2017). Although these documents include secondary-level students, they still apply in grades 4–5. Some reading assessments are based on students' demonstrating an understanding of longer works, such as a chapter book, whereas other assessments may only necessitate the reading of a poem, a pair of poems, a short complex text, or an excerpt from a longer literary work. Additionally, teachers must consider the text used as the basis for a response and whether the task is meant to measure reading or writing standards, or both. We touch on this assessment consideration in Discuss Options for Complex Texts (page 80).

Students need to be aware of the exact expectations of a writing task and be taught how to interpret what teachers ask them to do. Do they demonstrate an understanding of the content that they read and use textual evidence? What type of writing are they to produce—expository (such as an opinion or informational essay) or narrative? Or, are they writing to show they can adhere to a genre's characteristic elements and structure, such as writing a realistic fiction piece or a type of poem? Teachers can ask students to practice reading prompts and looking at key verbs (such as *explain*, *tell*, or *convince*) that give clues to the purpose of writing, which indicates text type and structure. For example, if teachers ask students to convince a reader of something, that would mean an opinion piece, which includes a claim, reasons, and evidence.

Teachers need to match the task with the amount of time they provide students to complete it. Some assessments ask students to respond in an on-demand situation within a compact period. Other assessments demand an extended time for completion as students learn and experience the steps of the writing process; and there are assessments that fall somewhere in between these time demands. To meet the rigor of priority learning standards, students must employ several skills and strategies, often simultaneously, across literacy-focused strands. Tasks that align with the complex processes of reading and writing, such as researching a topic to write an information essay or identifying a theme of a narrative, typically take longer to complete than those that don't require these core literacy skills. To determine a theme, for example, students first establish the setting, understand characters' roles and motivations, track the plot, and examine the interplay among these literary elements. Through this analysis, students begin to see a theme emerge, which they verify as the story unfolds and eventually resolves. Grasping and implementing the reading strategies that aid in comprehension can understandably be time-intensive. Add on a writing task for students to explain their understanding of the reading—and to do so with grammar and conventions intact—and the number of skills teachers are assessing multiplies.

Another assessment reality within literacy is the time it takes for teachers to score students' writing. You may have heard it said (or even said it yourself), "It is so much easier to assess students in mathematics because there's one right answer!" Additionally, the subjective nature of scoring certain skills—for example, *using sensory details to depict a character* or *constructing events to build suspense*—can present a challenge. Susan M. Brookhart (2013) refers to these types of items as *high inference*; they require assessors to make a decision and draw a conclusion about how to interpret criteria descriptions.

Having precisely scaled rubrics with scoring criteria and descriptions of each performance level addresses this type of subjectivity; these rubrics provide specific information not only for teacher teams but also for students and parents. In addition, participating in a collaborative-scoring process with grade-level teammates and establishing anchor papers—examples of student responses at each level of performance—will lead to more accuracy and consistency among teams when assessing and reporting on literacy tasks. (We discuss these topics in chapter 4, page 93.)

Assessment provides a clear snapshot of every student's progress at multiple points in an instructional unit. To demonstrate proficiency in the multifaceted areas of literacy, students need continuous practice to read and write well. As a result, teachers must purposefully conduct myriad assessments tied to standards. When teachers collect and score the assessments (see chapter 4), they provide their charges with timely, individualized feedback (see chapter 7, page 153) to help students progress. Assessments and data collection (see chapter 5, page 117) are invaluable because, without them, a teacher could not confidently identify the students struggling with specific concepts or the exact skills that present a problem. Similarly, the teacher would be unaware of those students who could benefit from learning extension. Although it may take time to score students' products in literacy, circling line items on a rubric to indicate students' proficiency at a point in time provides feedback and shows where they need to go next in their learning. Coupling rubrics with anchor papers concretizes the language on a rubric so students see examples of different levels, striving to aim higher on line items that reflect skills not yet mastered.

EXERCISE

Consider Assessment Types and Purposes

With your collaborative team, brainstorm and list various formative and summative assessments you might conduct for your unit. After reading about learning progressions in chapter 3 (page 59), return to this list and use it to identify specific literacy assessments that align with learning targets. For now, you should have a heightened awareness of the types of assessments and a healthy list of options to add to what you already conduct.

Use the following questions to guide this exercise.

★ What types of unobtrusive assessments can we conduct in our classrooms?

★ What formative and summative assessments can we administer to gain an accurate picture of what students can do?

★ What types of formal and informal data can we collect during instruction?

★ What does our journey of assessment look like, and what adjustments might we make to optimize data collection?

Summary

With unwrapped priority standards, knowledge items, key skills, and levels of rigor determined via the PREP process, teacher teams are well positioned to begin determining which assessments they will conduct. For each learning target, they can start to decide which types of assessments are ideal for appraising students' proficiency. With an understanding of assessment options in place, teams can turn their attention to how they will teach the standards they've identified as priority.

In the next chapter, teams create a learning progression to map out the stepping-stones of knowledge and skills that students must acquire on their journey toward mastery of both content-area and literacy standards. *What will students need to learn first? How will teachers build on that knowledge? And what data will they collect along the way to determine if students learned the knowledge and skills necessary to eventually demonstrate proficiency?* Continue reading to grasp the importance of learning progressions and how they steer effective instruction and assessment.

CHAPTER 3

Create a Learning Progression to Guide Instruction and Assessment

During the PREP process articulated in chapter 1 (page 9), teams unwrap priority standards and determine the specific learning targets (skills) that they need to teach. As teams analyze and discuss their specific learning targets, they use Webb's (1997, 1999) Depth of Knowledge levels to distinguish the targets that represent simple skills or concepts from those that are more complex for students to understand or perform. In doing so, they naturally begin organizing the knowledge and skills into an instructional sequence. This work sets the stage for creating a *learning progression*, which James Popham (2011) defines as:

> a sequenced set of subskills and bodies of knowledge (*building blocks*) a teacher believes students must master en route to mastering a demanding cognitive skill of significant curricular importance (a *target curricular aim*). . . . [It is a] formal, thought-through outline of the *key content of instruction*— what's pivotal to be taught and mastered, and in what sequence. As such, it's a foundation for sound instruction and effective planning. It's also the backbone of a sensible, *planned* approach to formative assessment. (p. 10)

By working together to sequence knowledge items and skills into a clearly articulated continuum of learning, teams essentially map out the step-by-step journey students will take toward proficiency. With rigor in mind, teachers list knowledge and skills in the order they will eventually teach them—from rudimentary to more complex—working up the proverbial ladder to mastery of the standard.

In developing learning progressions, which are each guided by one or more complementary priority standards, teachers catalog and design target-aligned assessments for students to demonstrate their understanding of knowledge and skills. The team-compiled list of myriad assessments from chapter 2 (page 37) completes and fortifies the learning progression. Then, teams plan high-quality instruction to move students forward in their learning.

This chapter provides a template your team can use to develop literacy-focused learning progressions for the priority standards your team has identified. We then use a literacy-based example to outline a six-step process that helps teams establish the foundational knowledge and skills the priority standards require. Finally, the chapter concludes with a section on how to set an instructional timeline for teaching learning progressions and assessing students' level of mastery in a unit.

A Template for Designing Learning Progressions

Teachers, and sometimes even collaborative teams, often neglect or overlook learning progressions as an essential step in instruction and assessment design. Despite the collaborative nature of a PLC culture, teacher teams often dedicate time to unwrap their standards, but jump to assessment writing without working together to determine the continuum of *how* learning develops as students strive to master a specific target. However, when teachers develop learning progressions, they can use them to help design assessments that emphasize literacy, pinpoint students' performance, and choreograph their instruction at each step toward meeting a standard. Doing this sets the stage for differentiated instruction.

For those students who are missing essential building blocks, including those who have low proficiency with essential literacy skills, teachers may need to backtrack along the continuum and reteach a concept or offer remediation on a particular skill. In other instances, students might already possess the knowledge and skills needed to advance further on the continuum, prompting teachers to increase the pace of instruction and provide extended learning opportunities for a target. In both situations, assessments guided by the learning progression provide data that allow teachers to appropriately match instruction to learners' specific needs (Heritage, 2008).

As a tool for designing a learning progression that drives instruction and assessment choices, teams use a template, such as the completed example for the dialogue unit featured in figure 3.1. (See page 237 for a blank reproducible version of this figure.) Notice how it establishes priority standards and then provides the option

Priority Standards:

- Use dialogue to develop experiences and events or show the responses of characters to situations. (W.4.3b [A])
- Use correct capitalization. (L.4.2a)
- Use commas and quotation marks to mark direct speech and quotations from a text. (L.4.2b)
- Choose words and phrases to convey ideas precisely. (L.4.3a)

Learning Progression Steps	Learning Progression Components	Assessments
Step 9	**Priority Standards** Use dialogue to develop experiences and events or show the responses of characters to situations. Use correct capitalization. Use commas and quotation marks to mark direct speech and quotations from a text. Choose words and phrases to convey ideas precisely.	***Common Summative Assessment: Constructed-Response Assessment (Dialogue Writing)** Write a final version of purposeful dialogue passages that develop a plot or show characters' reactions; include verbs that depict how characters speak, feel, or act; use proper mechanics. (Summative and formal)
Step 8	**Learning Target (Skill)** Use words and phrases to convey ideas in a dialogue tag.	**Short Constructed-Response Assessment (List)** Add to list of verbs and categorize them; use the list as a resource for writing dialogue tags. (Formative and formal)
Step 7	**Knowledge** Dialogue tag verbs provide description to indicate how characters speak to one another. (Connects to supporting standard L.4.6)	**Constructed-Response Assessment (Dramatic Enactment)** Find and circle dialogue passages from complex text where the author uses strong dialogue tag verbs. With a partner, act out a few of these passages using the dialogue tag verbs as a guide to show how characters speak to one another. Record verbs in academic notebooks or journals. (Formative and formal) **Selected-Response Assessment (Mini-Whiteboards)** Using mini-whiteboards, write dialogue tag verbs and chorally identify each verb. Record verbs in academic notebooks or journals. (Formative and formal)

Figure 3.1: Unit learning progression and assessments—Dialogue.   continued →

Step 6	**Learning Target (Skill)** Use proper conventions when writing dialogue.	**Constructed-Response Assessment (Dialogue Writing)** Revise dialogue passages within your story to ensure proper use of conventions. (Formative and formal)
Step 5	**Knowledge** Types of dialogue (or speaker) tags—beginning, middle, end, or no tag Punctuation and capitalization rules for the different types of dialogue or speaker tags	**Short Constructed-Response Assessment (Exit Slip)** Using proper conventions, write three sentences of dialogue: one with a beginning dialogue tag, one with a middle dialogue tag, and one with an end dialogue tag. Label each sentence appropriately as *beginning tag*, *middle tag*, and *end tag*. (Formative and formal)
Step 4	**Learning Target (Skill)** Write dialogue to develop a plot or to show characters' responses to situations.	***Common Formative Assessment: Constructed-Response Assessment (Dialogue Writing)** Write dialogue passages throughout a story draft that develop the plot or show characters' responses to situations. (Formative and formal)
Step 3	**Knowledge** Purpose and function of dialogue Brainstorming is a form of planning—an initial step in the writing process. (Connects to supporting standard W.4.5)	**Teacher Conference** Meet with the teacher to show your plans for inserting meaningful dialogue into your story draft, and provide a rationale. (Formative and informal) **Constructed-Response Assessment (Brainstorming)** Prepare for writing dialogue passages by brainstorming a plan for where to insert dialogue and for what purpose. (Formative and formal)
Step 2	**Knowledge** Dialogue is meaningful and serves a purpose—to develop the plot or to show characters' responses to situations.	**Constructed-Response Assessment (Annotation)** Read dialogue and the surrounding text, and underline what you think is meaningful. Explain the purpose of what you underlined, and provide your opinion about why it is important. (Formative and formal)

			Selected-Response Assessment (Hand Signals)
			Determine the purpose of each dialogue passage your teacher reads. If it moves the plot forward, signal with one finger. If it reveals characters' responses to situations, signal with two fingers. If you're unsure, make a fist. (Formative and informal)
Step 1		Knowledge Purpose and function of dialogue	Selected-Response Assessment (Voting Techniques) Determine to what degree a dialogue passage is important in developing the plot. For each passage your teacher reads, raise one hand if the dialogue is not very important, raise two hands if it is important, or stand up if it is extremely important. (Formative and informal)

*Grade-level teams will analyze and discuss data collected from common formative and summative assessments.

Source for standards: NGA & CCSSO, 2010.

of identifying a learning target (skill), knowledge, or both for each step in the progression. This indicates that each learning progression is distinctive because teams customize it for specific purposes.

This example is based on the integration of the following fourth-grade priority standards introduced in chapter 1's PREP template (figure 1.1, page 13).

▸ **W.4.3b (A):** "Use dialogue to develop experiences and events or show the responses of characters to situations."

▸ **L.4.2a:** "Use correct capitalization."

▸ **L.4.2b:** "Use commas and quotation marks to mark direct speech and quotations from a text."

▸ **L.4.3a:** "Choose words and phrases to convey ideas precisely" (NGA & CCSSO, 2010).

The common summative assessment linked to these standards asks that students write meaningful, purposeful dialogue with proper conventions and well-chosen words (also sometimes phrases) to convey ideas in the speaker tags. Note that in primary grades, many learning progressions address one standard. In upper elementary and beyond, sometimes teams deem it necessary to combine aligned standards. Our learning progression example reflects the integrated approach of the cited standards due to their natural interconnectedness and for instruction and assessment purposes. At another time in the unit, the team would also create a separate learning progression for RL.4.1: "Refer to details and examples in a text when explaining what the text says explicitly and when drawing inferences from the text" (NGA & CCSSO, 2010).

Although this example progression features nine steps, teams might elect to add or remove rows as necessary for their specific priority standards. As alluded to earlier, the arrow in the template reflects an upward trajectory since it mimics the graduated order in which teachers present instruction.

Ultimately, teams design a learning progression for each priority standard or a group of standards as in our fourth-grade example. They might choose to include supporting standards, as well.

In the following sections, we explain the process steps we recommend to develop a learning progression, including ideas for assessments, and suggestions for your team to build one.

Suggested Learning Progression Process

With so many options for and approaches to instruction, teachers might wonder, *How will we know that we got it right? Is our sequence for instruction correct?* According to W. James Popham (2007), with few exceptions, "there is no single, universally accepted and absolutely correct learning progression underlying any given high-level curricular aim" (p. 83). Popham (2007) argues that separate teams of committed educators can unwrap identical standards and generate diverse learning progressions, and that is perfectly acceptable. Some teams are new to creating learning progressions and don't feel as confident with their final product. Indeed, teams continue revising learning progressions over time. What matters most is that when collaborative teams take the time to think deeply about learning and discuss each learning target's nuances, it benefits students more than not making the attempt. Therefore, read this section for guidance to create a learning progression suitable for students at your site. If your team uses a purchased literacy program that includes a prepared progression of lessons, review the document together to ensure that the program addresses the unwrapped priority standards and aligns with the true intentions of the unit your team plans to teach. If it doesn't, make the necessary adjustments to achieve your team's predetermined learning outcomes.

With the completed PREP template and a blank version of the learning progression and assessments template (pages 234 and 237) accessible—plus any accompanying resources to support the unit, such as textbooks, complex text, and internet links—the team begins to construct a learning progression. We recommend the following process; however, teams can choose to reverse steps 2 and 3 if that appears more prudent as they are devising their learning progressions.

1. Select priority standards.

2. Sequence the learning targets (skills).

3. Sequence the knowledge items.

4. Determine all assessments.

5. Identify and design common assessments.

6. Discuss options for complex texts.

Read further to understand our fourth-grade team's thinking behind each step of creating the dialogue learning progression we used to develop assessment ideas. Additionally, we include our team's discussion of possible complex texts to use within instruction and ways to research other text options suitable for this grade.

Select Priority Standards

Recall from earlier in this chapter that, depending on needs, teams may select just one priority standard to develop a learning progression, or they may choose several interconnected priority standards. When our fourth-grade team discussed which priority standards about writing dialogue to include in our learning progression, we acknowledged that dialogue comprises many skills that work in concert with one another. Ultimately, students will incorporate dialogue into a well-developed, logically sequenced story they write. However, dialogue in and of itself requires a combination of priority standards. Therefore, we decided to group together those reflecting the content of the dialogue (to develop plot or show characters' responses to situations), the manner in which characters speak (verbs used in the tags), and as the conventions required when using dialogue (capitalization, commas, quotation marks).

Since a learning progression builds in sophistication to meet the curricular outcome of one or more priority (and likely some supporting) standards, teams record their selected standard or standards in the top row of the template to represent the overarching goal. They input it again on the top rung of the learning progression ladder (the last step in students' learning) because an eventual end-of-unit summative assessment must align to it. Our fourth-grade team illustrates this top-level step for dialogue in figure 3.2 using dark gray shading. We will continue to expand on this figure over the rest of this chapter.

Priority Standards:

- Use dialogue to develop experiences and events or show the responses of characters to situations. (W.4.3b [A])
- Use correct capitalization. (L.4.2a)
- Use commas and quotation marks to mark direct speech and quotations from a text. (L.4.2b)
- Choose words and phrases to convey ideas precisely. (L.4.3a)

	Learning Progression Steps	Learning Progression Components	Assessments
	Step ____	**Priority Standards** Use dialogue to develop experiences and events or show the responses of characters to situations. Use correct capitalization. Use commas and quotation marks to mark direct speech and quotations from a text. Choose words and phrases to convey ideas precisely.	

Source for standards: NGA & CCSSO, 2010.

Figure 3.2: Establishing the priority standard for a learning progression.

Sequence the Learning Targets (Skills)

When the team approaches this learning progression within the dialogue unit, students will have produced their first story draft. With this established at the forefront of the conversation, the team can more accurately generate the steps within the learning progression that build to the integrated standards. In unwrapping them (see PREP template, figure 1.1, page 13), we identified three specific and aligned skills that represent learning targets inherent in each of the priority standards listed in figure 3.2.

1. Write dialogue to develop a plot or to show characters' responses to situations. (DOK level 2)

2. Use proper conventions when writing dialogue. (DOK level 1)

3. Use words and phrases to convey ideas in a dialogue tag. (DOK level 1)

To determine how to sequence these items, teachers engage in *backward planning* or *backward analysis*, a process that means beginning with the end goal in mind and then determining the steps necessary to reach it. Previously, the team assigned a DOK level to each skill. Teachers might be inclined to begin with DOK 1 and then graduate sequentially to more complex levels, although this isn't always the case (and is not the case here). Ultimately, our team applied a combination of all skills—along with addressing knowledge items—to aid students in writing dialogue within their original stories, a DOK 3 task.

In our unit, although the first learning target on the list focuses on students writing dialogue, which is DOK level 2, they accomplish this skill after they address knowledge items (explained in the next section). Doing so enables students to examine dialogue passages to determine their purpose. This analysis of published work prepares them for writing dialogue in their stories that moves the plot forward or reveals how characters react to situations. After they focus on the content of dialogue and write passages for their stories, they learn about proper writing mechanics and apply the skill related to dialogue conventions (the second and third items on our skills list). The team felt that homing in on the meaning and purpose of the dialogue first was beneficial; then students would concentrate on conventions. The team decided to teach strong verb usage in speaker tags last; this skill enhances the words and even phrases students use in their writing for when characters speak to one another.

Based on this analysis, we input these learning targets on the metaphorical ladder in the teaching order that we decided to follow, sequenced from the bottom up. Since learning targets represent crucial skills needed for mastering the priority standard, these rows are lightly shaded on the learning progression to indicate their significance, as shown in figure 3.3 (page 68).

Learning Progression Steps	Learning Progression Components	Assessments
Step ____	**Priority Standards** Use dialogue to develop experiences and events or show the responses of characters to situations. Use correct capitalization. Use commas and quotation marks to mark direct speech and quotations from a text. Choose words and phrases to convey ideas precisely.	
Step ____	**Learning Target (Skill)** Use words and phrases to convey ideas in a dialogue tag.	
Step ____	**Learning Target (Skill)** Use proper conventions when writing dialogue.	
Step ____	**Learning Target (Skill)** Write dialogue to develop a plot or to show characters' responses to situations.	

Figure 3.3: Learning progression work in progress—Learning targets.

The learning progression captured so far reflects a work in progress. At this point in the process, the team has yet to add any knowledge items, which are essential to assisting students to grasp skills. Once teams record all building blocks onto the template, they can review and look at it critically to settle on the exact number of learning progression line items, as well as the sequence. For this reason, wait to number the learning progression steps until team members agree with the order of all the learning targets and knowledge items. When working through the remaining steps, teams might decide to shuffle what they input in light of any new thinking or ideas. Constructing the progression using a shared electronic document assists with manipulating the entries to reorganize them or add and delete rows, as needed.

As stated earlier in the chapter, there is no ideal or prescribed learning progression associated with each priority standard. Teams can fashion it in various ways, so the key is to engage in discussion to arrive at a plan that supports your students and your team members' teaching styles.

Sequence the Knowledge Items

As a reminder, knowledge comprises facts, dates, people, places, examples, and vocabulary and terms—including concept words. Knowledge items reflect what students should know so that they can perform the skills (learning targets) we want them to acquire.

Because knowledge items indicate important steps on students' learning journey, teachers refer again to the PREP template (figure 1.1, page 13) and determine where to position the established items within the learning progression. Review figure 3.4 (page 71) to see how our team added knowledge items to the in-progress learning progression. Again, the learning targets remain shaded in light gray, while the knowledge items have no shading. To review, our team sequenced the learning targets (skills) in this way to reflect an order of teaching that leads to the priority standard of using dialogue to develop experiences or events or show the responses of characters to situations.

The first two knowledge items (the bottom two rows of the figure) involve students examining published work to discover the purpose and function dialogue serves as well as to what degree it is meaningful to the narrative. Specifically, dialogue can fuel plot development and reveal the circumstances that arise. Dialogue can also expose characters' reactions to various situations, such as to a setting that lands them in the center of a conflict, or to interactions between characters, which might be contentious, puzzling, or touching. Reviewing conversations between characters within complex text—which doubles as mentor texts—will guide students as they write their own intentional and compelling dialogue. (See chapter 7, page 153, for a discussion about mentor texts.) Once they experience how authors integrate dialogue authentically, they can consider ways to use this narrative technique within their own stories, which signifies the third knowledge item moving up the ladder related to brainstorming. Note here that our team referenced this related supporting standard—W.4.5, "With guidance and support from peers and adults, develop and strengthen writing as needed by planning, revising, and editing" (NGA & CCSSO, 2010)—since brainstorming and conferring with teachers constitute aspects of the writing process. In addition, we added supporting standard L.4.6 regarding words and phrases since it aligns with choosing words and

Learning Progression Steps	Learning Progression Components	Assessments
Step ____	**Priority Standards** Use dialogue to develop experiences and events or show the responses of characters to situations. Use correct capitalization. Use commas and quotation marks to mark direct speech and quotations from a text. Choose words and phrases to convey ideas precisely.	
Step ____	**Learning Target (Skill)** Use words and phrases to convey ideas in a dialogue tag.	
Step ____	**Knowledge** Dialogue tag verbs provide description to indicate how characters speak to one another. (Connects to supporting standard L.4.6)	
Step ____	**Learning Target (Skill)** Use proper conventions when writing dialogue.	
Step ____	**Knowledge** Types of dialogue (or speaker) tags—beginning, middle, end, or no tag Punctuation and capitalization rules for the different types of dialogue or speaker tags	
Step ____	**Learning Target (Skill)** Write dialogue to develop a plot or to show characters' responses to situations.	
Step ____	**Knowledge** Purpose and function of dialogue Brainstorming is a form of planning—an initial step in the writing process. (Connects to supporting standard W.4.5)	

		Knowledge Dialogue is meaningful and serves a purpose—to develop the plot or to show characters' responses to situations.	
	Step ____		
	Step ____	**Knowledge** Purpose and function of dialogue	

Figure 3.4: Learning progression work in progress—Knowledge items.

phrases to convey ideas precisely (priority standard L.4.3a). Therefore, we adapted the standard and recorded it as a knowledge item. Together, these steps prepare students for writing dialogue.

The team then discussed the remaining knowledge items from the PREP process. After focusing on the dialogue content, we decided to address knowledge items for speaker tags (such as *he shouted, she replied,* or *they exclaimed*), their placement (before, in the middle, or at the end of the dialogue), and the mechanics of writing dialogue. Once teachers deliver instruction around these knowledge items, students can revise their dialogue to reflect what they've learned.

Lastly, the team planned to teach that the verbs used in speaker tags can add dimension to what characters say by showing reactions and revealing emotions, so we added the item about verbs to our learning progression. Since connecting literacy standards to a complex text is optimal, we use a mentor text to provide students with strong examples that illustrate these knowledge items regarding dialogue tag position and speaker tag verbs.

When perusing figure 3.4, notice the team's decisions to list the same knowledge item in steps 1 and 3 (bottom to top). As we discussed how the unit might unfold, we decided to launch it by inviting students to explore the purpose, function, and meaning of dialogue and then cycle back through areas more deeply to prepare them for the first learning target (step 4).

With this prerequisite knowledge in place to support learning targets, teachers can number the steps, as shown earlier in the completed figure 3.1 (page 61). This sequenced learning progression establishes a thoughtfully articulated and logical plan for undertaking the next stage of the learning progression—assessment design. Remember, however, that since a learning progression reflects the work of a particular team engaged in this process, another team implementing these same standards might decide to fashion the same unit in a different way.

Determine All Assessments

In the beginning of the chapter, we quoted Popham's (2008) definition of *learning progressions* as a sequenced set of subskills and bodies of knowledge, which we term *learning targets (skills)* and *knowledge items*, respectively. These components are what he refers to as *building blocks*:

> Each of the building blocks you identify . . . should be so unarguably important that a student's status regarding every building block must be and will be verified via formal or informal assessment. You are not trying to locate "nice to know" building blocks here. Rather, you are isolating "need to know" building blocks. (Popham, 2008, p. 37)

As detailed in chapter 2 (page 37), teachers use a variety of formative assessments to collect data on student progress that serve to drive instruction forward. They administer many of these check-ins through classroom obtrusive assessments, like asking students to complete exit slips, quick writes, or graphic organizers. They also unobtrusively formatively assess by observing students and listening to them as they participate in a group activity, engage in discussion with a partner, or contribute to a class discussion. At this point of the learning progression process, teams determine all assessments for each step on the ladder so students can demonstrate what they have learned. To accomplish this task, the teams return to the brainstormed list of formative and summative assessments that they generated as a result of the exercise at the end of chapter 2 (page 56).

For classroom assessments, individual teachers have the freedom to choose how they want to meet a particular skill or knowledge item. They might all plan an assessment together and issue the same one, but that is not mandatory. Individual teachers also decide how long to spend on a particular step since students in some classrooms might progress at a faster or slower pace than those in another. This exemplifies the flexibility—or loose aspect—of PLC culture. The tight, non-negotiable aspect of PLCs means that all members of a team must develop and issue common formative assessments, as well as a common summative assessment at the end of the learning progression. Typically, these common assessments are more formal, consisting of selected-response items, constructed-response items, a combination of both, or sometimes a performance assessment. Teams identify which assessments are common in the next step.

To design valid assessments for each learning progression step, teams must consider the level of rigor for the intended learning target and choose an assessment method that matches the cognitive demand of the learning. They take into account the knowledge items and design pertinent assessments to measure students' take-away of factual information, as well. For example, if teachers use only the selected-response format (multiple-choice and true-or-false items) to assess the learning target, *Describe the similarities and differences among different levels of government*, it wouldn't allow a teacher to confidently ascertain that students can describe what is similar and different about local, state, and federal government. Selected-response items could, however, uncover whether students can name these three levels of government and individuals who serve in office. But the selected-response format would be too narrow in giving students a proper avenue with which to demonstrate their understanding of the rigorous task this particular learning target requires. However, the constructed-response format could more aptly assess to what degree students can *describe* the similarities and differences of the government structure since this learning target necessitates providing a description. A combination of selected- and constructed-response items, or a constructed-response task alone, would allow students to paint a more exacting picture of their capabilities. Remember that an assessment is valid only if it measures what it is intended to measure; therefore, align the learning target's rigor with the assessment format.

In addition to designing a valid assessment, teachers must consider the reliability factor. Reliable assessments mean that teachers can trust that the results indicate which students have and have not reached proficiency based on the learning target an assessment is meant to gauge. In their book *Simplifying Common Assessment*, authors Bailey and Jakicic (2017) explain two aspects that contribute to reliability:

> The first is to make sure to include enough questions for each of the assessed learning targets. While there is no one piece of research that supplies the answer to how many questions this would be, most researchers suggest that at least three to four selected-response questions per learning target will eliminate lucky guessing (Gareis & Grant, 2008). For constructed-response questions, one well-written question should instill confidence in a team that it can decide on next steps. (p. 70)

The other reliability component involves writing the question or task in language accessible to students so they clearly understand what they are supposed to do. If the language in assessment directions hampers students, their misinterpretation can skew the results.

With the array of assessments in mind, the fourth-grade team decided which assessment types best reflect what students can show they learn for each building block. Some line items on the learning progression included two different assessments that teachers felt were necessary to scaffold instruction to teach knowledge or skills in an intentional way. To make this decision with your own team, ask and discuss the following questions.

- "What types and formats of assessments can we use from the list we generated earlier?"

- "What evidence will each assessment yield that will reveal whether students are achieving mastery?"

- "Do any assessments seem like candidates for a common assessment that we can flag and revisit to develop them as a team?"

Later, teachers use the assessments as a guide to find or design comprehensive lessons; additionally, they agree as a team what constitutes mastery for each assessment (see chapter 4, page 93). For now, peruse figure 3.5 to learn about which assessments our fourth-grade team chose for each knowledge item and learning target and its rationale for each chosen assessment. Teams do not need to write detailed explanations as reflected in the figure. However, some may choose this option so they can refer to this work as a reminder of their thinking when the time comes to design or revise assessments for validity and reliability. This is particularly helpful if teams meet and plan the unit long before teachers actually conduct it (perhaps during the summer) or if new teachers join the team throughout the year. As a reminder, read from the bottom rung up since this represents the order of teaching. Again, combining learning targets (skills) with knowledge items or knowledge items with each other—as in steps 3 and 5 in this example—allows teachers to assess them together. For example, when students complete an exit slip asking them to write and label sentences of dialogue with beginning, middle, and end tags, they show how well they can differentiate among types of dialogue tags as well as use proper dialogue mechanics for each version.

Identify and Design Common Assessments

With a list of assessments determined, the collaborative team reviews it and identifies which ones become the common formative assessments (CFAs) and common summative assessments (CSAs) that all grade-level teachers will administer at agreed-on steps in the learning progression. Although individual teachers issue formative assessments that provide timely feedback and valuable data to both teachers and students, these data alone "cannot become a catalyst for improvement" (DuFour, DuFour, Eaker, & Many, 2010, p. 184).

Learning Progression Steps	Learning Progression Components	Assessments
Step 9	**Priority Standards** Use dialogue to develop experiences and events or show the responses of characters to situations. Use correct capitalization. Use commas and quotation marks to mark direct speech and quotations from a text. Choose words and phrases to convey ideas precisely.	***Common Summative Assessment: Constructed-Response Assessment (Dialogue Writing)** Write a final version of purposeful dialogue passages that develop a plot or show characters' reactions; include verbs that depict how characters speak, feel, or act; use proper mechanics. (Summative and formal)
Optional explanation: This assessment reflects a synthesis of all the learning targets and knowledge items pertaining to dialogue.		
Step 8	**Learning Target (Skill)** Use words and phrases to convey ideas in a dialogue tag.	**Short Constructed-Response Assessment (List)** Add to list of verbs and categorize them; use the list as a resource for writing dialogue tags. (Formative and formal)
Optional explanation: Students examine published and student narrative samples and add salient verbs used in dialogue tags to the list from step 7. Then they categorize the words; for example, they might group their verbs under these four headings: (1) Answer (inquire, respond, reply); (2) Say (state, explain, comment); (3) Persuade (convince, encourage, plead, beg); and (4) Cry (scream, whimper, shriek, weep).		
Step 7	**Knowledge** Dialogue tag verbs provide description to indicate how characters speak to one another. (Connects to supporting standard L.4.6)	**Constructed-Response Assessment (Dramatic Enactment)** Find and circle dialogue passages from complex text where the author uses strong dialogue tag verbs. With a partner, act out a few of these passages using the dialogue tag verbs as a guide to show how characters speak to one another. Record verbs in academic notebooks or journals. (Formative and formal) **Selected-Response Assessment (Mini-Whiteboards)** Using mini-whiteboards, write dialogue tag verbs and chorally identify each verb. Record verbs in academic notebooks or journals. (Formative and formal)
Optional explanation: Teachers read aloud dialogue excerpts from a complex text and ask students to write on individual mini-whiteboards the verb used in each dialogue tag. Additionally, teachers can feature dialogue excerpts on an interactive whiteboard or document camera and ask students to chorally say on cue which word is the verb in each tag. Additionally, students identify passages in mentor text that contain descriptive dialogue tag verbs. To experience the effect these verbs have on the way characters interact, they participate in a dramatic enactment. If verbs are coupled with adverbs to further reflect how characters speak (such as *carefully explained* or *sharply questioned*), teachers point this out. Students then (or during these activities) record verbs in their academic notebooks or journals.		

continued →

Figure 3.5: Learning progression with rationale for assessments.

Learning Progression Steps	Learning Progression Components	Assessments
Step 6	**Learning Target (Skill)** Use proper conventions when writing dialogue.	**Constructed-Response Assessment (Dialogue Writing)** Revise dialogue passages within your story to ensure proper use of conventions. (Formative and formal)
	Optional explanation: Students return to the dialogue passages that they wrote (step 4) and revise them to ensure proper use of conventions for all types of dialogue—those with beginning, middle, and end tags. Teachers conduct writing conferences and arrange peer review sessions to provide feedback to students about their dialogue passages in preparation for their final version in the last step.	
Step 5	**Knowledge** Types of dialogue (or speaker) tags—beginning, middle, end, or no tag. Punctuation and capitalization rules for the different types of dialogue or speaker tags	**Short Constructed-Response Assessment (Exit Slip)** Using proper conventions, write three sentences of dialogue: one with a beginning dialogue tag, one with a middle dialogue tag, and one with an end dialogue tag. Label each sentence appropriately as "beginning tag," "middle tag," and "end tag." (Formative and formal)
	Optional explanation: After conducting lessons about the position of dialogue (or speaker) tags and the mechanics involved in writing dialogue, teachers instruct students to complete an exit slip. They collect students' slips and separate them into three piles: (1) those who have mastered this knowledge, (2) those who haven't, and (3) those who can somewhat apply the knowledge but still have some difficulty. The next day in class, teachers work with those who need support to gain proficiency.	
Step 4	**Learning Target (Skill)** Write dialogue to develop a plot or to show characters' responses to situations.	***Common Formative Assessment: Constructed-Response Assessment (Dialogue Writing)** Write dialogue passages throughout a story draft that develop the plot or show characters' responses to situations. (Formative and formal)
	Optional explanation: Students write purposeful dialogue at strategic points throughout their story drafts.	

Step 3

Knowledge

Purpose and function of dialogue

Brainstorming is a form of planning—an initial step in the writing process. (Connects to supporting standard W.4.5)

Teacher Conference

Meet with the teacher to show your plans for inserting meaningful dialogue into your story draft, and provide a rationale. (Formative and informal)

Constructed-Response Assessment (Brainstorming)

Prepare for writing dialogue passages by brainstorming a plan for where to insert dialogue and for what purpose. (Formative and formal)

Optional explanation: Transferring what they learn from previous lessons, students explain to teachers during a brief conference where and how they can use dialogue in their stories that they previously drafted. To prepare for this conference, teachers provide time for students to brainstorm, which is an initial step in the writing process and addresses supporting standard W.4.5.

Step 2

Knowledge

Dialogue is meaningful and serves a purpose—to develop the plot or to show characters' responses to situations.

Constructed-Response Assessment (Annotation)

Read dialogue and the surrounding text, and underline what you think is meaningful. Explain the purpose of what you underlined, and provide your opinion about why it is important. (Formative and formal)

Selected-Response Assessment (Hand Signals)

Determine the purpose of each dialogue passage your teacher reads. If it moves the plot forward, signal with one finger. If it reveals characters' responses to situations, signal with two fingers. If you're unsure, make a fist. (Formative and informal)

Optional explanation: First, teachers informally assess students' understanding of the purpose of dialogue to identify whether specific passages are used to advance the plot or to reveal characters' responses to situations. Next, students complete a formal annotation assessment to explain their thinking about what specifically makes dialogue important.

Step 1

Knowledge

Purpose and function of dialogue

Selected-Response Assessment (Voting Techniques)

Determine to what degree a dialogue passage is important in developing the plot. For each passage your teacher reads, raise one hand if the dialogue is not very important, raise two hands if it is important, or stand up if it is extremely important. (Formative and informal)

Optional explanation: Throughout the dialogue unit, teachers use short stories or a novel (or both) as complex texts. These published works also serve as mentor texts for students to discover how authors use dialogue. For an assessment aligned to step 1 in this learning progression, teachers find several dialogue passages from the complex text and ask students to vote on the level of importance of each one. This informal assessment allows teachers to ascertain students' impression of the importance of dialogue and its role in plot development as a launching pad for the unit.

For teachers to use the data to spur students toward growth and achievement, there must be a basis for comparison. Therefore, teams collaboratively take the following steps for grading calibration.

1. Design common assessments.

2. Collect students' work (data).

3. Analyze students' work together against a common rubric.

Teams should carefully consider which steps along the learning progression will require the focus and attention of a common formative assessment and which ones teachers can individually assess. Most likely, teams will choose to develop common formative assessments to measure students' progress on critical and more complex learning targets that students often find difficult to learn rather than on knowledge items, which teachers can typically measure using informal check-ins. In addition, teams should consider the realistic conditions of how frequently they can meet and how much time they have available because engaging in data analysis and collective reflection takes dedicated, uninterrupted time together. We address this later in this chapter, in the Learning Progression Timelines section (page 83).

As our fourth-grade team worked, a discussion ensued about which assessments would become common. Although all steps of the learning progression represent key building blocks of student knowledge and skills, the team decided that step 4—*Write dialogue to develop a plot or to show characters' responses to situations*— is a critical learning target for students' overall mastery of the priority standard. Therefore, the team planned to create, administer, and analyze a common formative assessment for it. When choosing the type of assessment to use, our teachers decided on a constructed-response assessment in which students would write dialogue passages within their story drafts. If some students had already included dialogue, they would revisit their passages with the new learning in mind and revise. This allowed all students to share their learning authentically and reflect on the multifaceted function of dialogue in creating a well-developed story.

In meeting to analyze the common formative assessment results, our team could respond accordingly to students' needs before reaching the final step of the progression. To do so, we would individually collect data, gauge students' learning, and calibrate instruction for the remaining steps. With the building blocks strategically mounted in place, we had students embark on the final rung of the ladder (the common summative assessment) to demonstrate their understanding of the full list of priority standards in the learning progression (step 9). After identifying step 4 as a common formative assessment and step 9 as a common summative assessment—

and labeling them as such on the template in figure 3.5 (page 75)—the team discussed plans for how to uniformly administer the assessments in each classroom in terms of manner, format, and time. Specifically, all teachers on the team assign the same common assessments, provide consistent directions for them, and administer them within a day or two of the rest of the team. Our team also talked about plans for developing common analytic rubrics, preparing students' data, and meeting to engage in data analysis. (See chapter 4, page 93, regarding rubrics and collaborative scoring; see chapter 5, page 117, for a discussion about data analysis.)

As part of this process, our team decided to participate in an exercise to determine where students within a classroom and across the grade level might experience hurdles. Teachers assumed the role of the student and wrote dialogue passages just as the team expected students to do. The entire teacher team should engage in this work and bring the adult work to a team meeting to discuss what the team members notice. Looking at the assessment in this way implies more than a glance or preview. By simulating what students will do to demonstrate mastery, teachers can fully understand and appreciate the expectations they place on students. Acting as a student and participating in the assessment helps teachers uncover mistakes or unclearly written tasks or directions. Additionally, this exercise pinpoints where students might struggle the most so teachers can align their instruction accordingly.

EXERCISE

Develop a Learning Progression and Assessment Plan

With your collaborative team, sequence the knowledge items and skills for one or more related priority standards from your PREP template into a learning progression that reflects how you want to sequence lessons for this part of the unit. Each step in the learning progression acts as a touchstone for formative assessments and an opportunity for teams to discuss the best type of assessment to check in on student learning.

Use the following questions to guide this exercise.

★ What priority standard or aligned standards in the unit form the basis for the learning progression we will build first?

★ How can we sequence the skills and knowledge items? Should we merge any of these skills and knowledge items into a single step in the learning progression?

★ What types and formats of assessments will we conduct?

★ As a team, what common formative assessments will we issue? What will the common summative assessment be?

Discuss Options for Complex Texts

Even though we do not list them on the learning progression template (although some teams may opt to), teachers plan for students to interact with grade-level complex texts. Regardless of the subject area, these texts should be rich in content, hold students' attention, elicit critical thinking, and include relevance. To choose such texts for instructional and assessment purposes, teams consider three criteria that gauge a text's complexity level: (1) the quantitative features of the text, (2) the qualitative features of the text, and (3) the reader and task considerations (NGA & CCSSO, n.d.).

1. *Quantitative* refers to text features and properties that can be counted, like word length and frequency, word difficulty, sentence length, and number of syllables. To calculate a text's quantitative readability level, schools typically rely on computer programs, for example, the Flesch-Kincaid Grade Level test or the Lexile Framework for Reading by MetaMetrics.

2. *Qualitative* refers to text features that include the sophistication of the language (literal and clear language versus figurative, archaic, or unfamiliar language); the knowledge demands concerning the extent of readers' life experiences, subject-matter content (typically for informational texts), and depth of cultural and literary knowledge (mostly for literary texts); and the text's structure, levels of meaning, and purpose. Refer to appendix A (page 233) for rubrics teams can use to ascertain the qualitative nature of literary and informational texts.

Quantitative and qualitative measurements are closely aligned; one without the other will render measurement incomplete and perhaps invalid when selecting the right text. For example, the quantitative text features of John Steinbeck's (1939/1993) *The Grapes of Wrath* measure at a second-to third-grade level, yet clearly, the qualitative and reader considerations would dictate that this text be read at a much higher grade level than grades 4–5 due to its sophisticated content.

3. *Reader and task considerations* refers to the particular composition of the students in a classroom (specifically, these readers' cognitive abilities, motivation, knowledge, and experiences). It also entails the purpose for reading, including the task students complete based on the text. Teachers use their professional judgment and expertise, coupled with what they know about their students, when attending to this area of text complexity. (Refer to chapter 9, page 217, for a discussion about equity and culturally relevant texts.)

In addition to considering the three aspects of text complexity, teams should be cognizant that students must understand texts of steadily increasing difficulty as they progress through grade levels. By the time they graduate, they must be able to independently and proficiently read and comprehend the kinds of complex texts commonly found in college and the workplace. (To augment this discussion, see the sections Close Reading of Complex Texts [page 158] and Mentor Texts [page 171] in chapter 7.)

As teams secure the learning progression for students, they should discuss and commit to complex text that would best address the demand of the knowledge and skills they will assess. Since our featured fourth-grade writing standard requires students to write dialogue in a narrative, a longer text or a collection of shorter works used during instruction should feature this literary device. For example, students might read a novel like *Wonder* (Palacio, 2012) or *Tuck Everlasting* (Babbitt, 1975). Or, they might read several short stories such as "The Marble Champ" (Soto, 1990), "Breaker's Bridge" (Yep, 1989), or a host of other options that contain dialogue and represent strong narratives as mentor texts. To support them in selecting appropriately challenging text, teams can search for potential titles in the following resources (Glass, 2015) and then check any contenders using the three complexity criteria described in this section.

▸ **The California Department of Education's Recommended Literature List (www.cde.ca.gov/ci/cr/rl):** This webpage features a list of recommended preK–12 literature across content areas. A customizable search tool aids users in finding appropriate texts to suit their criteria.

▸ **Appendix B of the Common Core State Standards for English language arts (www.corestandards.org/assets/Appendix_B.pdf):** This appendix includes complex text suggestions for grade-level bands (including 4–5) across content areas and categorized by text type. Some entries appear as titles only and others are excerpts taken from whole works, so educators can find and expose students to the original text sources. In addition, this source includes sample performance tasks that educators might issue.

▸ **National Council of Teachers of English award winners (NCTE, https://ncte.org/awards/ncte-childrens-book-awards):** Each year, the NCTE grants the Orbis Pictus Award (for children's nonfiction) and the Charlotte Huck Award (for children's fiction) and lists the winning titles on its website.

▸ **The International Literacy Association's Choices Reading Lists (www.literacyworldwide.org/get-resources/reading-lists):** This organization offers three collections of reading lists: Children's Choices (grades K–6), Teachers' Choices (grades K–8), and Young Adults' Choices (grades 7–12) each year. Each resource provides annotated lists of literary titles.

Teacher teams must select their resources carefully. When they issue assessments aligned to reading standards, they need to use texts at the appropriate complexity level. Otherwise, an assessment may yield very different results when analyzing data and ultimately determining proficiency and mastery of learning targets. For example, although a student might be able to demonstrate a reading skill when using simpler text, the student may actually struggle to independently show proficiency when he or she applies that skill to an appropriate grade-level complex text. In his blog post "If Students Meet a Standard With Below Grade Level Texts, Are They Meeting the Standard?" Timothy Shanahan (2020) states:

> If a student is able to identify a main idea in a second-grade text, then he is meeting the second-grade standard. Students need to be able to demonstrate that they can make sense of texts in the ways described in the standards, but they have to be able to do this with texts commensurate with their grade levels.
>
> At the end of the year, they'll be tested on fourth grade, not second grade, texts. And, of course, if they continually are working with texts that are a year or two behind their grade level, when they leave high school they'll be at a horrible disadvantage. . . .
>
> We need to teach students to make sense of grade-level texts. If we don't, then no matter how skilled students may seem to be, they will not be meeting our educational standards and they won't be on track for literacy-enriched lives.

EXERCISE

Consider Options for Complex Texts

Teachers must be aware of what qualifies a text to be complex. Review this chapter's three criteria for text complexity—and the qualitative rubrics in appendix A (page 233)—to ascertain the complexity level of any text your team has under consideration for classroom instruction. Make plans as a team to select appropriately challenging texts or review current texts for this purpose.

Use the following questions to guide this exercise.

★ What texts do we already use? Do we need to re-evaluate any to ensure appropriate complexity levels?

★ Have we considered culturally responsive texts? (See chapter 9, page 217.)

★ Which complex texts can we use as mentor texts (or exemplary models) to align to learning targets in the unit? (See chapter 7, page 153, for a detailed discussion about mentor texts.)

Learning Progression Timelines

After completing a learning progression and selecting or designing assessments, teams begin planning the execution of the unit. In doing so, they generate a team calendar that pinpoints dates for instruction and assessment (both formal and informal) around the standards. Some building blocks might take two or more days to teach; if this is the case, teams reflect this in the team calendar. In fact, in the dialogue unit, the fourth-grade team decided to allot two days also for teachers to complete the common formative assessment. Additionally, they reserve time for intervention—offering corrective instruction for students who have yet to master standards and providing extension for those who have achieved mastery. Teams anticipate these assessment and intervention dates and incorporate them within the unit's time frame.

As mentioned in the Identify and Design Common Assessments section (page 74) and described more thoroughly in chapter 5 (page 117), assessments guided by the learning progression provide data that allow teachers to appropriately match their instruction to their learners' specific needs. It stands to reason that the more common assessments teams conduct, the more data they collect and analyze together. But the team calendar must also reflect a *realistic and attainable* timeline of instruction, interventions of corrective instruction and extension, and all that pertains to assessment, such as team meetings devoted to writing an assessment, developing a rubric, and analyzing data. To accomplish this, team members must take into consideration aspects of the unit, such as its length, the number of priority and supporting standards, and the complexity of those standards.

As a reminder, teams should plan for approximately five or fewer priority standards per unit. Essentially, every unit should have mid-unit check-ins, and longer units will have more, but brief, check-ins. For example, if a unit is twelve weeks long, the team might issue a common formative assessment every three weeks. For a short three-week unit, issuing a common formative assessment each week may not work. Additionally, team members should recognize time issues, such as how often the team meets and the length of these meetings. If a team has limited opportunities to convene, it needs to take that into account when creating a timeline.

Using the learning progression for dialogue (see figure 3.1 on page 61), along with the District 96 assessment continuum (figure 2.5, page 52) as a resource, our fourth-grade team strategically mapped out instruction, assessment, and intervention onto the team calendar shown in figure 3.6. It includes indications of standards, learning progression steps (marked *LP*), assessments that guide instruction, and time allotted for interventions (both corrective instruction and extension) and team meetings. Although the learning progression is designed to be read from the bottom up, like walking up the steps of a ladder, for those days where there are two assessments, this calendar lists them in order of instruction.

The entire team regularly accesses and utilizes this calendar. As the teachers teach, they make notes to use for a team discussion and for possible revision the next time this unit occurs. If students struggle at any point within the unit, teachers re-evaluate this original timeline to cater to students' needs in real time. Since individual teachers regularly conduct in-class assessments, they might consider making a copy of the team calendar and inputting interventions to conduct on any assessment they issue in class. For example, the exit slip provides teachers with valuable information about students' understanding of dialogue mechanics. Even though it is not a common assessment, teachers must intervene, as needed, based

Unit 2: The Role of Dialogue Within a Narrative

Time Frame: Approximately two weeks in October | **Grade:** 4

Monday, 9/16	Tuesday, 9/17	Wednesday, 9/18	Thursday, 9/19	Friday, 9/20
Instruction for the current unit takes place while the team engages in the PREP process for the upcoming 9/30 dialogue unit. Teams might also engage in the PREP process during the summer or at another mutually agreed-on time.				

Monday, 9/23	Tuesday, 9/24	Wednesday, 9/25	Thursday, 9/26	Friday, 9/27
Instruction for the current unit takes place while the team continues to engage in the PREP process for the 9/30 dialogue unit.				Preassessment

Monday, 9/30 — Day 1	Tuesday, 10/1 — Day 2	Wednesday, 10/2 — Day 3	Thursday, 10/3 — Day 4	Friday, 10/4 — Day 5
W.4.3b (A)—LP Step 1 **Selected-Response Assessment (Voting Techniques)** Determine to what degree a dialogue passage is important in developing the plot. For each passage your teacher reads, raise one hand if the dialogue is not very important, raise two hands if it is important, or stand up if it is extremely important. (Formative and informal)	W.4.3b (A)—LP Step 2 **Selected-Response Assessment (Hand Signals)** Determine the purpose of each dialogue passage your teacher reads. If it moves the plot forward, signal with one finger. If it reveals characters' responses to situations, signal with two fingers. If you're unsure, make a fist. (Formative and informal) **Constructed-Response Assessment (Annotation)** Read dialogue and the surrounding text, and underline what you think is meaningful. Explain the purpose of what you underlined, and provide your opinion about why it is important. (Formative and formal)	W.4.3b (A) and supporting standard W.4.5—LP Step 3 **Constructed-Response Assessment (Brainstorming)** Prepare for writing dialogue passages by brainstorming a plan for where to insert dialogue and for what purpose. (Formative and formal) **Teacher Conference** Meet with the teacher to show your plans for inserting meaningful dialogue into your story draft, and provide a rationale. (Formative and informal)	W.4.3b (A)—LP Step 4 **Common Formative Assessment: Constructed-Response Assessment (Dialogue Writing)** Write dialogue passages throughout a story draft that develop the plot or show characters' responses to situations. (Formative and formal)	

continued →

Figure 3.6: Team calendar showing a timeline for unit instruction and assessment.

Monday, 10/7 Day 6	Tuesday, 10/8 Day 7	Wednesday, 10/9 Day 8	Thursday, 10/10 Day 9	Friday, 10/11 Day 10
L.4.2a and L.4.2b—LP Step 5 **Short Constructed-Response Assessment (Exit Slip)** Using proper conventions, write three sentences of dialogue: one with a beginning dialogue tag, one with a middle dialogue tag, and one with an end dialogue tag. Label each sentence appropriately as "beginning tag," "middle tag," and "end tag." (Formative and formal)		L.4.2a, L.4.2b, and W.4.3b (A)—LP Step 6 **Constructed-Response Assessment (Dialogue Writing)** Revise dialogue passages within your story to ensure proper use of conventions. (Formative and formal) **Team Meeting: Data Inquiry** Teachers bring scored student work from the 10/4 CFA to the meeting and enter data on the team data tool before the meeting.	L.4.3a & supporting standard L.4.6—LP Step 7 **Selected-Response Assessment (Mini-Whiteboards)** Using mini-whiteboards, write dialogue tag verbs and chorally identify each verb. Record verbs in academic notebooks or journals. (Formative and formal) **Constructed-Response Assessment (Dramatic Enactment)** Find and circle dialogue passages from complex text where the author uses strong dialogue tag verbs. With a partner, act out a few of these passages using the dialogue tag verbs as a guide to show how characters speak to one another. Record verbs in academic notebooks or journals. (Formative and formal) **W.4.3b (A) Intervention** Corrective Instruction or extension for standard	L.4.3a—LP Step 8 **Short Constructed-Response Assessment (List)** Add to list of verbs and categorize them; use the list as a resource for writing dialogue tags. (Formative and formal) **W.4.3b (A) Intervention:** Corrective instruction or extension (continued)

Monday, 10/14 Day 11	Tuesday, 10/15 Day 12	Wednesday, 10/16 Day 13	Thursday, 10/17 Day 14	Friday, 10/18 Day 15
W.4.3b (A), L.4.2a, L.4.2b, and L.4.3a—LP Step 9 **Common Summative Assessment: Constructed-Response Assessment (Dialogue Writing)** Write a final version of purposeful dialogue passages that develop a plot or show characters' reactions; include verbs that depict how characters speak, feel, or act; use proper mechanics. (Summative and formal)	Instruction for the next learning progression within the dialogue unit or another unit takes place while the team scores this learning progression's CSA in preparation for data inquiry.		**Team Meeting: Data Inquiry** Teachers bring scored student work from the 10/14 CSA to the meeting and enter data on the team data tool prior to the meeting.	

on their classroom data. Inputting time for classroom corrective instruction or extension will prove valuable to students' learning curve.

While teaching the unit, teachers make notes about possible calendar adjustments and discuss suggestions for revisions at a team meeting. We recommend your team use or adapt the following steps when devising a calendar.

1. Begin constructing unit calendars by indicating any days off school or other important events like field trips.

2. Note team meetings to appropriately pace common formative assessments and data-inquiry conversations.

3. Indicate when to administer a preassessment prior to the unit to plan instruction.

4. Fill in standards and assessments based on learning progressions in a realistic time frame for the unit.

The process of creating and adhering to the team calendar allows teachers to both coordinate the curriculum and pace instruction. Although teams assign specific dates for issuing a common formative assessment plus calibrating and scoring it, teachers must realize the imperative of also collecting classroom data that may not be common with teammates. In particular, they gather unobtrusive, informal assessment data that they use to drive instruction and tailor learning experiences to individual students. As teachers progress through the overall instructional plan, they proactively allot intervention time in recognition of those who learn the material in different ways and at varying paces. This includes students still seeking avenues to master a standard and others who benefit from deeper engagement with it.

When generating a calendar with your team, peruse and discuss the sample calendar in figure 3.6 (page 85) concurrently with these points.

▶ One to two weeks before a unit starts, teams should engage in the PREP process articulated in chapter 1 (page 9) to gain clarity and prepare for teaching the unit, plus design a preassessment. Teams might even elect to work together in the summer to plan.

▶ Not all instruction within the instructional time frame will center on priority standards. Teams will want to build in instructional opportunities for nonpriority (supporting) standards as well.

▶ For more robust learning progression steps that take two days or more to teach, teams can merge cells in their calendar to indicate the necessary allocation of time.

▶ In a well-functioning PLC culture, teams meet for different purposes. Teachers need time to participate in a team data-inquiry meeting (see chapter 5, page 117) where they can analyze and discuss the collected results from common formative assessments. Teams also get together to collaboratively score assessments (see chapter 4, page 93), which helps inform the data-inquiry meetings. During some units of instruction, teams will input collaborative scoring on their calendars to be sure they carve out time to interpret the rubric uniformly and collect anchor papers. This helps ensure they are consistent in their scoring, which contributes to accurately analyzing data.

▶ *Intervention* and *responsive teaching* are interchangeable umbrella terms that encompass both corrective instruction and extension. *Corrective instruction* speaks to PLC critical question 3, as it services students who have yet to master a standard. *Extension*, which appeals to critical question 4, refers to those who have successfully mastered a standard and thus need extended opportunities. Although teachers responsively teach in that they cater to students' needs and provide necessary support daily based on classroom formative assessments, corrective instruction and extensions are built into the team calendar. This ensures teachers directly make the instructional moves that need to occur based on the data-inquiry meeting's review of the common formative assessment.

▶ While providing an intervention, which could last one to three days, teachers continue to teach other standards within the learning progression unless they determine that most students have not shown mastery. If this is the case, teachers must critically examine their instruction and teaching practices to provide alternative strategies that will help students succeed. Just because they have taught a standard does not necessarily mean that students have learned it.

▶ Teachers also calibrate the common summative assessment, take it to a team meeting for data analysis, and account for corrective instruction of this assessment in the subsequent unit's calendar.

▶ Teams should group together standards as makes sense for assessment purposes. This serves to maximize class time. While assessments are both valuable and essential to student growth, teachers must aim to provide and protect ample time for instruction and intervention, when the learning and growing takes place. Ultimately, we want students to be able to synthesize information, make connections between the standards, and think critically to draw conclusions about the unit's overarching concepts. In grouping standards—especially in the common summative assessment—teachers give students opportunities to demonstrate a wealth of new knowledge and skills.

EXERCISE

Map Out Instruction and Assessment Dates

At this junction, work with your team to produce a team calendar. Consider the suggestions in the preceding list to assist each other in completing this work.

Use the following questions to guide this exercise.

★ In what ways might we prepare for our team meeting to make efficient use of our time? (For example, teachers can research preassessments to share with the team, draft ideas for the assessment tasks, research a tool or format for the team calendar, and so on.)

★ Who will be responsible for creating a calendar template that the team can fill in together during discussion? Where will this document live for all to access?

★ How can we pace instruction so that we account for data-inquiry meetings, enabling us to be responsive in our teaching?

Summary

It is critical that teacher teams carefully design a learning progression that sequences the step-by-step instructional moves teachers take to teach the skills and knowledge necessary for students to attain mastery of priority standards in any given unit. This crucial aspect of curriculum design also provides teachers and teams with guidance in developing assessments, gathering evidence of student performance, and adjusting instruction to meet the specific needs of students.

When teams develop a learning progression, they also take into account the complex text students will experience as the vehicle to meet expectations. Such works can also serve as reading and writing mentor texts. Since choosing complex text can prove challenging, teachers implement a three-part model to assist them in selecting appropriate fiction, nonfiction, and informational texts. It involves examining the quantitative and qualitative aspects of prose or even poetry, as well as considering students' characteristics and the tasks the team will ask students to perform.

Once teams build a learning progression and determine assessments, they fashion a team calendar. On it, they record dates for instruction, assessments, interventions, and data analysis. Individual teachers can duplicate the team calendar and input their classroom assessments on it, as well, to be sure to intentionally map out all that is required to assist all students toward mastery of priority standards.

After teams participate in the exercise to map out instruction and assessment dates, the next chapter supports teams in understanding and designing rubrics and student checklists and using them as instructional tools. Additionally, teams will learn a process for consistently scoring student work so all teachers assess uniformly.

CHAPTER 4

Develop Collective Understanding of Learning Expectations

With a solid learning progression in place, teachers position themselves to deliver a guaranteed and viable learning journey for every student. Thus far, teams have mapped the steps students will take to acquire the knowledge and skills needed to master targeted literacy standards. Additionally, they have determined how to assess students along the way. In doing this work as a team, teachers put in place a secure progression of literacy-focused learning in all classrooms. Yet as part of a PLC culture, the commitment to collaboration continues. Teachers must collectively understand what it means for a student to master each standard and not just what type of data to collect to measure students' progress. Without this collective understanding, there is no assurance that teachers will evaluate all students similarly and hold them to the same learning expectations. What does mastery look like? How will teachers know when a student has mastered a learning standard? How will teachers measure student proficiency and do so uniformly?

Despite the necessity of discussing and scoring student work together, many teams fail to collaborate on this critical aspect of PLCs. Teams successfully prepare for instruction, but often, each teacher evaluates student performance in isolation. Consequently, teachers come to realize that, just down the hallway, colleagues lack clarity on what mastery looks like. Or, they happen into a conversation that reveals a notable difference in their and other teachers' evaluation of student performance. Upholding a commitment to collaboration helps teams avoid this common setback as they work together to promote continued clarity and solidify consistent expectations in specific ways. As teachers implement literacy standards across content areas, this work is important for evaluating reading comprehension and writing in social studies, science, and other disciplines so that all high-inference rubric items are also interpreted and scored uniformly.

This effort is the focus of this chapter, which covers rubrics (understanding rubric types, rubric development, and using them as instructional tools), student checklists (creating a list of items an assignment requires), and collaborative scoring (scoring consistently and collecting anchor papers).

Rubrics

Teachers of any grade likely come across a medley of rubrics—also called *rating scales*—with different point scales, formats, and purposes used to assess students' performance on a variety of artifacts. Susan M. Brookhart (2013) articulates the value of rubrics:

> Rubrics are important because they clarify for students the qualities their work should have. This point is often expressed in terms of students understanding the learning target and criteria for success. For this reason, rubrics help teachers teach, they help coordinate instruction and assessment, and they help students learn. (p. 11)

The goal is to create standards-focused rubrics teams can use in multiple assessment situations throughout the year, whenever students must demonstrate their understanding of a particular standard or set of standards. If constructed and used well, rubrics should benefit both teachers and students to assess performances—that is, what students do, make, say, or write—across content areas (Brookhart, 2013).

With these factors in mind, this section examines types of rubrics, common analytic rubrics and their development, and the use of rubrics as an instructional tool.

Types of Rubrics

The most common types of rubrics are holistic and analytic, although sometimes educators use other kinds, like task-specific rubrics. In *The Fundamentals of (Re)designing Writing Units*, author Kathy Glass (2017) describes holistic rubrics:

A holistic rubric might include a broad entry about the use of proper writing conventions instead of specifying which particular convention is the focus (such as proper use of subject-verb agreement or quotation marks in dialogue). Usually, holistic-scoring systems are used with an on-demand prompt for a school, district, or state summative assessment. They are efficient and useful when scoring student products on a large scale and can even work well for some classroom assessments to determine how the class performs as a whole to inform instruction. Although these rubrics do reflect students' strengths and weaknesses, they often provide a single score without feedback to identify specific areas that need attention or demonstrate where a student shows mastery. (p. 60)

Holistic rubrics typically group more than one skill, revealing a general picture of student performance. For a concrete example, review the following grade 3 narrative writing rubric excerpt from the Smarter Balanced Assessment Consortium (2014):

The organization of the narrative, real or imagined, is fully sustained and the focus is clear and maintained throughout:

- an effective plot helps to create a sense of unity and completeness
- effectively establishes setting, and narrator/characters
- consistent use of a variety of transitional strategies to clarify the relationships between and among ideas; strong connection between and among ideas
- natural, logical sequence of events from beginning to end
- effective opening and closure for audience and purpose

This excerpt groups a series of skills together as meeting level 4 out of four levels for the trait (category) *Organization/Purpose*. A list of these skills at level 3 includes the same number of items but with descriptors reflecting an *adequate* and *generally maintained* performance.

Unlike holistic rubrics, *analytic* rubrics are educative in that each criterion is devoted to a specific skill that students need to master. Consequently, these rubrics provide teachers, as well as students, with feedback for improvement. In this regard, analytic rubrics are a highly effective tool for classroom instructional purposes and for scoring skills both formatively and summatively. Figure 4.1 (page 96) illustrates how a rubric can treat separately two discrete skills related to a narrative's plot.

	4.0 Extends	3.5	3.0 Mastery	2.5	2.0 Developing Mastery	1.5	1.0 Novice
Plot development and event sequence: Create original, well-paced, and developed plot; sequence events in a logical order.	Highly original and clearly well-paced and developed plot; logically sequenced events; may effectively include plot techniques, like flashbacks		Original, well-paced and developed plot; logically sequenced events		Plot original in some places and predictable in other places; somewhat paced and developed; somewhat logically sequenced		Restates existing plot; halted pace; undeveloped with many holes; weak or haphazard sequence; difficult to follow
Resolution: Resolve the central conflict and answer questions readers might have.	Central conflict resolved completely with no unanswered questions; might even have a creative ending; no rambling or abrupt ending		Central conflict resolved with no unanswered questions; satisfying conclusion		Central conflict mostly resolved, but some questions remain; somewhat rambling or abrupt		Weak ending with many unanswered questions; too abrupt or rambling

Figure 4.1: Analytic rubric examples.

A *task-specific* rubric details criteria specific to a particular assignment, such as the following items for a science writing task: *accurately details the characteristics of ecosystems, thoroughly reveals the differences between two ecosystems*, and *correctly explains the similarities in changes between ecosystems*. This type of rubric assesses knowledge pertaining to a specific unit topic; it measures performance for a single point in time, and it is often only applicable to one assignment. Due to its temporary application to one assignment or one unit, the feedback provided to the student doesn't typically allow for the tracking or monitoring of long-term goals. The student knows how he or she performed on this one assignment but has limited information about how to improve his or her skills for the next unit of study. Given these limitations, we focus our efforts in this chapter on analytic rubrics, which can be used for common and in-class assessments.

Common Analytic Rubrics

Since analytic rubrics target and isolate specific skills that are typically taught and assessed, teacher teams benefit from using this type of rubric. When they agree on adopting the same analytic rubric, it's called a *common* analytic rubric, which, not surprisingly, they use to score *common* assessments. With this tool, teams collect information for gleaning strengths and weaknesses in students' performance to move their learning forward (Jonsson & Svingby, 2007).

Common analytic rubrics fit the bill of addressing the second critical question of a PLC: *How will we know if our students have learned the knowledge and skills we want them to?* (DuFour et al., 2016). Teams use this type of rubric to assess student performance based on set criteria that align to standards. Relative to our discussion of learning progressions in chapter 3 (page 59), rubrics set the learning expectations for students so the success criteria that they need to achieve are transparent. In this way, teachers also utilize the rubric as an instructional tool so students can be advocates for their learning, including their literacy-skill development. (See the section Rubrics as an Instructional Tool, page 102.)

Regardless of its visual format, an analytic rubric encompasses three common components: (1) scoring criteria, (2) levels of performance, and (3) criteria descriptors. Figure 4.2 (page 98) shows an example of our fourth-grade team's common summative rubric for the featured learning progression in chapter 3 that addresses the following integrated priority standards (NGA & CCSSO, 2010).

- ▸ **W.4.3b (A):** "Use dialogue to develop experiences and events or show the responses of characters to situations."

- ▸ **L.4.2a:** "Use correct capitalization."

- ▸ **L.4.2b:** "Use commas and quotation marks to mark direct speech and quotations from a text."

- ▸ **L.4.3a:** "Choose words and phrases to convey ideas precisely."

In reviewing this rubric, notice how the criteria descriptors illustrate the justification behind a particular score and indicate to students what they can do to improve and move closer to mastery. Also, recognize how this rubric indicates the opportunity to assign half-values for students who demonstrate some characteristics found in two adjoining columns. In that case, teachers may prefer to assign and mark on the rubric an in-between score to reflect the student's performance in each of the two adjacent columns. Teams collaboratively make the decision whether to utilize a half-value, and as such, all members should consistently implement this option (or not implement it) for scoring and reporting purposes.

When assessing literacy skills across disciplines, teachers in various content areas can select line items from an ELA team's common analytic rubric for scoring products, making certain each criterion is potentially applicable to multiple assessment

Levels of Performance

Scoring Criteria	4.0 Extends	3.5	3.0 Mastery	2.5	2.0 Developing Mastery	1.5	1.0 Novice
Dialogue to develop plot: Write dialogue to develop a plot or to show characters' responses to situations.	Completely meaningful and sophisticated dialogue moves the plot forward and enhances story development.		Dialogue moves the plot forward and meaningfully adds to the story development.		Weak dialogue somewhat moves the plot forward; some dialogue is unnecessary.		Little, if any, dialogue is used; dialogue might confuse readers.
Word choice for dialogue tags: Use words and phrases to convey ideas in a dialogue tag.	Descriptive and sophisticated word choice for dialogue and dialogue tags deeply enhances what characters say and how they say it.		Strong and varied verb use for dialogue tags conveys characters' feelings or reactions.		Somewhat repetitive verb use for dialogue tags sometimes conveys characters' feelings or reactions.		Repetitive and weak verb use for dialogue tags makes how characters feel or react unclear.
Dialogue mechanics: Use proper conventions when writing dialogue.	Minimal or no errors in dialogue mechanics		Minor errors in dialogue mechanics		Some errors in dialogue mechanics		Serious errors in dialogue mechanics, which might make reading or what speakers say difficult to understand

Criteria Descriptors

Figure 4.2: Dialogue common analytic rubric.

situations. For example, if the targeted skills revolve around using key details to identify a text's main idea, students can complete a graphic organizer, annotate text, and respond to a writing prompt. This literacy-focused practice contributes to the assurance of proficiency. Additionally, it allows teams to gain comparative data and students to observe their progress across a building. Many teachers can then identify skills for students to work on and even set personal growth goals. In this regard, common analytic rubrics support teacher teams to obtain several data points from which to assess students' proficiency, check their progress over time, and thoughtfully plan instruction and interventions.

The following section explains and explores each of the three sections we highlight in this rubric.

Common Analytic Rubric Development

When teachers collaboratively design a common analytic rubric, they must clarify and agree on expectations for student mastery, in addition to descriptors for other performance levels. To make rubrics instruments that guide them in fairly and accurately measuring students' performance and achievement, teachers participate in calibration sessions, which are discussed later in this chapter (see Collaborative Scoring, page 107). For now, review the following four general steps for rubric generation. As you read these steps, consider the example rubric in figure 4.2 (page 98), as well as the line items in figure 4.1 (page 96), as a guide while designing rubrics or revising existing ones.

1. **List the scoring criteria:** For standards-aligned rubrics, the learning targets (or skills) are the elements to be measured, so list them on the rubric's left-hand side to indicate the scoring criteria. Some discrete literacy-focused criteria might include *draw inferences using key details*, *use sensory details to describe a setting*, *differentiate between fact and opinion*, and *use correct punctuation*.

   To avoid overlap, which would only create confusion when scoring, ensure that each criterion is dedicated to a separate skill and positioned in its own row. For example, in figure 4.2, there are three distinct skills focusing on these areas: (1) dialogue to develop the plot, (2) word choice for dialogue tags, and (3) dialogue mechanics.

2. **Determine the levels of performance and the terminology:** Most rubrics have between three and six levels of performance. If possible, teams should use the same number system as reflected in the school or

district report card. This is particularly important in a standards-based grading system where report cards list the same learning standards to report on learning outcomes (Townsley & Wear, 2020). Some rubrics include numbers and terms; others include one or the other. If using terms, just as the point scale should reflect the school's or district's grading system, so, too, should the terms coupled with each score, such as *advanced* or *extends* for level 4; *proficient* or *mastery* for level 3; *developing mastery* or *partially proficient* for level 2; and *basic* or *novice* for level 1. Some schools may need to revise their rubrics to adopt growth language, so that they avoid judgmental language (for example, *excellent*, *fair*, and *poor*), or create terms, if desired, where they currently are absent. For performance label ideas or suggestions, consult curriculum products or standardized tests. Enter these performance levels across the top row of the rubric, as shown in figure 4.2 (page 98).

3. **Craft criteria descriptors:** With the assessment criteria and performance levels in place, teams collaborate to write descriptors that match each level of performance. Rubric designers begin in one of two ways. In one approach, begin with the Mastery (proficient) column, which represents the grade-level expectations and aligns with the standard. Then build up or down from there. Others take the approach of beginning with the Extends column, describing what student work looks like when they move beyond the grade-level mastery expectation, which is more sophisticated. From this point, describe performance levels moving down.

Consider the following examples for the skill *Use transitional words and phrases to show the logical sequence of events.*

- *Level 4 (Extends)*—Consistently uses a variety of transitional words, phrases, and clauses appropriately to show the logical sequence of events; some sophisticated transitions.

- *Level 3 (Mastery)*—Uses a variety of transitional words and phrases appropriately to show the logical sequence of events.

- *Level 2 (Developing mastery)*—Uses transitions somewhat appropriately.

- *Level 1 (Novice)*—Uses weak transitions; transitions are missing or repeated; uses no phrases, only transition words.

4. **Test the rubric:** Once done, teams should test the rubric by analyzing and scoring actual student work or teacher-created exemplar pieces.

The goal is to ensure sufficient clarity in the language among all team members so that they can effectively implement the rubric. Even though teachers try it out, once they score actual student work, the rubrics often need tweaking and revision, which could conceivably occur during the collaborative-scoring session. Nevertheless, simulating using the rubric is a proactive measure that could lead to identifying and avoiding mistakes that may arise as teams analyze student work.

Crafting descriptors—the most involved of these steps—warrants further exploration. Therefore, teachers should consider the following definitions of performance levels when writing them. Even though teachers might devise these descriptors together, to accurately score students' work, they should participate in collaborative scoring to ensure that all team members interpret them consistently. While reading these explanations, use figure 4.2 (page 98) as a reference.

- ▶ The Extends column serves a distinct purpose since, in a PLC, a teacher's obligation is to push or encourage students who already know a skill to extend their learning. Providing students who have already mastered a standard with a descriptor dedicated to extending performance beyond proficient-level expectations upholds this commitment.

- ▶ The Mastery column signifies the goal for all students, as it reflects grade-level expectations articulated in the standards. To construct this descriptor, teachers use the language of the standard as a guide and discuss what proficiency should resemble.

- ▶ The Developing Mastery column identifies what the initial stages of proficiency look like for a student. Early in the instructional cycle, many students will be at this level, as it demonstrates a partial understanding of the standard progressing toward mastery. Students who are developing mastery typically require prompting and support from the teacher because they are not yet independently demonstrating proficiency.

- ▶ The Novice column reflects when students are still unable to demonstrate a partial understanding of the standards, despite adult guidance and prompting. The descriptions tend to be far from proficient and typically indicate deficits, as a student's responses are inaccurate or missing. This student still needs additional differentiated opportunities to learn and master the material.

By creating a common analytic rubric, teachers can evaluate student performance aligned to specific learning targets. Using this tool, teachers can more capably ascertain students' performance—particularly their development of essential grade-level literacy skills—against learning criteria and support students in moving their achievement forward in the specific key areas. Once your team has a completed rubric, turn your attention to the ways you can effectively use the rubric as an instructional tool for students.

EXERCISE

Develop a Common Analytic Rubric

Using the steps from this section, work as a team to design a grade-level common analytic rubric. Then try out the rubric prior to scoring students' work.

Use the following questions to guide this exercise.

- ★ What point scale will we use on the rubric?
- ★ Do the rubric's performance levels include numbers as well as phrases, such as *novice, developing mastery, mastery,* and *extends*?
- ★ What are the scoring criteria and associated descriptors for the common formative and common summative assessments?
- ★ Is there a rubric we currently use that we can adjust to ensure the rubric includes the essential components?

Rubrics as an Instructional Tool

Utilizing rubrics during instruction can allow students to assume responsibility for their learning and contribute to achievement. To ready them to address the full scope of a rubric, teachers conduct a series of direct instruction lessons yielding formative assessments that focus on specific learning targets represented as line items on the rubric. During instruction, teachers can isolate these learning targets by asking students to locate and circle them to direct their focus. To capitalize on using the rubric as an instructional tool for improvement, teams can review the following suggested student actions together and determine how they will have students exercise them. Teams might decide that teachers use selected suggestions for in-class formative assessments in preparation for the common assessments.

▶ **Set goals and track progress:** Rubrics can equip students with the information necessary to make strides in their learning by setting goals over time and tracking their progress. Students, teachers, and parents or guardians can review a student's past performance and celebrate growth throughout a unit, semester, or school year. By using the rubric as an instructional tool, teachers provide students with consistent feedback and growth opportunities throughout instruction and prior to a summative assessment. Self-monitoring enables students to take charge of their learning and advocate for themselves as they progress.

▶ **Understand task expectations:** As previously stated, rubrics communicate success criteria to students so they are aware of the expectations of assignments they complete. Popham (2007) writes that it is essential that students understand the evaluative criteria the teacher team will judge them on, stating, "How can students make decisions about the effectiveness of their progress in mastering a particular curricular outcome if they don't know the factors by which their performance is to be evaluated?" (p. 80). Having criteria foremost in their minds early in the unit via a rubric sets the stage for success, as students progress with a keen focus on desired outcomes.

▶ **Discern strong from weak writing samples:** During instruction, teachers deliver learning experiences in which students compare strong and weak anonymous student writing samples based on specific target areas. For instance, in a lesson focusing on sentence variety, teachers present students with writing samples that include fluid prose because of a combination of sentence structures as well as papers that are halting to read due to many simple sentences. Students score the papers against the line item on the rubric for sentence variety only and notice what constitutes proficiency. This exercise of using rubric sections to assess writing allows students to discover what qualities constitute optimal performance so they can strive to achieve it. Matching criteria with concrete examples helps students understand how the rubric supports their growth.

▸ **Self-assess:** To help students self-assess, teachers familiarize students with the rubric elements and format, plus model how students can optimally use rubrics. After students complete a first writing draft, they can use the rubric to assess their efforts and realize which areas of their papers need attention. They can then make adjustments and prepare another draft before submitting it for a teacher's assessment.

▸ **Conduct peer feedback:** Rubrics also serve as a tool that classmates use to give feedback to each other. Teachers must show students how they can engage in peer review for the express purpose of providing constructive feedback that will steer revision. To do so, teachers focus on a specific skill in the rubric and use an anonymous student sample to model for students how they can give input to one another. When students review each other's papers, they can apply what they learn to improve their own papers. (See the Feedback section in chapter 7, page 166, for additional feedback discussion.)

▸ **Solicit teacher feedback:** Rubrics allow teachers to note areas where students must stretch or make improvements, then they offer pertinent strategies to this end. Students record these strategies and practice applying the necessary skills to their drafts; the teacher feedback acts as a revisionary tool during the writing process.

For rubrics to be effective as an instructional tool, the language in them must be accessible to students. Typically, primary teachers create a student version of their rubrics, but grades 4–5 teams may be able to use the teacher rubric with students. This requires careful assessment of how teams have crafted their descriptors. If teams feel the need to create a student-friendly version, they should be cautious to ensure that the rigor and intention of the criteria mirror the original at each proficiency level. To make the rubric a powerful instrument for growth, teachers conduct lessons that introduce the rubric's academic vocabulary and format and familiarize students with how to use the rubric. They also isolate and chunk specific line items to focus lessons and formatively assess students.

Student Checklists

Checklists are companion pieces to the scoring criteria in a rubric. Whereas a rubric defines the quality of each scoring criterion, a checklist itemizes an assignment's requirements. Teachers can refer to items on the rubric and the checklist as they conduct lessons to make a connection between learning experiences and expectations. Unlike a rubric, teachers do not use a checklist for scoring or reporting purposes; rather, the list serves as a guide and self-checking tool for students as they work to complete a task to demonstrate their learning. Figure 4.3 shows an example checklist that might accompany the rubric from figure 4.2 (page 98) for incorporating dialogue within a story.

Dialogue Assignment Checklist

Task: Write meaningful dialogue between characters that develops a plot or shows characters' reactions. Remember to include verbs that show how characters speak, feel, or act. Also, make sure to use proper mechanics.

☐ I write meaningful dialogue to develop my story's plot or to show characters' reactions.

☐ My dialogue tags include descriptive verbs to convey characters' feelings and reactions.

☐ When I write dialogue, I use quotation marks, commas, and other conventions properly.

Figure 4.3: Checklist for writing dialogue.

With a definitive checklist in place, both teacher and students maintain parallel expectations for the requirements of students' end product. Teachers conduct lessons around most items on the checklist since they match the learning targets on the rubric. This isn't necessarily the case for all line items. Some requirements might be reminders for students of what to include in their writing and represent skills previously taught, like *I spell words correctly* or *I include a creative title*. Rather than using checklists as an afterthought, they serve as a guide for students while they work. Therefore, teams should write checklist line items using first-person pronouns and present-tense verbs.

Once teams create a checklist, they should present it to students in an engaging way to generate student ownership and familiarity with items. Consider the following exercise to effectively share it. This process serves a dual purpose: (1) it exposes students to elements of the writing that they will produce (regardless of content area), and (2) it sets up the expectations for their task (Glass, 2017).

1. To small groups of students, distribute anonymous exemplary writing samples that are representative of what students will ultimately produce. Note that you can use samples reflecting what students will write in a variety of content areas, which enhances literacy growth. For example, teachers can share a research report students might create in social studies or a lab report in science.

2. Ask students to read and compare these samples to identify elements that are common among them. For example, a teacher could pose this group task: *I will pass out two stories that students wrote. Read both of them once. Then read them again to figure out what common elements you notice among them. Ask yourselves the following: What makes these both a story? What characteristics do they each share that tell you these are stories? Make a list of these elements to share with the class.*

3. Have groups share their ideas to create a class-generated list. The class should then review the master list to collapse items, delete unnecessary ones, and add other items, as needed. Next, ask students what all writing should have in general: "When we write, what should we all pay attention to so that others can easily read our paper? In addition to the story elements that we wrote on our list, what does all good writing include?" Then, add these items—such as *correct spelling*, *complete sentences*, and *unit vocabulary*—to the list.

4. Distribute the teacher-prepared checklist. Have the student groups compare this checklist with the class-generated one and identify what is missing on either list. Discuss whether items should be added to or deleted from the teacher-prepared checklist. In doing so, use textual evidence from an exemplary writing sample to justify the addition or deletion.

5. Have students store the teacher-prepared student-writing checklist so they can later use it as an instructional tool to guide them while writing.

After some practice with teacher-generated checklists and even rubrics, students may cocreate either tool prior to writing. Doing so promotes critical thinking as students glean the requirements of completing a complex task consistent with the expectations of the grade-level team.

Whether they have a rubric, a checklist, or both, students must be keenly aware of learning expectations. This way, they know what it takes to produce quality products that demonstrate their literacy skill growth, and, depending on the task, they also understand what content-area knowledge they must accumulate. Students can use checklists as a guide while they write to ensure they are including the designated items in their work. Rubrics make them cognizant of the criteria, including the levels of performance, for a given assignment. In addition, rubrics are tools to formatively and summatively assess students' work. Explicitly modeling how to use these instruments throughout instruction can contribute to student improvement.

The following section illustrates how teams conduct a collaborative scoring session to ensure that they consistently evaluate students' work in accordance with the rubric.

EXERCISE
Create Student Checklists

Once your team's common rubric is complete, collaborate to design an accompanying student writing checklist for a common assessment. Write items in first-person point of view with present-tense verbs and accessible language so students can use the checklist as a guide while they address the formative or summative writing task. The questions that follow can guide you in revising an existing checklist or steer you in creating a new one.

Use the following questions to guide this exercise.

★ Are items on the checklist aligned to standards and the rubric?

★ Is each sentence written in first-person point of view and present-tense verbs?

★ Is the assessment task written at the top of the checklist? (See figure 4.3, page 105, for an example.)

★ How will we introduce the checklist so it captures students' attention and they use it as a useful tool to guide their writing?

Collaborative Scoring

Just as team members must collaborate to determine priority standards, assessment types, and learning progressions, they must also work together to ensure consistency of scoring. This requires that teams calibrate *how* they will score students' work. We refer to this process as a *calibration session*.

While scoring, all teachers aim to arrive at the same score for each criterion. However, this does not always occur. Distribute identical copies of a student-completed assessment and its accompanying rubric to a team of teachers, and it is possible that teachers' scores may vary. While rubrics certainly promote more accurate and informative evaluation of student work, teachers may also interpret the rubric somewhat differently or embrace expectations of student mastery that deviate from each other. To close the evaluation gap, teacher teams participate in a calibration session to align their scoring practices.

When teams convene for a calibration session, they collectively score student work for the same assessment task using an agreed-on common analytic rubric they've designed together. Additionally, uniform scoring requires that teachers administer the task consistently; otherwise, it will have unfair, skewed results. For example, if one teacher assists students with the introduction of an informational writing task and other teachers do not, this support—or lack thereof—will impact student performance, causing an uneven playing field. Use figure 4.4 as a team checklist for the collaborative-scoring process to ensure that team members are aligned in the benefits of calibration.

Calibration Checklist

When we collectively calibrate our team's scoring of students' work, we:

☐ Engage in discussion with colleagues to achieve a common understanding of expectations for student work

☐ Help ensure that team members interpret each level of the rubric consistently and apply the rubric uniformly

☐ Interpret high-inference rubric items using evidence from students' work

☐ Enable reliability and confidence when scoring independently

☐ Collect anchor papers to show levels of performance featured in the rubric

☐ Tap the expertise and input of colleagues

☐ Suggest changes to prompts or rubrics as needed

Figure 4.4: Checklist to calibrate the team-scoring process.

*Visit **go.SolutionTree.com/literacy** for a free reproducible version of this figure.*

During team time, the goal is to reach consensus about student examples of proficiency for each criterion so teachers have consistent impressions of what each level on the rubric means. This ensures that all those scoring student work interpret and apply the rubric uniformly, which increases the assessment data's reliability. To support this endeavor during calibration, teachers collect anchor papers, establish a process for collaborative scoring, and fulfill post-calibration tasks.

Anchor Papers

When teachers review student work as a team in calibration sessions, they determine *anchor papers*—examples of student work that align to each performance level on a rubric. Because teachers can interpret items differently, these anchors give expression to a rubric so that, together, the rubric and anchor papers form a clear picture of what writing at different performance levels looks like.

Since writing-focused rubrics, in particular, contain high-inference items that teachers find difficult to interpret, anchor papers serve as a best representation of what each scoring criterion means. In this way, they serve as benchmarks for assessing students' writing that contribute to reliability when teachers independently score their students' work. They also aid conversations during parent conferences, as they make family members and guardians aware of how to interpret rubric scores.

Teacher teams can also use their inventory of anchor papers, categorized by levels of performance, for instructional purposes. When teachers conduct lessons using anchor papers, students can capably determine where their writing meets the standard and where they need to focus their attention for improvement. Specifically, students critique and score anchors against the rubric, which challenges them to identify strengths and weaknesses pertinent to targeted writing skills. Teachers also model how to use these sample papers to self-assess and give peer feedback so students can apply these strategies on their own. Teams deem anchors papers that reflect high-quality characteristics that meet or exceed criteria on the rubric as *exemplars*. Along with devising learning activities that ask students to examine weak examples to detect deficiencies and possibly revise them, teachers should also design lessons that give students the opportunity to read, analyze, and emulate exemplars so they can apply elements of good writing to their own work (Graham & Perin, 2007).

The Collaborative-Scoring Process

By participating in a collaborative-scoring process, teachers establish and maintain a shared understanding of the rubric, consistency in their evaluation of student work, and common expectations of mastery for all students in every grade-level classroom. We recommend collaboratively scoring student work at least three times a year for each text type in the curriculum—such as narrative writing, explanatory and informational writing, and opinion writing—or more throughout an instructional cycle, if time permits. Even singletons (teachers who are without grade-level or content-aligned teammates) can participate in the collaborative-scoring process with colleagues from another grade level, as it is just as important to vertically align student expectations from one grade to the next.

The following sections detail the five steps involved in the collaborative-scoring process that teacher teams should engage in as part of a calibration session.

1. Preselect student samples prior to meeting as a team.

2. Review the task and common rubric.

3. Score the first paper.

4. Discuss scores and arrive at a consensus.

5. Repeat the process, collect anchors, and take notes.

Preselect Student Samples Prior to Meeting as a Team

In advance of the team meeting, teachers review their students' papers. They preselect samples that holistically represent a variety of achievement levels, even though the team will ultimately score each line item on the analytic rubric. Specifically, each teacher collects two or three papers at each level—those meeting overall grade-level expectations, those approaching mastery, and those not yet progressing toward mastery—to share with colleagues. If such a sample is available, this collection should also include a paper that extends beyond grade level. Teachers can optionally affix sticky notes to label each pile—*extends, mastery, developing mastery,* and *novice.* Additionally, they should conceal students' names to avoid bias and preserve anonymity during the calibration process. Teachers should devise a system for identifying these papers after collective scoring, such as writing numbers or letters on each paper and generating a class list that matches the code to the students. Teachers then either make enough copies of each sample for every team member or send electronic copies of these preselected papers in advance of the meeting. They will use them to select anchor papers that ground the team in maintaining consistent expectations at each level of proficiency. Teachers should bring the following to the calibration session.

▸ Copies of preselected samples to share with team members (unless they send electronic versions prior to the meeting)

▸ Their entire class set of papers in case there is time to score more than the preselected papers or in the event that the team needs other samples during the discussion

▸ A copy of the common analytic rubric that the team will use to score the assessment

▸ Notetaking tools to collect information about student performance

▸ Charged electronic devices (such as laptops or tablets) to take notes, and to review the papers if everyone is reviewing them electronically

Review the Task and Common Rubric

To begin the calibration process, all teachers review the writing prompt or task that students completed along with the accompanying rubric used for scoring. With a clear understanding of the assessment, teams discuss any high-inference or subjective items on the rubric to clarify expectations. During scoring, a discussion will likely ensue to reach consensus; however, at this point, teachers clarify dubious meanings of any criteria to determine intent.

For example, with the standard "Use dialogue to develop experiences and events or show the responses of characters to situations" (W.4.3b [A]; NGA & CCSSO, 2010), our fourth-grade team expressly looked for students to write dialogue so that what characters say to one another has purpose. We asked ourselves questions, such as "Will students who write dialogue that features extraneous content that fails to develop the plot or show characters' reactions at all receive a score of 1.0?" and "How does that differ from students whose stories contain no dialogue?"

As another example, for the standard "Choose words and phrases to convey ideas precisely" (L.4.3a; NGA & CCSSO, 2010), our team sought for students to use strong action verbs to articulate the emotion characters feel as they speak. For this, we asked, "What if students write a couple of strong verbs but use them repetitively? Do we give high credit for the strength of the verbs or mark down for lack of variety?"

Determining what teachers expect before scoring as a team well positions them to more accurately and consistently assess students' work.

Score the First Paper

At this step, teams benefit by appointing a facilitator—a teacher on the team or perhaps an instructional coach—who is familiar with the process. The facilitator asks any teacher for a paper preidentified as *extends* (or *mastery*, if no student preliminarily scored in the *extends* level) and reads it aloud. Or, all teachers can read this paper silently since everyone should have a hard or electronic copy. Next, teachers independently score the paper using all criteria on the team's common rubric while taking mental or physical notes about what they notice from the descriptors that match the performance on the student's paper.

Discuss Scores and Arrive at a Consensus

When everyone is ready, the facilitator asks each teacher to share his or her score for one line item at a time. In large teams, the facilitator can record and tally these scores for all to see. If all teachers agree on a score for a criterion, they move on to the next item and repeat the process. The facilitator leads a discussion only for discrepancies in scoring. In these situations, teachers share their impressions of each line item, citing distinct performance indicators from the rubric with textual evidence from the student's work. The team engages in conversation until all teachers agree on a definitive score for the item in question. During this collaborative discourse, rich conversations emerge about student proficiency and expectations of mastery. This dialogue is a necessary and valuable part of the scoring process. As it develops, teachers often find themselves rethinking and refining their understanding of student mastery and aligning it with their teammates'. If differences of opinion occur, teams should use the rubric language to guide their evaluations, and they may elect to examine additional student examples to make comparisons and further calibrate their scoring practices.

Repeat the Process, Collect Anchors, and Take Notes

Teachers repeat this process for each remaining student paper, forever mindful that the goal is to reach consensus as well as determine which ones qualify as anchors at different performance levels. Sometimes, teams naturally discuss which ones are candidates for anchors as they score papers. Teachers will use these papers when they individually score their class sets of papers after the calibration session.

During the calibration process or after scoring all the preselected papers, teachers need to take notes about how the team can use the selected anchors during instruction. As mentioned previously, teachers may use anchor papers to create learning opportunities where students examine strong and weak samples and notice the elements that account for these differences. They may also have students study exemplars—those papers that are excellent examples—and focus on what makes them stellar so they can emulate the skills the student writer exhibits. Therefore, teachers should leave a calibration session with plans for incorporating anchors into their instructional program, and of course, determine how each teacher can obtain electronic or print copies of these papers. Since it is best to share anonymous student samples, when teachers use these samples for a lesson, they should take off students' names and switch papers with a teacher from another classroom. Or, teachers save the papers to use for the following school year.

While participating in this collaborative process, teachers will also find themselves reflecting on the reliability and validity of the assessment and what changes, if any, the rubric needs. Does the assessment task elicit adequate evidence to determine if a student mastered the standard? If it poses questions, are they framed in a way that prompts students to make detailed and accurate responses? Is the assessment formatted in a student-friendly manner? As teachers consider these factors, they may collectively decide to adjust the assessment for future use or to collect additional formative data so they gain a clearer snapshot of the students' abilities. Either way, participating in the collaborative-scoring process allows teams to develop shared expectations for student achievement and refine assessments to make them as efficient and informative as possible.

Although this process focuses on collaborative scoring of written work, teams can also adapt it for reading or performance tasks in all disciplines. For instance, when teams assess comprehension, teachers can record students reading excerpts. Or, when assessing safety procedures in a science lab, they can videotape precautions students take. These audios or videos then function as the student samples. Using an analytic rubric they have customized for this task, the teacher team members can participate in a modified version of the collaborative-scoring process this section articulates.

Post-Calibration Tasks

After teachers collect anchors during calibration and achieve clarity about student work that aligns to the rubric's proficiency levels, they score the full set of their students' papers. Likely, they need to finish this independently, but teachers might find time available during the team meeting to finish scoring. Afterward, they record their students' strengths and areas for growth to guide future instruction. Additionally, they input all their students' scores onto a spreadsheet or other data-collection tool and reconvene as a group to discuss findings across the grade level and at the classroom level. Read The Data-Inquiry Process section in chapter 5 (page 118) to learn more about how teams use the data from common formative assessments.

EXERCISE
Participate in Collaborative Scoring

Once your team develops a common analytic rubric and issues an accompanying common assessment, engage in collaborative scoring so all team members can independently score their students' papers with consistency against the agreed-on rubric. Then, all team members enter their class set of scores onto a data-collection tool (discussed in chapter 5, page 117) in preparation for a team meeting in which they further analyze the scores.

Use the following questions to guide this exercise.

★ Are all members aware of the team's calibration session protocol? If not, how can the points in this section be communicated to everyone? (For example, members should know the team's logistic plans for meeting to discuss common formative assessment scores after they issue the assessment.)

★ Who will facilitate our collaborative scoring session?

★ Will we share preselected student writing samples in hard-copy form or electronically?

★ After the calibration session, what are our plans for collecting and sharing anchor papers among team members so we use them within instruction?

Summary

Assessments play a critical role in the progression of learning in all classrooms, and to further augment assessments' value, teams in a PLC design effective rubrics and collaboratively score student work to ensure accuracy and consistency when measuring learning. Holistic rubrics serve a purpose when assessing student performance on a large scale across a school building, district, and state or province. They group together many criteria into an overarching description making scoring faster, but perhaps more confusing since they combine criteria. Analytic rubrics include criterion items separately that each focus on a discrete learning target. This allows teachers to identify students' strengths and weaknesses in specific skills. Therefore, teams design and use common analytic rubrics to assess students' work since they can provide specific feedback and steer instruction based on the findings of where students excel or need support. Teachers also use analytic rubrics for scoring classroom assessments. To share the requirements of a particular task with students, teachers devise a checklist that students use as they write to guide their work. The rubric and checklist can both serve as instructional tools during a lesson; communicating clear expectations and requirements sets students up for success.

When scoring student work, teams participate in a collaborative scoring session so that all teachers reach agreement about how they interpret criterion items on the rubric. They collect anchor papers to reflect what constitutes examples of student work for each level of proficiency according to a task. Once they reach this collective understanding, they can independently score individual students' work with consistency. If, perhaps the following year, teams conduct the same assessment and score with the same rubric, they can use these anchor papers and modify the calibration sessions accordingly.

Yet, a team's commitment to student growth doesn't end there. Teachers working in collaborative teams must analyze and respond to the data they collect to determine every student's specific needs in literacy within ELA and across content areas. In chapter 5, the link between data and intervention takes center stage. What do our data tell us about the learning needs of our students? What scaffolds, supports, and other learning opportunities do students need to reach proficiency? How will we appropriately challenge students who are already mastering content? Considering these questions will help sharpen teachers' already-attuned focus on student learning and achievement.

CHAPTER 5

Respond to Student Data to Ensure All Students Learn

A fundamental underpinning of the PLC process centers on the first big idea of a PLC—the belief that all students are capable of learning at high levels. Within this idea reside the two critical questions (questions 3 and 4) that represent this chapter's primary focus: *How will we respond when some students do not learn?* and *How will we extend the learning for students who are already proficient?* (DuFour et al., 2016). To attend to these questions, this chapter demonstrates how teams can use data analysis to determine how they can ensure all students progress in their learning with particular respect to literacy skill development.

As teachers, we are obligated to address each student's unique learning needs. The reality of a heterogeneous classroom is that some students already possess the skills we will teach, while others will require additional time or practice to become proficient. A one-size-fits-all instructional approach does not cater to the needs of all students. Such an approach hinders the learning of students who are ready for more or, conversely, leaves behind students who depend on additional support to learn.

Achieving the fundamental tenet of the PLC process that all students can and will progress in their literacy skill development, as well as in the rest of the curriculum, requires that educators use data to determine when and how to engage in intervention. This signifies responsive teaching. As we explain in the Learning Progression Timelines section in chapter 3 (page 83), we define *intervention* as the opportunity to remediate skill gaps for students as well as extend learning for those who have already acquired skills. Although the term *intervention* often carries a negative connotation that implies attending only to those who struggle, we assert that it encompasses both reteaching *and* extension. Therefore, when educators engage in intervention, they meet the needs of learners at all levels of proficiency—those who already demonstrate mastery and are candidates for extension or acceleration and those who haven't yet achieved mastery and benefit from corrective instruction.

In an effort to close achievement gaps and make a profound and long-lasting impact on students' development, educators within a PLC work together to analyze data and use them to provide high-quality, timely, and systematic instruction that targets students' specific needs—in this case, literacy. The team data-inquiry process—a team meeting expressly dedicated to analyzing students' common assessment results—proves essential to this collaboration. Therefore, we begin with this topic, explaining how to implement and prepare for collective data inquiry, and sharing guidelines teachers abide by to respond to data proactively. We address what to do once you have determined when a student or a group of students requires learning extensions or additional time for reteaching.

The Data-Inquiry Process

A recurring public conversation relative to education centers on the amount of time schools devote to assessing students during the school year. When not done well, assessments detract from learning. As a result, critics—including parents and educators—refer to *assessment* as detrimental to students and consider it a distasteful word. However, as discussed in chapter 2 (page 37), when educators issue and use assessments as an effective instructional tool, they can benefit students. Specifically, when teachers systematically collect data, analyze the results, and respond to the ever-shifting instructional needs of students as they strive toward mastery of unit standards, assessment is an altogether powerful contributor to growth. So, it is critical that teams participate in collaborative data inquiry to examine assessment results and use this information to steer instruction intentionally so they push student learning even further.

This section will help guide your understanding of the conversations teacher teams ought to have and the actions they should undertake to further student learning. We support this effort by explaining the team data-inquiry process, establishing how to prepare for a data-inquiry meeting, and providing guidelines for using students' data.

The Purpose of the Team Data-Inquiry Process

Collaborative data inquiry is the foundation of high-performing PLCs, and without it, we cannot ensure high levels of learning for all students. The research of Ronald Gallimore, Bradley A. Ermeling, William M. Saunders, and Claude Goldenberg (2009) finds that when collaborative teams implement an inquiry-focused protocol to address issues with instruction, student achievement significantly increases. This growth only occurs when teams persevere in working on a learning problem until they solve it and realize the correlation between how they teach and positive student gains.

As Jenni Donohoo and Steven Katz (2017) contend, collaborative inquiry helps build teachers' sense of collective efficacy—"the belief that, together, they can positively influence student learning over and above other factors and make an educational difference in the lives of students" (p. 21). Teams that routinely engage in cycles of collaborative data inquiry continuously deepen their knowledge, improve their practice, and impact student success. When teachers can attribute student success to their instructional practices, rather than to outside factors, they shift from the assumption, "I planned and taught the lesson, but they didn't get it," to beliefs, such as, "You haven't taught it until they've learned it" (Gallimore et al., 2009, p. 553). Without evidence, teachers simply hope students learn what they teach rather than guarantee it.

In general, through the data-inquiry process, teachers capitalize on their team members' expertise and learn about instructional experiences in using scaffolds and other strategies that resulted in success for many students. As teams move through the instructional unit, they continuously collaborate around the informal observational and formal data they collect to refine instruction as needed for students.

Preparation for a Data-Inquiry Meeting

As discussed in chapter 3 (page 59), teams set the stage for their data-inquiry meetings by using their learning progressions to map out core instruction, assessment, intervention, and data-inquiry meeting dates on their team calendar. To ensure your team is prepared for a data-inquiry meeting, use the checklist in figure 5.1 (page 120) to complete the tasks it lists. Note that you will learn about developing a team data-collection tool in the next section.

Data-Inquiry Meeting Preparation Checklist

☐ Identify the common assessment to be discussed.

☐ Ensure each team member administers and scores all his or her students' assessments in a logical and feasible time frame. (All team members should administer the assessment in their classrooms within a defined and agreed-on window of time; generally, teachers each conduct the assessment within a day or two of their teammates.)

☐ Guarantee all team members have access to the team data-collection tool and are proficient in using it.

☐ Verify all team members enter data (students' results) onto the data-collection tool prior to the meeting. (Teams must be invested in using data-inquiry meeting time to analyze students' results rather than input scores or grade papers. Therefore, teams must emphasize that each teacher enter data prior to the meeting.)

☐ Remind teammates to bring the actual assessments (the task and students' work) to the data-inquiry meeting so teachers can refer to them in conversation.

Figure 5.1: Data-inquiry meeting preparation checklist.

*Visit **go.SolutionTree.com/literacy** for a free reproducible version of this figure.*

Guidelines for Using Student Data in a Data-Inquiry Meeting

To help teachers manage, process, and discuss their results, Tom Many (2009) recommends committing to a set of guidelines, or rules, for using data. Based on his suggestions, we developed three criteria to assist teachers during the data-inquiry process.

1. The data are accessible, easy to manage, and purposefully arranged.

2. The data are publicly discussed.

3. The data are action oriented.

When a teacher team ensures its data meet these criteria, it increases the productivity and utility of the inquiry meeting. The following sections elaborate on each of these criteria.

The Data Are Accessible, Easy to Manage, and Purposefully Arranged

To make data accessible, teams choose and devise a data-collection tool (such as using a print or computer-generated table, chart, graph, or spreadsheet) for sharing and displaying students' results. By serving as a collected representation of data, it is sometimes called a *data wall*—a metaphorical reference if, for example, teachers view data on a computer spreadsheet, or literal if displayed on a wall. Authors and experts on data-based interventions Austin Buffum, Mike Mattos, and Janet Malone (2018) recommend teams format their data-collection tool to include both individual student results and classroom results for each of an assessment's targets and accompanying scoring criteria.

This tool must also make data easy to manage during the meeting to ensure the inquiry process doesn't become cumbersome and hinder teachers from engaging in the analysis process. Teachers must also purposefully arrange data in a format that is complete, accurate, and straightforward (Many, 2009). If not, the team might spend the majority of its meeting working to organize data rather than engaging in the meeting's most critical purpose—collaboratively determining the next steps in instruction for student learning.

Teams grant all members—including other professionals who support the students, such as special education teachers, related service providers, teachers of English learners, principals, and assistant principals—access to the data-collection tool. These educators may already be a part of your teacher team and participate in decision making; however, collaborative teams in a PLC can vary depending on the needs of the school. So, inviting invested educators who may not be part of your team to examine the data guarantees that they can responsively support students through their lens.

As discussed in chapter 4 (page 93), teams collaboratively design an analytic rubric that reflects the scoring criteria for a common assessment. In our dialogue unit, step 4 of the learning progression includes a common formative assessment that addresses one significant skill: *Write dialogue to develop a plot or to show characters' responses to situations* (see figure 3.1, page 61). Figure 5.2 shows a portion of our data wall, which includes our fourth-grade team's common formative assessment and the criteria from our team analytic rubric for the administered assessment. Formatting the data-collection tool as we did helped us clearly display each student's proficiency level for the scoring criteria, highlighting the specific strengths and weaknesses in learning.

Team Common Formative Assessment Data
Priority standard: Use dialogue to develop experiences and events or show the responses of characters to situations. (W.4.3b [A])
Learning target: Write dialogue to develop a plot or to show characters' responses to situations.
Assessment task: Write dialogue passages throughout a story draft that develop the plot or show characters' responses to situations.

Figure 5.2: Team data-collection sample for grade 4.

continued →

Student	Teacher	Scoring Criteria Dialogue to Develop Plot: Write dialogue to develop a plot or to show characters' responses to situations
Carlos	Teacher A	3.0 (Mastery)
Suzy	Teacher A	2.0 (Developing Mastery)
Latisha	Teacher A	2.0 (Developing Mastery)
John	Teacher B	1.0 (Novice)
Rohan	Teacher B	3.0 (Mastery)
Anna	Teacher B	4.0 (Extends)
Ritika	Teacher C	2.0 (Developing Mastery)
Kyle	Teacher C	3.0 (Mastery)
Ramon	Teacher C	3.0 (Mastery)

Source for standard: NGA & CCSSO, 2010.

Accessible, manageable, and purposefully arranged data help teachers maintain focus on student results and limit potential distractions from a faulty or complicated presentation format.

EXERCISE
Design a Data-Collection Tool

With your collaborative team, review an upcoming common formative assessment and its common analytic rubric to guide you in designing a data-collection tool that allows for easy management and purposeful arrangement of your team's data.

Use the following questions to guide this exercise.

★ What type of data-collection tool will we devise (for example, a sticky note chart, table, or Excel spreadsheet)?

★ How will we display our data?

★ How will we ensure all team members can access the data-collection tool?

The Data Are Publicly Discussed

Teams embark on the process of publicly discussing students' results after all teachers enter their data on the tool. To help teammates cultivate a safe, supportive environment conducive for sharing data, education expert and consultant Joellen Killion (2008) suggests using a data-analysis protocol that "keeps the focus on issues rather than people, engages people in an appreciative inquiry approach rather than a deficit approach to a situation, and results in a plan of action that energizes and motivates people" (p. 7).

When teams interact to discuss data, they must determine a set of norms to engage thoughtfully and productively. According to Richard DuFour, Rebecca DuFour, and Robert Eaker (2008), norms represent "commitments developed by each team to guide members in working together. Norms help team members clarify expectations regarding how they will work together to achieve their shared goals" (p. 471). To guide a team meeting on developing data-discussion norms that lead a conversation toward efficacy, teams can complete figure 5.3.

Goals of Data Analysis	Avoid This	Try This (Norms)
Keep the focus on issues rather than people		
Engage people in an appreciative inquiry approach rather than a deficit approach to a situation		
Develop a plan of action that energizes and motivates people		

Source for protocol guidelines: Killion, 2008.

Figure 5.3: Tool for creating data-discussion norms.

*Visit **go.SolutionTree.com/literacy** for a free reproducible version of this figure.*

In the first column, teams jot down the overall goals of their data discussions. In figure 5.3, we input the guidelines Killion (2008) recommends from the paragraph at the start of this section. Then, in the Avoid This column, teachers brainstorm behaviors that might prevent them from reaching each goal. For instance, to achieve the desired goal of "keep the focus on issues rather than people," team members might decide that *Blaming each other*, *Criticizing a teacher's instructional strategies*, or *Refusing to share their data with a teammate* are behaviors to be avoided and therefore add them to the column. Next, team members discuss how to rewrite the list of Avoid This behaviors into productive actions members might try instead to attain the desired goal. The outputs of this discussion become the norms. In this instance, teachers might suggest changing *Criticizing a teacher's instructional strategies* to *Reflect on the effectiveness of a teaching strategy*. By turning negatives into positives, teams establish a clear and affirming list of commitment statements all teammates will be inclined to adopt (DuFour et al., 2016).

In addition to norms, which include guidelines for communication reflected in the Try This (Norms) column, teams use protocols for examining student data. These protocols delineate procedures that teachers use to examine strengths and weaknesses of their instruction and include time frames for meetings. To determine how long teachers convene, they take into account the length of the assessment and the number of criteria to be assessed. In grades 4–5, a team data discussion of a literacy-based common formative assessment typically takes forty-five to sixty minutes.

In Kildeer Countryside Community Consolidated School District 96, team members analyze data using the Here's what, So what? Now what? protocol. Through this procedure, teachers identify data trends, determine what led to the results, and ultimately develop an intervention plan to responsively teach particular students by providing corrective instruction for those struggling to meet standards, or extension for those ready for more. The following list breaks down each of this protocol's components.

- ▸ "Here's what" means that teachers focus on the strengths and weaknesses that the data and student work reveal.

- ▸ Once teachers critically look at how students perform, they ask, "So what?" to interpret the results and uncover what led some students to succeed and others to miss the mark. Since all teachers strive to gain better results, they endeavor to learn from each other. So this part of the meeting relies on collegial openness and support as teammates share ideas and respond to the following kinds of questions.

  - • "Does a teammate have ideas that will enhance instruction for students who are still unclear?"

- "Is there a scaffold another teacher used in class that seemed to provide just the right amount of support?"

- "What extension opportunities have helped push students' thinking? Perhaps a teammate might suggest a graphic organizer, visual, or hands-on cooperative learning structure that yielded positive results."

Teachers also examine what might have derailed learning or produced less than desirable results. They might ask these questions to probe for insights.

- "Did our instruction truly align with the priority standards?"

- "Did teachers proactively catch students before they failed?"

- "Did our lessons follow the gradual release of responsibility model to slowly and deliberately hand over responsibility to students when they were ready?" (See chapter 6, page 137.)

▶ Teams conclude by asking, "Now what?" to determine and make a concrete plan for intervention. This section of the protocol is inspired by Buffum and his colleagues (2018) in *Taking Action*. In this part of the data-inquiry discussion, analysis uncovers which students struggle and need more assistance than others, as well as those who might need extension. Therefore, our fourth-grade team indicated how we can differentiate to attend to the needs of students who score in the *novice* and *developing mastery* categories on the rubric, as well as those who score in the *mastery* and *extends* levels. By virtue of attaining the learning target, we coupled *mastery* and *extends* together, although teachers may need to differentiate learning based on students' current level of understanding.

The organizer in figure 5.4 (page 127) features a template with guiding questions—modeled after Kildeer's protocol—that teams can use to capture the notes from their data discussion. Since teams participate in a continuous cycle of assessment and acting on the data that teams analyze, they can also use this protocol for both common formative and summative assessments.

By working together to analyze student data, teachers are more likely to benefit from the collective wisdom of their teammates, develop new instructional approaches and strategies, and turn their data into action.

Data-Inquiry Discussion and Recording Template

Learning Target

Here's What

Based on the student data and work samples for this assessment, identify specific trends, observations, or outcomes. (Five minutes)

What strengths do students demonstrate that reflect proficiency?

What weaknesses do the data reflect?

So What?

Interpret the results, and determine what led to the results. (Fifteen minutes)

What instructional strategies help proficient students master the learning target?

Why might some students struggle with these concepts or skills?

Now What?

Develop an intervention plan to address the trends or patterns in the data that you've collected. (Thirty minutes)

What will our team do next to address the trends or patterns in the data that we collected? (Use the following columns to answer.)

Scoring Criteria	Novice	Developing Mastery	Mastery and Extends
Criterion:	Students:	Students:	Students:
Criterion:	Students:	Students:	Students:
Criterion:	Students:	Students:	Students:
	Instructional Plan:	Instructional Plan:	Instructional Plan:

Figure 5.4: Data-inquiry discussion and recording template.

Visit go.SolutionTree.com/literacy for a free reproducible version of this figure.

The Data Are Action Oriented

As the term explicitly states, *action oriented* simply means that teachers proactively support students based on the data they collect and analyze because, frankly, that is our job, and it is what common sense dictates. Otherwise, why collect the data? The whole crux of the data-inquiry conversation is to ascertain the next steps in instruction for students, knowing they are each at varying levels of proficiency. As Thomas Guskey (2010) argues, "It would be foolish to charge ahead knowing that students have not learned key concepts or skills well" (p. 55), just as it would be a shame to hold students back knowing they have already mastered the learning.

Therefore, as part of the unit-planning process discussed in chapter 3 (page 59), teams embed dedicated time for responsive teaching into their unit calendar to address the needs of struggling learners and to extend the learning of those students who are ready for more advanced coursework. They indicate this time on the team calendar by inputting *Intervention: Corrective instruction or extension* (see figure 3.6, page 85). Instruction continues during this time; however, teachers must be cognizant of students who need more scaffolding as well as challenge.

To make prudent instructional decisions and select appropriate support for students, teams should also consider alternate forms of data to augment the common assessment results. This means utilizing formal or informal literacy-connected data from across disciplines to ascertain students' performance and to assist with planning scaffolds and extensions. Since students experience a wide range of texts across content areas and write for myriad purposes, teachers can, for example, analyze data from a social studies assessment to predict what support students might need to master a reading or writing standard. As well, teachers may utilize previous writing data from an assignment other than the common assessment to inform their next moves. Considering these results enables teachers to amass a more complete picture in which to create a well-constructed plan for supporting, scaffolding, and individualizing learning, and for forming small groups of students with similar needs.

Figure 5.5 shows entries our fourth-grade team recorded onto the Data-Inquiry Discussion and Recording Template for the common formative assessment we issued in the dialogue unit. In the *Here's What* section, although we kept our focus on the purpose for dialogue—which is the learning target for this common formative assessment—we noted deficiencies in other skills we tackle later in the unit. Specifically, we input that students overuse the verb *said* and need help to properly use writing mechanics when inserting dialogue. In this regard, we took advantage

Data-Inquiry Discussion and Recording Template

Learning Target: Write dialogue to develop a plot or to show characters' responses to situations.

Here's What

Based on the student data and work samples for this assessment, identify specific trends, observations, or outcomes. (Five minutes)

What strengths do students demonstrate that reflect proficiency?

– *Many students include sufficient dialogue in their stories, and the dialogue serves a purpose and is intentional.*

What weaknesses do the data reflect?

– *Some students are still unclear about how dialogue functions in a story since some include extraneous, inconsequential dialogue.*

– *Novice students have scant dialogue since their story is underdeveloped in general.*

– *Many students use "said" repeatedly and need extra practice to use quotation marks for inserting dialogue, although these are upcoming skills in the unit that we will address later.*

So What?

Interpret the results, and determine what led to the results. (Fifteen minutes)

What instructional strategies help proficient students master the learning target?

– *Annotation—students underlined textual evidence of meaningful dialogue in a complex text and wrote in the margin what purpose the dialogue served*

– *Color-coding—students highlighted parts of the dialogue and dialogue tags in yellow to show plot development; they used pink highlighters for dialogue and dialogue tags that reveal characters' reactions*

Why might some students struggle with these concepts or skills?

– *Writing dialogue presents a problem if students' story drafts are weak and underdeveloped.*

Now What?

Develop an intervention plan to address the trends or patterns in the data that you've collected. (Thirty minutes)

continued →

Figure 5.5: Completed fourth-grade data-inquiry discussion and recording template.

What will your learning team do next to address the trends or patterns in the data that you've collected? (Use the following columns to answer.)

Scoring Criteria	Novice	Developing Mastery	Mastery or Extends
Criterion: Dialogue to develop plot—Write dialogue to develop a plot or to show characters' responses to situations.	**Students:** John	**Students:** Suzy Latisha Ritika	**Students:** Carlos Rohan Kyle Ramon Anna
	Instructional Plan: Teachers work with students to develop their stories and to include dialogue so their drafts are complete. They ask the following. − "Who are the characters in your story?" − "What is the setting?" − "Who is the narrator that tells the story?" − "What central conflict sets the story in motion?" As they discuss the storyline, teachers help students fill out a story map. Then the teacher asks what conversations characters might have that move the events in the story along or that show how characters react to one another or a situation. Students add this information to their maps, then further develop their stories using what they recorded.	**Instructional Plan:** Isolate a dialogue exchange in a familiar mentor text. Ask students for (or supply) a brief summary of what is happening in the story leading up to the dialogue. Ask students to explain in their own words what the dialogue tells readers. Then ask them if this purpose advances the plot or shows how a character reacts. To verify a character's reaction, consider how the dialogue can be acted out. Then, instruct each student to read his or her dialogue to self-reflect and get feedback from the group using these questions. What is the purpose of the dialogue? Is there dialogue that is unnecessary that can be deleted? Is there dialogue that should be added? After collecting input, students delete, add, or revise dialogue to their stories.	**Instructional Plan:** Tell students they will add purposeful dialogue in their stories that both advance the plot and show characters' reactions. Have students recap the differences between these two functions of dialogue. Then, students form pairs to give each other feedback on the dialogue they each wrote. Students form new pairs and collect feedback from a different partner. Using this input, they improve the dialogue in their stories. For those needing more challenge, discuss ways they can include figurative language and descriptive words in their dialogue and tags. Show excerpts from mentor text to provide examples for students.

of using this tool to record brief preassessment data for future reference. It may not always be the case to enter such information, but if it occurs, embrace this opportunity.

Students Who Need Extension

The teacher team discusses steps for students who demonstrate a clear understanding of essential learning standards that teachers have addressed or are currently addressing during instruction. As Buffum et al. (2018) explain, teachers can provide extended learning opportunities to encourage advanced learners to dig deeper into current content based on standards. To accomplish this differentiated approach, teachers challenge students to:

> look at things from different perspectives, apply skills to new situations or contexts, look for many different ways to solve a problem (not just looking for the correct answer), or use skills learned to create a new outcome or product. (Buffum et al., 2018, p. 180)

For example, in our fourth-grade team's dialogue unit, teachers encouraged students who master and need extension for using verbs in the dialogue tag to go deeper with this skill rather than move to another topic of instruction. To facilitate this, teachers can show them mentor text passages by authors who employ detailed dialogue tags to reveal in what manner characters are speaking, such as "He cried while hugging his stuffed toy." To differentiate for students who can tackle even more sophisticated ways of thinking, teachers might show published examples that incorporate figurative language, such as "Stomping his feet, Joey roared like an angry guard dog and shrieked . . . "). Students then return to their stories to apply this skill. No matter your approach for providing ways to extend learning, keep in mind that all students deserve the opportunity to achieve at high levels.

Students Who Need Additional Time and Support

For students who lack mastery, teams spend additional time implementing an instructional scaffold, or temporary support structure, to help them understand a concept or perform a task they could not typically achieve on their own (Northern Illinois University, n.d.). When implementing scaffolds, teachers break down concepts into comprehensible chunks and implement strategies, perhaps offering a structure or a tool of some kind, to guide students in achieving the expected outcome.

Providing scaffolds during the reading process helps readers shift from experiencing frustration with a text to feeling successful and capable, thus building their perseverance for when they encounter complex text. In her article "Building Stamina for Struggling Readers and Writers," Paula Bourque (2017) poses these questions to guide teachers in choosing appropriate scaffolds for students that build stamina for reading engagement.

▸ Does the scaffold encourage students to employ stamina to stick to a complex text?

▸ Does the scaffold allow students the opportunity to struggle a bit but still find success?

▸ Does the scaffold invite problem solving, or does it require continued support?

▸ Will the scaffold allow for transfer of a strategy to another text or task?

▸ Will the scaffold eventually fade or become obsolete with experience and practice?

Additionally, teachers use gradual release of responsibility, a sound instructional framework presented in chapter 6 (page 137), to scaffold reading across the disciplines. Plus, they can implement the following research-based suggestions. Doing so can support students in becoming more proficient readers with a heightened sense of comprehension across different text genres they will experience with other subjects.

▸ **Listen-read-discuss (Manzo & Casale, 1985):** The teacher chooses a text passage. Before students read it, he or she uses a short summary or engages in discussion to present key ideas and vocabulary that are essential for students to comprehend the material. Students then read the selection independently. Afterward, the teacher facilitates conversations in which students seek clarification and discuss complex issues connected to and arising from the text to better understand complicated portions.

▸ **Laddering texts or the use of text sets (Lupo, Strong, Lewis, Walpole, & McKenna, 2018):** Building background knowledge helps students access a complex text. To support this endeavor, teachers provide a series of texts along a continuum of varying difficulty levels based on the same subject. Since concepts and vocabulary are likely to appear repeatedly across these selections, they assist students in increasing their knowledge of the subject and eventually gaining access to the targeted text.

▸ **Partner reading (Meisinger & Bradley, 2008):** In partners, students engage with a text by each reading half of the selected text while the other listens and follows along; then, the two swap roles. When the reader confronts difficulties, his or her partner provides assistance. Teachers check in on pairs and provide scaffolding support, as needed.

Understanding unknown words in texts is critical for all students but especially those who struggle. As we write in chapter 7 (page 153), teachers preview a text to determine which words are essential to comprehension and, therefore, must be taught. They expressly identify those without context clues. For words with context clues, teachers give students tools to ascertain words' meanings where the authors supply such information. In chapter 8 (page 193), we discuss that teachers can teach words before, during, or even after reading a complex text, so avoid front-loading all vocabulary lest it overwhelm students. Review strategies in chapter 8, in particular, to devise scaffolding ideas for teaching vocabulary with a direct instruction construct. Additionally, review figure 5.6 (page 134), which features general interdisciplinary suggestions, many of which are successful scaffolding tools. Share these ideas among team members, then sample and implement different strategies, making sure they match the right scaffold to a student's characteristics and needs related to learning a specific skill. Afterward, discuss as a group how well a particular strategy worked or what teachers might recommend changing.

As students acquire a skill and learning continues, teachers remove the scaffolds to advance pupils to the next level in the learning progression. The key is to select the appropriate scaffold to facilitate productive struggle and then gradually release the scaffold so that students do not become too dependent. Over time, students should be able to employ the strategy or perform the skill without the need for additional support; however, for students with a severe disability, the scaffold can stay in place and serve as an accommodation.

If a scaffold allows the students to accomplish a task too easily, the support is probably too enabling. In a classroom where teachers promote productive struggle, students feel empowered to persist despite a healthy struggle since the teacher encourages determination and curiosity. Students gain a sense of accomplishment as they try and try again to tease out something challenging. They feel the struggle is worthwhile because they can sense that by pushing through, success will come. Teachers offer cues and prompts to support students without giving them the answer outright. If this sounds like a learning environment that adopts the growth

Scaffolding Strategies

Use any of these alone or in combination based on students' characteristics and needs.

Let Them See It

- Show visuals, or point to something in the classroom environment, like a word wall or chart.
- Provide graphic organizers.
- Show a timeline to provide context.
- Use realia (objects or activities that relate what you are teaching to real life).
- Use gestures and animation.

Let Them Hear It

- Model how something works or how to do it; use the think-aloud strategy so they hear your brain at work.
- Rephrase it into simpler language or paraphrase.
- Read the text aloud or furnish an audio recording or video.
- Use verbal cues, prompting, or questioning to elicit responses or elaboration, or to redirect.

Break It Down

- Divide the task or directions into manageable parts or steps.
- Create a calendar or timeline to plot milestones.
- Check students' progress after each part or step.
- Convert a text portion or a set of directions into a bulleted list.

Give a Clue or Use Manipulatives

- Teach mnemonic devices for rote memorization (for example, use acronyms like HOMES to remember the Great Lakes or chants like "Thirty days hath September . . ." to remember the number of days in the months).
- Provide templates, sentence frames, or sentence starters.
- Offer hints to the solution.
- Partially complete a graphic organizer.
- Create manipulatives, such as words, sentences, or pictures on cards, that students physically maneuver, for example, to sort, sequence, or match.

Figure 5.6: Interdisciplinary scaffolding strategies.

*Visit **go.SolutionTree.com/literacy** for a free reproducible version of this figure.*

mindset philosophy—believing that intelligence is something that can be developed, rather than a fixed trait (Dweck, 2016)—it is.

The absence or mismatch of scaffolds or supports can lead to destructive struggle for students. Subsequently, no learning occurs due to missed learning opportunities. When confronted with this type of struggle, students feel overwhelmed and frustrated. As a result, they feel disengaged and ill-equipped to arrive at a solution. Sensing the learning target is out of their grasp, and with failure in sight, they shut down. Overcoming these consequences requires immense teacher effort in terms of reteaching students and likely rebuilding their self-efficacy. To be clear, teachers are obligated to ensure productive struggle with students so they have the opportunity to grow academically and become more confident in general. To accomplish this, we position our students for success through teaching and assessing at rigorous levels, mindful that scaffolds might be necessary.

Given intense focus of instruction from the classroom teacher for multiple purpose, there might still be situations in which a student needs more. In that case, we suggest consulting dedicated RTI resources such as *Taking Action* (Buffum et al., 2018) as essential for implementing intervention practices to both support and extend learning.

EXERCISE

Participate in a Team Data-Inquiry Discussion

After entering common formative assessment data into your data-collection tool, you and your team are ready to discuss student results, share instructional strategies and ideas, and develop a responsive teaching plan.

Use the following questions to guide this exercise.

★ What are our logistics for meeting as a team? For example, have we set a date and location for our team data discussion?

★ How will we guarantee all team members complete the necessary steps prior to the meeting?

★ Which data-discussion protocol will we use to help each other focus on student results in a safe, nonthreatening environment?

★ Where will we record ideas for providing scaffolds for students who need additional support to master skills and extended opportunities for those who have already mastered them?

Summary

In a PLC, collaborative teams are committed to finding ways to support all students in achieving at high levels. To uphold this promise, teams review and analyze data from a common assessment to find trends in students' performance. With this information, they capitalize on the findings and each other's expertise to devise ways to support struggling learners and extend the capacity of those who have achieved mastery. To help ensure that teachers speak candidly and feel comfortable to share and discuss data in a safe place, they establish norms. Additionally, teams must develop a robust and systematic data analysis protocol—like Here's What, So What?, Now What?—so they have a procedure for sifting through, analyzing, and acting on what the data reveal.

When a team meets to analyze data and ultimately draws the conclusion that some students struggle with a particular target or skill, team members must dig deep into the reasons for this struggle and develop a concrete action plan. As well, they must formulate learning opportunities for students ready to broaden and deepen their understanding of a skill. By working through an ongoing, continuous cycle of data inquiry, teams deliver the quality core instruction and targeted interventions needed to ensure all students can read and write at grade level, fostering a love of literacy to carry them throughout their school-age years and beyond.

In chapter 6, readers will learn how to reach these goals by designing high-quality lessons using *gradual release of responsibility*, a research-based instructional model. When teachers devise lessons through this framework, they position students well to achieve desired goals.

Design Lessons Using the Gradual Release of Responsibility Instructional Framework

Teachers' commitment to their students' reading and writing skills necessitates the planning and delivery of a literacy-focused, guaranteed, and viable curriculum (DuFour & Marzano, 2011). In the preceding chapters, collaborative teams engaged in a deep-dive process to determine priority standards, developed a literacy-focused learning progression (complete with accompanying assessments and rubrics), and established a process to gather and collaboratively assess data. This work is all vital to offering the curriculum grades 4–5 students deserve, but ensuring that all students learn depends on more. It requires that teachers use the data they collect to inform their classroom instruction each day. Figure 6.1 (page 138) illustrates how each step in this process has brought us to this point.

Dovetailing from chapter 5's focus on collecting and responding to data, this chapter continues with a focus on how teams use the assessment data they gather to inform instruction that addresses critical questions 3 and 4 (*What will we do when students haven't learned it?* and *What will we do when students already know it?*; DuFour et al., 2016). To attend to these queries, this chapter explores gradual release of responsibility as an ideal model for providing differentiated instruction that, used appropriately, enhances students' growth when learning any new skill, strategy, or procedure. We begin by introducing this instructional framework, then follow with a discussion of the model's flexibility; we conclude with an example of gradual release of responsibility in action for a literacy skill.

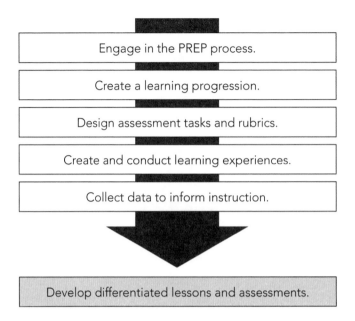

Figure 6.1: Overview of the curriculum-design process.

Gradual Release of Responsibility

Teachers have at their disposal an array of strategies but should judiciously employ appropriate ones for the express purpose of meeting learning outcomes. During instruction, teachers must collect evidence of student learning via formal and informal formative assessment (as discussed in chapter 2, page 37) and adjust their teaching based on how well students grasp the targeted skills. As straightforward as that seems, it is no easy task to implement effective instruction for students to demonstrate clear understanding of a learning target on an assessment. Therefore, to design and execute effective lessons, we recommend teams use *gradual release of responsibility*, an instructional framework that originated with P. David Pearson and Margaret C. Gallagher (1983). It involves an orchestrated, graduated cognitive shift from teachers modeling new learning to students employing the new skill, strategy, or process independently:

> When the teacher is taking all or most of the responsibility for task completion, he is "modeling" or demonstrating the desired application of some strategy. When the student is taking all or most of that responsibility, she is "practicing" or "applying" that strategy. What comes in between these two extremes is the gradual release of responsibility from teacher to student. . . . The hope in the model is that every student gets to the point where she is able to accept total responsibility for the task, including the responsibility for

determining whether or not she is applying the strategy appropriately (i.e., self-monitoring). But the model assumes that she will need some guidance in reaching that stage of independence and that it is precisely the teacher's role to provide such guidance. (Pearson & Gallagher, 1983, p. 35)

Douglas Fisher and Nancy Frey (2014c) identify the following four phases of gradual release of responsibility inspired by Pearson and Gallagher's (1983) model. Together they contribute to an effective and fluid learning experience that can yield student achievement and contribute to high-quality instruction.

1. Focused instruction ("I do it.")

2. Guided instruction ("We do it.")

3. Collaborative learning ("You do it together.")

4. Independent learning ("You do it alone.")

When introducing a new learning target, lessons must include all four components of gradual release of responsibility—focused and guided instruction and collaborative and independent learning—to maximize its effect and to increase the likelihood that students will achieve mastery. However, there is flexibility in how teachers use it. For example, they can rearrange or repeat parts of the model based on their expertise of how the lesson should unfold, taking into account their students' needs. For more simplistic skills, teachers can incorporate abbreviated forms of the four components within a typical class period. When addressing more sophisticated learning targets, such as *quote accurately from a text when drawing inferences* or *support reasons with facts and details*, teachers will likely need to extend the model across two or more days. Teachers might omit parts only if they are reinforcing or reviewing a learning target for which students have received direct instruction in a previous or current school year.

Timothy Shanahan (2018) humorously, albeit realistically, addresses decisions about how quickly or gradually teachers relinquish support to students. He also illustrates the potentiality of this model to be iterative:

Those decisions are hard because they need to be made on the spot. And, when they are wrong—that is, when it turns out that the kids can't take the reins successfully—the teacher has to take back the responsibility, for the time being, that is.

That's why I think of gradual release as: I do it, we do it, I do it again, we try to do it again but this time a little differently, we do it, we do it, oops, I have to do some of it with more explanation, you do it (no, not quite like that), you do it, we do it again, okay now you can do it. (I know it isn't catchy, but it is more descriptive of how the process really tends to work.) (Shanahan, 2018)

Teachers must use their professional expertise and knowledge of their students' characteristics to determine how to choreograph the steps of this model so they best suit the needs of all students in their classrooms.

The following sections explain each of the four phases of the gradual release model, adapting the concepts laid out in Pearson and Gallagher (1983) and Fisher and Frey (2014c).

Focused Instruction—"I Do It"

During focused instruction, teachers take on most of the responsibility, which accounts for the first-person phrasing of "I do it." They establish the learning target, provide context, and show students what the skill, strategy, or process entails. While conducting focused instruction, teachers unobtrusively assess to determine how best to support students later during guided instruction. This portion of the lesson might last around fifteen minutes.

1. **Set the purpose for learning:** Teachers state the lesson's purpose at the outset by posing and posting the learning target (using an *I can* statement) and perhaps a guiding question in student-friendly language. Or, teachers might wait to reveal the learning target and guiding question after teachers engage students in a brief activity. For example, in a lesson that focuses on using sensory details to describe a narrative's setting, teachers might read two paragraphs—one rich with imagery and the other blandly written. They ask students to identify which one is more effective and to justify that choice. After students respond—for example, by articulating that the stronger paragraph has descriptive details, uses sensory words, and helps them visualize the setting—teachers confirm the students' impressions. The teachers then present the goal for the lesson: "Today, we will focus on the guiding question, *How do writers use sensory details to describe settings?* and address the learning target, *I can use sensory details to write descriptive settings for my story.*" To provide context for the work, teachers connect the learning to what students have done previously, what they already know, or how they will use the new learning.

2. **Model or demonstrate and think aloud:** After teachers establish the purpose, they model or demonstrate the new learning to present how to perform the task and what constitutes quality. For clarification, there's a technical difference between modeling and demonstrating. When teaching

cognitive processes, like reading, writing, or performing mathematical computations, teachers employ *modeling* to illustrate how to produce high-proficiency work. When showing students how to perform physical tasks, such as swimming using the butterfly stroke or filling a test tube, teachers employ *demonstration* (Fisher & Frey, 2014c). Concurrent with modeling or demonstrating, teachers employ the think-aloud strategy to reveal what goes on in their heads as they perform the task. This self-talk makes their thoughts transparent to students. Teachers also describe certain pitfalls to avoid, misconceptions to fend off when the task might be difficult, and how to deal with the challenging aspects of the task.

3. **Invite minimal participation:** Teachers check for understanding at this early stage in the lesson. While modeling or demonstrating the task, they unobtrusively observe students. Additionally, they might invite students to actively respond to a question or prompt by signaling with a thumbs-up (*yes* or *true*), a thumbs-down (*no* or *false*), or a fist (*I am not sure*). Or, to allow time for students to process and synthesize the new learning taking place, teachers might ask students to turn and talk with a neighbor or elbow partner. All the while, teachers collect information to lead guided instruction.

During focused instruction, teachers provide context by presenting the learning target to students and connecting it to what they will be doing. They explicitly show and narrate what proficiency looks like to prepare students for what they will eventually do on their own. They also reveal any errors students might be prone to make so they avoid these mistakes. Teachers attentively assess, albeit informally, in preparation for guided instruction.

Guided Instruction—"We Do It"

During guided instruction, teachers differentiate by arranging students purposefully in pairs, trios, or small groups of four based on similar needs. They work on a different task from the one they previously modeled so that students can practice the new learning and apply it in a novel situation. While students practice how to transfer this skill, teachers supervise and provide guidance. They circulate around the classroom, constantly formatively assessing and offering pointed feedback by way of questioning, prompting, and discussing, to support students in achieving mastery. They differentiate to redirect, remediate, or repeat information, as needed. Additionally, they might scaffold instruction, which serves myriad purposes: "to provide support, knowledge, strategies, modeling, questioning, instructing, restructuring, and other forms of feedback, with the intention that the student comes to 'own' the knowledge, understanding, and concepts" (Hattie, 2012, p. 144). For scaffolding suggestions, review the section Students Who Need Additional Time and Support (page 132). Teachers might also differentiate by offering extension opportunities for those who would benefit from an additional challenge. If need be, teachers regroup students and allow them to work at different paces. Teachers also refer students to the learning progression so they can monitor their own learning and gauge their status. In fact, some students might move on to collaborative learning while teachers continue to support others with guided instruction.

Collaborative Learning—"You Do It Together"

By discussing and actively engaging in a task with peers, students derive deeper meaning and perhaps new insights based on the learning target. Together, they seek validation and clarification, articulate their thoughts, and question each other (Fisher & Frey, 2014c). This collective involvement spurs students toward clarity and understanding and develops critical-thinking and communication skills.

Collaborative learning is an opportunity for students to work with partners or in small groups around targeted skills. When they do, students' output becomes stronger than what they would have produced on their own. To be clear, it represents an important component of gradual release of responsibility that teachers should not overlook:

> When done right, collaborative learning is a way for students to consolidate their thinking and understanding. Negotiating with peers, discussing ideas and information, and engaging in inquiry with others gives students the opportunity to use what they have learned during focused and guided instruction. (Fisher & Frey, 2014c, p. 7)

After students participate in a collaborative exercise, teachers determine the next instructional moves, such as lead a debriefing session, conduct another formative assessment, return to guided practice for particular students as needed, or move to independent learning.

Independent Learning—"You Do It Alone"

Within the gradual release of responsibility model, students eventually assume full responsibility for the cognitive load and independently demonstrate an understanding of their new learning. To accomplish this, each student applies the skill, strategy, or procedure in a unique situation to show that he or she can transfer learning and provide evidence of mastery. For example, if students practice writing dialogue that employs correct mechanics, they apply this skill of proper conventions usage in their own narratives. Or, when working to determine the meaning of figurative language, using the earlier chapters of a novel during the other phrases of gradual release of responsibility, they interpret similes or metaphors in later chapters of the same novel or in a new short story. If some students still exhibit difficulty with application, teachers reteach relevant phases of the instructional model accordingly or group students together to provide differentiated support.

An Example of Using Gradual Release of Responsibility—Dialogue Tag Verbs

This section provides a specific example of a gradual release of responsibility lesson that teachers can conduct to support students in generating a list of concrete verbs. It addresses step 8 in the learning progression from figure 3.1 (page 61), which is also excerpted in figure 6.2. This lesson prepares students to ultimately incorporate a variety of dialogue tag verbs into their own stories. We also provide suggestions for how it can be adapted to use with other learning targets.

Learning Progression Step	Learning Progression Component	Assessment
Step 8	**Learning Target (Skill)** Use words and phrases to convey ideas in a dialogue tag.	**Short Constructed-Response Assessment (List)** Add to list of verbs and categorize them; use the list as a resource for writing dialogue tags. (Formative and formal)

Figure 6.2: Learning progression excerpt—Step 8.

Here is a snapshot of the upcoming sample lesson.

1. **Focused instruction ("I do it"):** The teacher introduces the lesson's guiding question (What strong verbs do authors use in dialogue tags?) and the learning target (I can identify and list strong verbs to use in dialogue tags).

2. **Guided instruction ("We do it"):** With teacher support, the students identify verbs in published passages and begin a class-generated verb list.

3. **Collaborative learning ("You do it together"):** In small groups, students find other dialogue tag verbs and categorize the comprehensive list.

4. **Independent learning ("You do it alone"):** Individually, students select descriptive dialogue tag verbs to use in their original stories.

This lesson fosters critical thinking since students find and generate descriptive verbs themselves, rather than receiving a teacher-prepared handout that lists them. Teachers might feel compelled to distribute such a list to students. However, we suggest refraining from passing it out or waiting until after you conduct this or a similar lesson so students can compare words they compile with a teacher-supplied list. In doing so, students are more prone to use the verbs because they actively sought them out and recorded them. They can then incorporate strong verbs into their first writing draft or during the revision process.

With this philosophy in mind of designing a lesson where students take ownership to cull their own list rather than teachers furnishing it, let's consider how teachers might adapt it for these two learning targets: (1) use transitions to connect ideas, and (2) vary sentence beginnings using prepositional phrases.

1. **Focused instruction ("I do it"):**

   - *Example 1*—The teacher introduces the lesson's guiding question (What transitional words and phrases do authors use to connect ideas?) and learning target (I can identify and list transitional words and phrases).

   - *Example 2*—The teacher introduces the lesson's guiding question (How can authors vary the way sentences begin by using prepositional phrases?) and learning target (I can vary my sentence beginnings by using prepositional phrases).

2. **Guided instruction ("We do it"):**

   - *Example 1*—The students participate in a card sort consisting of words that are transitions along with other random words. After helping students to verify words that function as transitions, the teacher begins a class-generated list.

   - *Example 2*—With teacher support, the students engage in a scavenger hunt to find prepositional phrases at the beginning of sentences in published passages and start a class-generated list.

3. **Collaborative learning ("You do it together"):**

   - *Example 1*—In small groups, students find and record other transitional words and phrases and categorize the comprehensive list, such as transitions to indicate time or show location.

   - *Example 2*—In small groups, students find and record other prepositional phrases that begin sentences.

4. Independent learning ("You do it alone"):

- *Example 1*—Individually, students select and insert (or replace existing) transitions to improve their writing.

- *Example 2*—Individually, students revise their writing to add prepositional phrases to vary their sentence beginnings.

Returning to the initial example of teaching dialogue tag verbs using the gradual release of responsibility framework, consider that there are two schools of thought about the use of dialogue tag verbs. Some authors intentionally use simplistic ones like *said* or *questioned* repeatedly so that the dialogue itself—and even punctuation marks used in the dialogue—solely carries the meaning and receives prominent attention. Other writers believe the tags serve to extend the dialogue's meaning by showing how characters speak, feel, and react. In this case, authors pepper their work with a variety of descriptive verbs, like *squawked, murmured,* and *cried.* Perhaps there is an intermediate approach in which some authors primarily use *said* throughout their work, but interject adverbs (such as *quietly, haltingly,* or *sweetly*) to support dialogue. These are stylistic choices authors elect to adopt. By sharing these approaches before or during the lesson, students do not mistakenly believe that published authors who use simplistic and repetitive tags are less skillful in their craft. Teachers can communicate to students that when they become more sophisticated writers, they can choose to employ either method within their original stories. For now, the focus is on including various verbs to articulate how characters speak.

Before conducting this lesson, students uncover the meaning of the dialogue within the complex text at the center of instruction so that they deepen their understanding of the storyline. If your team were to adapt this lesson to focus on transitions or prepositional phrases, the same notion would apply. In any case, students return to the complex text with the purpose of examining specific aspects of its contents—in this case, the author's craft in using dialogue tag verbs.

Focused Instruction—"I Do It"

Write the learning target (and perhaps the guiding question) on the classroom whiteboard or easel. Feature and read aloud a passage of dialogue from a classroom complex text on an interactive whiteboard or under a document camera. Purposely choose a passage that contains a variety of verbs in the tags, like this one from *Holes* by Louis Sachar (1998). For your clarification, if needed, here are the dialogue tag verbs in this sample passage—*said, challenged, yelled, shouted:*

> "Teach the bully a lesson," said Mr. Pendanski.
>
> Zigzag hit Stanley on the shoulder with his open hand. "Teach me a lesson," he challenged.
>
> Stanley made a feeble attempt to punch Zigzag, then he felt a flurry of fists against his head and neck. Zigzag had hold of his collar with one hand and was hitting him with the other. . . .
>
> "That's enough!" Mr. Pendanski yelled.
>
> It wasn't enough for Zigzag. He jumped on top of Stanley.
>
> "Stop!" shouted Mr. Pendanski. (p. 135)

After reading it to students, say, "Today in our lesson, we will focus on the guiding question *What verbs do authors use in dialogue tags?* and address the learning target *I can identify and list strong verbs to use in dialogue tags.*" Point to the posted lesson goals—guiding questions, learning target, or both—as you say them. You might even have students recite them chorally with you.

Then, model what students will do, which is to underline each dialogue tag verb. Concurrently, think out loud to explain that although the task is to underline only the verbs used in dialogue tags, the author includes other verbs, so point them out. For example, *teach* is a verb; however, it is within the actual dialogue, so do not underline it. As you underline, solicit brief input from students by asking for a choral response or verification each time you focus on a sentence. Unobtrusively assess students to gauge their understanding. When finished with identifying the verbs, direct students' attention to the dialogue tags and ask, "Does the author write the same verbs, or does he write different ones?" Then, briefly ask volunteers to share how the passage would change if the author repeatedly used *said* instead of the other verbs.

Teachers can adapt this same strategy if focusing on using transitions to connect ideas or prepositional phrases to begin sentences. Merely feature passages from a complex text that contains these words and phrases.

Guided Instruction—"We Do It"

To prepare for this guided instruction exercise, do the following.

1. Find a combination of dialogue passages from complex text students have read that include strong dialogue tag verbs like *screamed, whispered, bragged,* or *whined* as well as *said.* In our team's practice, we found examples from *Holes* by Louis Sachar (1998), which furnishes a wide variety of tags within a single work; however, you may find you must cull passages from several texts familiar to students. Find a variety of passages differentiated by readiness levels.

2. Type or copy each passage on a separate card, and place three excerpts in an envelope. Differentiate the cards by levels and make enough sets for each group of three students who share common needs. For example, you might have two groups that are on the same level, so make two duplicate sets to distribute to each group.

3. Arrange students into trios based on readiness levels, which you determine from any preassessments and from observing students during focused instruction. Distribute an envelope containing the three passages (cards) to each group.

When you are ready to conduct the exercise with students, do the following.

1. **Assign the task, instructing each group member to take one card from the envelope:** Essentially, students underline verbs in three separate passages, one at a time. Tell students, "Each of you select a card from the envelope. Read it silently, and find the verbs used in the dialogue tags. Underline each dialogue tag verb as I showed you earlier from the passage I modeled. When I call time, pass your card to the left so that another group member can verify that what you underlined is correct. You'll pass it again and repeat so that you all check and agree on the dialogue tag verbs in all three passages."

2. **Observe student groups and move between them, offering scaffolding or extensions as needed:** For example, some groups may need more teacher support to identify the words that are verbs. In this case, teachers can probe and question without furnishing the answer, such as by saying, "Put your finger where you find dialogue that shows a character is speaking. Who is doing the talking? How do you know? What word explains how the character is speaking?" For students who need extended learning, ask them to find and write synonyms for the verbs the author uses. They can write these synonyms directly on the card or on a sticky note.

3. **Invite each group to share the verbs to make a class-generated list:** Once students have underlined and agreed on the dialogue tag verbs, teachers ask each group to share their words to generate a class list. Once completed, the whole class reviews it, adds other verbs they might now consider, and deletes words that are not verbs.

If adapting this activity to focus on using transitions or prepositional phrases, teachers would prepare sets of cards accordingly.

Collaborative Learning—"You Do It Together"

Next, have students work collaboratively to add to the class-generated list. To do so, they can participate in a scavenger hunt of published works to find other dialogue tag verbs. They could search in the same text used earlier in the lesson, provided students look at different dialogue passages within the text, so they practice applying what they are learning to new material. Otherwise, use a different text. As students find words, group members confer with each other and agree on which ones to add to the master list.

Once students finish the inventory of words, they collaborate to sort this master list. They push each other's thinking to determine how many categories of verbs they should have and which verbs belong in each one. They also identify a heading that helps them see larger concepts. In fact, some words on the master list might qualify as a heading. For students who struggle, teachers can narrow down the verb lists and provide headings. When finished, students report their category headings to the class with some examples and any additional verbs they found or added on their own.

As an option, after students compile their inventory of verbs, teachers can share a handout like the one in figure 6.3 before students categorize the words. Students can cross-reference the two lists and add words to their own list. If, however, the lesson yields already-lengthy lists, teachers need not distribute a handout since students have successfully produced their own.

asked	hesitated	roared	threatened
continued	hollered	sang	urged
cried	joked	screamed	whimpered
demanded	laughed	shouted	whined
exclaimed	murmured	sighed	whispered
explained	questioned	stuttered	yammered
giggled	recalled	suggested	yelled

Figure 6.3: Partial verb list for dialogue tags.

In thinking of adaptations for this exercise, consider how it might apply for teaching transitional words and phrases. Figure 6.4 illustrates this. Teachers can find or compile a similar handout for prepositions, if needed.

Show Location		
Above	Beside	Near or nearby
Across	Between	Off
Adjacent to	Beyond	On top of
Against	By	Opposite to
Along	Down	Outside
Among	Here	Over
Around	In back of	Throughout
Behind	In front of	To the right
Below	Inside	Under
Beneath	Into	

Indicate Time		
About	Following	Subsequently
After or afterward	Later	Then
Always	Meanwhile	Third
As soon as	Never	Today
At	Next	Tomorrow
Before	Once	Until
During	Second	When
Earlier	Simultaneously	Whenever
Finally	Sometimes	Yesterday
First	Soon	

Compare Items		
Also	In the same way	Similarly
As	Like or likewise	In similar fashion

Show Differences		
Alternatively	However	Otherwise
Although	In contrast	Rather than
But	Nevertheless	Still
Contrary to	Notwithstanding	Whereas
Even though	On the other hand	Yet

Figure 6.4: Transitional words and phrases.

continued →

Emphasize a Point		
Again	In fact	To reiterate
By all means	Indeed	To repeat
Certainly	Of course	Undoubtedly
For this reason	Surely	Without a doubt
Add Information		
Again	As well	Further or furthermore
Along with	Besides	In addition
Also	For example	Moreover
Another	For instance	Next
Summarize or Conclude		
As a result of	To conclude	To summarize
Finally	In short	Last
In conclusion	In summary	Therefore

Independent Learning—"You Do It Alone"

Individually, students review the class list and record pertinent verbs they might use in their stories; they may record these verbs in their writing resource binders, their journals, or another notetaking device. Teachers launch this task by stating, "Think about the characters you've invented for your stories and the dialogue you have written. Review the collective class list of verbs, and record those that strengthen how the characters in your story speak to one another."

Students will select verbs from this annotated list to revise their drafts (now or at another time) to replace repetitive or existing weak verbs with new ones or add verbs where needed to complement dialogue. To prepare students for success with this revision task, teachers model and use the think-aloud process beforehand. In doing so, they remind students that they will insert or change dialogue tag verbs to aptly reveal emotions, responses, beliefs, and so on in their characters' exchanges. They identify the dialogue section or sections of a sample draft by placing sticky notes in the margins or highlighting or circling the passage by hand or through an electronic editing tool. Then, they write on the sample while concurrently thinking out loud to show where they would revise to strengthen any portion of the writing that needs attention.

Summary

When acquiring a new skill, strategy, or procedure, any learner benefits from a direct instruction model, such as gradual release of responsibility. This instructional framework is predicated on four components that teachers use to plan lessons in an orchestrated way that promotes successful mastery. Although teachers can change the order of these phases, when teaching something new, educators must capitalize on each of them to cement learning. In the subsequent chapters, readers will shore up their toolbox for teaching literacy. Once armed with a collection of effective ways to instruct and assess, teachers will use gradual release of responsibility to work with team members to design solid, cohesive lessons that address learning targets.

CHAPTER 7

Plan High-Quality Literacy Instruction

Teachers of all academic disciplines in grades 4–5—or those in a self-contained classroom who teach all subjects—should emphasize literacy skill development since it remains a goal of *every* teacher to further students' capabilities in this area. This practice can augment dedicated literacy time within the school day for delivering high-quality and comprehensive literacy instruction that interweaves the domains of reading, writing, speaking, and listening. In developing these essential skills, teachers guide students to naturally make connections among them and honor the reciprocity of these literacy strands.

Teaching to accomplish these lofty goals occurs during a dedicated segment of the school day. In grades 4 and 5, some schools refer to it as a *literacy block* or *ELA*. Others may teach reading and writing separately at different times within the school day. As mentioned in this book's introduction (refer to the list on page 3), with the interconnected and complementary nature of reading and writing, cleanly dividing the two areas of literacy proves difficult and not necessarily in students' best interest. Furthermore, in *Writing to Read* authors Graham and Hebert (2010) assert that "writing about a text should enhance comprehension because it provides students with a tool for visibly and permanently recording, connecting, analyzing, personalizing, and manipulating key ideas in a text" (p. 13). Therefore, it behooves schools that have separate reading and writing sections or periods to intertwine both subjects in certain instances. For example, in reading class, students should write to demonstrate comprehension; in a writing period, students read to find evidence in fiction and nonfiction texts to use for various writing purposes.

(For more information about the interrelated benefits of these literacy strands, see Writing Instruction Recommendations, page 164.)

No matter its name or configuration, schools build a specific and sacred period into the daily schedule for literacy. *Specific* implies that this particular chunk of time is intentionally devoted to the teaching, refinement, and practice of literacy skills and standards. *Sacred* refers to the utmost priority assigned to this endeavor; accordingly, literacy remains protected as a fundamental part of a student's day, like mathematics and science.

Teachers must intentionally map out the learning that takes place by maximizing every minute of literacy instruction. Students participate in activities and assessments, articulate the purpose of their learning, and work as a classroom community toward the common goal of becoming independent interpreters of complex text, communicators, and crafters of written works within a high-quality learning environment. Though the structures, timing, and procedures may vary by classroom, school, and district, teachers strengthen literacy skills during a language arts block. Teachers of other subjects incorporate pertinent literacy goals within their content areas, as well.

To support teams in strengthening students' literacy, this chapter focuses on how teachers can effectively address the following components in the classroom.

- Literacy instruction in a PLC
- Reading instruction recommendations
- Close reading of complex texts
- Writing instruction recommendations
- Feedback
- Mentor texts
- Spelling instruction
- Vocabulary instruction

Literacy Instruction in a PLC

Delivering a guaranteed and viable curriculum that meets the needs of all students requires a well-thought-out, collaborative plan. In a PLC, teams work closely together to construct and uphold a daily time for deep and intentional teaching, thinking, and practice dedicated to literacy. They meet regularly—weekly if schedules permit—to discuss forthcoming curricular materials and instructional plans. Together, they participate in the PREP process (chapter 1, page 9) and establish learning progressions (chapter 3, page 59) as they develop a curriculum to ensure they meet the demands of the learning standards and overall objectives. They familiarize themselves with the complex texts they deliberately chose and identify the elements of the texts that will lead to authentic teachable moments in developing reading, writing, vocabulary, and foundational skills.

Teams discuss plans for explicit teaching, modeling, differentiating, and assessing, as well as possible scaffolds, extensions, and opportunities for student engagement. Teachers will undoubtedly apply their own unique teaching styles within their individual classrooms and adapt instruction to meet their students' diverse needs. However, working as a team allows teachers to capitalize on each other's expertise and collective thinking so they plan high-quality instruction that ensures advantageous learning experiences for all students.

Reading Instruction Recommendations

In their report *Reading Next*, Gina Biancarosa and Catherine Snow (2004) assert that it is more challenging to secure adequate literacy development for students in grades 4–12 than it is to provide primary students with solid reading education. Why? First, students in the former group grapple with more complex literacy skills that are incorporated in various subjects. Second, as students progress from upper elementary to high school, they often lack the motivation to improve their reading or maintain an interest in school-based reading as compared to when they were in primary school.

Biancarosa and Snow (2004) compile a list of reading instruction recommendations, which are featured in table 7.1 (page 156) alongside ideas for how each might play out during classroom instruction in various subject areas. They assert that these instructional methods effectively support students in transitioning from the basic literacy tasks they experienced in primary years to the more challenging tasks required in grades 4–12.

When reviewing the research-based recommendations in table 7.1, recognize that any of them in isolation will not suffice. Therefore, teachers must use them in combination within instruction to optimally service students, as well as collect assessment data to gauge students' performance and respond accordingly.

Table 7.1: Reading Instruction Recommendations and Examples

Recommendations From *Reading Next*	Examples for Implementation
Direct, explicit comprehension instruction, which is instruction in the strategies and processes that proficient readers use to understand what they read, including summarizing, keeping track of one's own understanding, and a host of other practices (such as teaching modeling, reciprocal teaching, and scaffolded instruction)	Using the components of the gradual release model described in chapter 6 (page 137), teachers conduct a series of lessons that explicitly and systematically support students in producing objective, brief summaries of narrative and informational text. By capturing the main idea and key details, students gain a better understanding of how an author develops his or her work, which serves to deepen students' comprehension.
Effective instructional principles embedded in content, including language arts teachers using content-area texts and content-area teachers providing instruction and practice in reading and writing skills specific to their subject area	When ELA teachers introduce a strategy, like outlining or paraphrasing, they expect students to apply the new skill not only with fictional works but with content-area texts, as well. This facilitates comprehension across disciplines. Additionally, subject-area teachers encourage students to read and write like experts in a field do, such as scientists, historians, and mathematicians. To teach this disciplinary literacy in science, for example, teachers focus instruction on how diagrams, drawings, and photographs help readers gain meaning.
Motivation and self-directed learning, which includes building motivation to read and learn and providing students with the instruction and supports needed for independent learning tasks they will face after graduation	In chapter 9 (page 217), a discussion about culturally responsive texts helps teachers consider how to select appropriate reading material that resonates with students. Another way to foster engagement is when teachers provide opportunities for students to choose their own texts to read from a list of appropriately challenging works. Or, they allow students to select topics for a writing task, such as for a research report or an opinion essay. (Additionally, see the ideas in the Diverse Texts section of this figure.)
Text-based collaborative learning, which involves students interacting with one another around a variety of texts	To increase students' comprehension and critical-thinking skills, teachers can organize collaborative opportunities that compel students to interact with one another around complex texts. For example, instruct students to participate in a jigsaw activity or form literature circles to work together to complete various tasks. Teachers can pose these types of questions, for example, as the basis for collaborative discourse during a narrative unit: "What evidence in the text reveals characters' traits?" "How do characters' beliefs impact their actions?" "What qualities do protagonists possess that make them similar across stories?" "How could the protagonist handle the situation differently?" "How does the dialogue in this section of the story move the plot forward?" "What does the dialogue reveal about characters, such as their motivations, beliefs, or actions?" "Is there a place in the narrative where an exchange of dialogue would be effective, and how so?"
Strategic tutoring, which provides students with intense individualized reading, writing, and content instruction as needed	After a data-inquiry meeting, teachers provide interventions based on the learning targets to address the needs of learners who struggle. Additionally, teachers meet with students to provide individual support based on in-class assessments. Refer to figure 5.6 (page 134) for scaffolding ideas for literacy instruction.

Diverse texts, which are texts at a variety of difficulty levels and on a variety of topics	Teachers can provide a list of texts pertaining to a unit of instruction in any subject area that is differentiated by readiness level, topical interest, and genre (mystery, fantasy, historical fiction, and so on). Conduct a brief book talk about each text, and invite students to list their top three choices on scratch paper. Review these choices, and assign each student to read a book at his or her appropriate challenge level. Teachers might organize literature circles for students who are reading the same fiction or nonfiction books to meet together to discuss the common text and to complete various tasks tied to learning targets. (Also see the ideas in the Text-Based Collaborative Learning section of this figure.)
Intensive writing, including instruction connected to the kinds of writing tasks students will have to perform well in high school and beyond	When students write about what they read, it improves their comprehension. For instance, have students write an opinion essay based on a narrative, such as in the following example: *Would you recommend living forever? After reading* Tuck Everlasting *by Natalie Babbitt (1975), write an essay to argue whether you would want to be immortal. Use evidence from the book to support your opinion.* Students can also write informational pieces connected to texts, as in the following example: *Write an informational essay that compares the perspectives of two different historical figures about the same event. Within your essay, cite textual evidence from resources.* Additionally, teach students the stages of the writing process to aid them in producing quality pieces; give them clear expectations for their writing.
A technology component, which includes technology as a tool for and a topic of literacy instruction	Technology complements and furthers literacy instruction in various ways. For example, students can use it to find synonyms, define unknown vocabulary (www.vocabulary.com), or look up a grammar rule. Students can also produce writing electronically, share and collect feedback from peers, and research various topics to collect evidence for a report or essay.
Ongoing formative assessment of students, which is an informal, often daily, assessment of how students are progressing under current instructional practices	Teachers can issue exit slips with open-ended prompts (such as the questions in Text-Based Collaborative Learning) or ask students to write a brief summary to reflect their understanding of content. They can lead an active-participation session in which students use thumbs-up or thumbs-down to respond to foundational prompts related to key details—for example, characters' actions, events in a historical event, or steps in a process (see figure 2.4, page 47).

Source for recommendations: Biancarosa & Snow, 2004.

Additionally, Biancarosa and Snow (2004) suggest providing infrastructure supports that align well to PLC culture, such as the following.

▸ Extended time for literacy (approximately two to four hours for literacy-connected learning daily within language arts and other subject areas)

▸ Long-term and ongoing professional development

▸ Ongoing summative assessments of students and programs

▸ Teacher team meetings

▸ Leadership commitment (principal as instructional leader and teachers who spearhead curricular improvements)

▸ Implementation of a comprehensive literacy program across content areas

Close Reading of Complex Texts

Teachers carefully select and expose students to complex texts of varying lengths and across multiple topics that align to each curricular unit of study. Students experience prose—fiction, nonfiction, and informational texts—as well as poetry. With the focus skills and learning standards top of mind, teams select complex texts by utilizing the three criteria of complexity described in chapter 3 (page 59). These criteria have teacher teams examine text by quantitative and qualitative measures, as well as consider students' characteristics and the tasks teachers ask them to address. Quantitatively, teachers rely on computer software to calculate the text's word and sentence lengths. Qualitatively, they look closely at the language, syntax, vocabulary, and levels of meaning. Additionally, teachers rely on their professional judgment to align the texts to the assignments they issue and their particular students.

With these carefully selected complex texts, teachers engage students in close reading, which the Partnership for Assessment of Readiness for College and Careers (2011) describes as follows:

> Close, analytic reading stresses engaging with a text of sufficient complexity directly and examining meaning thoroughly and methodically, encouraging students to read and reread deliberately. Directing student attention on the text itself empowers students to understand the central ideas and key supporting details. It also enables students to reflect on the meanings of individual words and sentences; the order in which sentences unfold; and the development of these ideas over the course of the text, which ultimately leads students to arrive at an understanding of the text as a whole. (p. 6)

When teachers guide students through a close-reading experience, they invite them to carefully examine the text to address specific learning targets. Perhaps a text necessitates a close read because of subtleties, sophisticated or archaic language, complicated structures, advanced vocabulary, keenly composed elements, or the elaborateness of the topic. Frey and Fisher (2013) emphasize the benefits of close reading in acknowledging that "students do not arrive already knowing how to interrogate a text and dig down into its deeper meaning. Teachers have to teach students how to do this, in both informational and literary texts" (p. 46). Through such texts, we explicitly teach our students to develop their knowledge, skills, comprehension, and vocabulary.

Teachers must prepare ahead of a close-reading lesson to maximize time and amplify the learning experience. They must have a well-orchestrated plan for delivering purposeful, robust, and engaging instruction. If a district uses a purchased reading program, teams carefully review each text prior to teaching it and ensure that plans and instruction laid out in the program's teachers' manual directly correlate with the targeted literacy standards and lesson objectives.

As teams collectively devise a distinct plan for using the text at the center of instruction, the following suggestions (in addition to the other chapters in this book) can serve as a useful guide to effectively enlist students in close reading.

- ▸ Determine the text's complexity level and core ideas.
- ▸ Identify purposes for reading, and chunk the text.
- ▸ Flag key vocabulary.
- ▸ Develop text-dependent questions.
- ▸ Ensure a unit connection.
- ▸ Introduce the text.

The following sections examine these suggestions in detail.

Determine the Text's Complexity Level and Core Ideas

Teachers determine the challenge level of a text by using the three criteria described in chapter 3 (page 59) and summarized earlier in this section. They also identify the text's core ideas to be sure they understand its essence and plan with this focus in mind. For example, these essential themes can apply to *Tuck Everlasting* (Babbitt, 1975): *People search for a place to call home and a sense of family to foster security. Sometimes, the truth needs to be kept secret to protect people. Life experiences can foster growth and change. The courage to break free of familiar ways creates freedom and self-confidence.* Teachers refrain from stating these overarching ideas to students lest they reveal the themes without the advantage of students discovering them for themselves through strong lesson design and execution.

Identify Purposes for Reading, and Chunk the Text

Longer texts, and even shorter texts, must be taught in manageable chunks. Therefore, teachers divide the text into sections or passages according to the purposes for reading and the amount of text students can consume at one time. Use preassessment information coupled with the teachers' professional judgment to determine how much of a text to target for a particular lesson.

Let students know that, since the text is complex, they will dive back into it sometimes for two, three, or even more exposures to reread for explicit purposes. Explain that each time they read the text, they gain ground as readers and understand the author's work more powerfully and even differently. For example, students circle unknown words and underline surrounding text that reveals context clues. They share their words with a partner and together agree on definitions and confirm them with an outside source. To focus on what the text implicitly states, they annotate a passage by highlighting evidence that has an underlying meaning and writing an inference in the margin that corresponds to what they mark. In another encounter with the text, they may revisit a passage to examine the author's craft or purpose for writing.

Flag Key Vocabulary

While examining the text, teachers should also be mindful to flag vocabulary words students need to know. This applies to specialized terms used in content areas, such as science and mathematics, as well as general words that frequently appear across texts. If students must know these words to initially comprehend a text, teachers frontload instruction of these words before or at the beginning of the text. If the texts include context clues for these words, teachers can conduct instruction around using these clues to uncover the meaning of unknown words. Otherwise, teachers can wait to teach other words as they appear in the reading passage. (See the Vocabulary Instruction section on page 174 for a thorough discussion about this topic.)

Develop Text-Dependent Questions

Text-dependent questions draw students' attention to essential areas of the content-rich text, compel them to closely read, and require the use of textual evidence. Consequently, students derive more meaning, which improves their comprehension. When developing questions for this purpose, pose those that invite students to use details from the text as a basis for their responses. For example, while reading the book *Wonder* by R. J. Palacio (2012), a teacher might ask students, "What evidence from the novel supports author R. J. Palacio's decision to title her book *Wonder*?" This text-dependent question compels students to rely on excerpts from the novel to support their assertions. In contrast, the following questions, although thematically tied to the text, do not require that students actually read the story to respond: "How would it feel to befriend a person who has a disability?" and "What prevents some people from befriending those who are disabled?" Questions of this nature permit students to merely provide their own opinion completely separate from the text.

Teachers can certainly ask questions that contribute to a lively discussion with text-to-self connections if they so choose. However, they should save these questions (such as the preceding text-to-self connection questions about *Wonder*; Palacio, 2012) for after students tackle questions that necessitate delving into the content to think more critically about the author's work. This tactic of saving text-to-self questions for later will likely facilitate a discussion in which students might naturally reference the book and add depth to their conversation.

Ensure a Unit Connection

Teachers select appropriately challenging complex text that expressly aligns with the particular unit of study and addresses its learning goals. For example, in our dialogue unit, our team selected literature that incorporates dialogue as a narrative device so students have published examples of skills they will emulate in their writing. The selected text can also be used in another narrative-related unit to exemplify other focus areas, such as those related to figurative language, story elements, and literary devices besides dialogue.

Introduce the Text

Teachers must introduce a new text to students in a judicious and intentional way. They must take into account what students already know and use strategies that allow them to gain full advantage of the reading material, which teachers expressly select for its complexity, content value, writing structure and style, and so forth.

A text can prove challenging for students who lack the background knowledge (schema) to make sense of it. Timothy Shanahan (2019) states that teachers can guide students to use what they already know to scaffold what they will learn in a text. He admits that prior knowledge can help students with, for example, drawing inferences and clarifying information. However, he cautions that too much emphasis on building students' prior knowledge preceding the reading of a text can result in issues. For instance, it can reduce the cognitive work teachers expect students to do to grow as readers. Sometimes teachers frontload too much irrelevant information that strays from the elements that should be the focus to bolster comprehension. To effectively build background knowledge when introducing a text, Shanahan (2019) recommends the following dos and don'ts:

- Do reveal to your students the topic they will be asked to read about and/or the genre they'll be reading about.

- Do not spend extensive time reviewing what they may already know about a topic.

- Do tell students relevant information the author would have assumed them to know unless you think it can easily be inferred.

- Do not reveal information the author is going to provide.

- Do consider whether there are cultural gaps between what the student knows and what the text assumes.

- Do not select texts that require extensive amounts of prerequisite information to understand.

- Do teach students to use what they know when evaluating the truth or accuracy of what they are reading (does it make sense?).

Additionally, to build background knowledge, teachers might take one of the following approaches, if necessary, to help students appreciate a text.

▶ A teacher can plan activities using short supplementary text, either fiction (perhaps a short story) or nonfiction (such as an article), that serves to inform students about the unknown topic. Therefore, when students begin the complex text at the center of instruction, they have built some awareness.

▶ A teacher can explain to students that they are beginning a complex text, and they likely have questions about it right away. The teacher instructs students to think about and share questions they have based on the beginning passages that he or she reads. Then, he or she responds to these questions to build schema, which can include conducting a slide presentation or asking students to read a short text, watch a brief video, listen to an audio, or study artwork that exposes them to topics related to the complex text. Teachers can even design a jigsaw activity using several different reading pieces.

When introducing a text, teachers should refrain from providing a summary that gives away too much since students can arrive at realizations on their own and through intentional lessons that teachers conduct. If an author provides a summary on the back cover, or an editor does so within a textbook, teachers might conceal it. Later, at an appropriate point in the text, teachers ask students to create a brief summary. Afterward, they can share the author's or publisher's synopsis and compare it with the students' versions. This can be a useful activity in and of itself to see how students' initial assumptions of the text differ from the official summary.

Teachers can also frontload explanations of words that lack context clues that students must know to comprehend the beginning of the text, as mentioned earlier. Additionally, teachers could pose a guiding question that positions students to consider an overarching concept and read with more purpose, such as the following.

▸ How do authors develop characters?

▸ Is figurative language an effective writing technique?

▸ How does an author's perspective or a narrator's point of view influence you as a reader?

Notice that these questions prime students to notice the interplay among literary elements and devices so they can read with more insight. This approach is preferable to posing prereading questions that lead students and reveal too much. As an example, before reading *Tuck Everlasting* (Babbitt, 1975), teachers should refrain from asking, "Would you like to live forever?" This question exposes content and themes that students should discover through their own careful reading.

Additionally, teachers might mentally prepare students for complexity by stating that the upcoming text will challenge them in new ways. Further, this work will expand their thinking, illuminate their understanding, and help them improve as readers so they can handle increasingly more sophisticated text. If the learning becomes difficult at times, that is to be expected. Explain to students that, as a group (teacher and students), you will assist each other in this journey of growth.

By grades 4 and 5, students have been exposed to nonfiction text features—tables of contents, glossaries, indexes, captions, headings, and so forth—and ways to use them to locate information and understand a topic. During prereading, students can briefly preview the text using these features to get an overview of what they are about to read. For narrative, which typically lacks text features, teachers can ask students to make predictions based on the title or the cover. These activities, though, should not be so involved that they interfere with students' own meaning-making as they experience the complex text.

To access a rich resource of teacher-created lessons for complex text typically used in grades 3–5—which includes quality text-dependent questions, integrated writing tasks and assessments, and selected vocabulary—become a member of the Basal Alignment Project (BAP). To do so, sign up on Edmodo (www.edmodo .com) for free, and join the BAP group by entering this code: f4q6nm. You can also access BAP through Achieve the Core (www.achievethecore.org), an organization that provides a host of resources, including a step-by-step guide on how to develop text-dependent questions, student writing samples, lessons, assessments, and more.

Writing Instruction Recommendations

In their Carnegie Corporation of New York report *Writing to Read*—in which they present their findings on the correlative influence between writing and reading—authors Graham and Hebert (2010) recommend ways that teachers can use writing to bolster students' reading skills and comprehension, and help students learn about subject-matter content. They sort their findings into three categories.

1. **Teachers ask students to write about what they read:** When students write an extended response based on a text-based task—for example, a personal response, analysis, interpretation, or summary—reading comprehension improves. Additionally, taking notes about text results in positive gains, as this enables students to review the text, determine significant ideas, organize the material, and make connections. Collectively, these steps yield new insights. Further, when students answer text-dependent questions in writing or design and answer these types of questions, they also deepen their understanding of a text and increase their knowledge of the content.

2. **Teachers conduct lessons around writing skills and processes to create text:** Since writing and reading share common processes and knowledge, teaching students to write well improves their reading skills. Therefore, teachers conduct lessons on the process of writing (planning, editing, revision, and so on), text structures (such as compare–contrast, problem–solution, cause–effect, sequence, and description), sentence and paragraph construction, and spelling. (See the Spelling Instruction section on page 173 for more details on this area of literacy.)

3. **Teachers increase the amount of writing that students do:** Providing students with more time to write their own texts—such as texts on self- or peer-selected topics, letters to internet pen pals, and journal entries to themselves or peers—correlates with an uptick in reading comprehension.

In another Carnegie Corporation report, *Writing Next*, authors Steve Graham and Dolores Perin (2007) identify eleven elements of research-based instructional methods that contribute to writing achievement in grades 4–12 students. To arrive at these recommendations, the authors used statistical meta-analysis "to determine the *consistency* and *strength* of the effects of instructional practices on student writing quality and to highlight those practices that hold the most promise" (Graham & Perin, 2007, p. 4). Although the following elements are intentionally ordered by effect size to list those with a higher influence first, only minimal differences occur among their effect sizes. The authors admit that additional research could uncover more of what can successfully increase writing skills.

1. **Writing strategies:** Explicitly teach each step of the writing process—prewrite, draft, revise, edit, publish, and reflect—and show students how to apply the steps independently. (This links with element 7.)

2. **Summarization:** To provide instruction to students about how to write strong summaries of texts, explicitly and systematically teach the characteristics and structure of a summary.

3. **Collaborative writing:** Devise activities throughout the writing process in which students support each other with at least one aspect of their writing; for example, they could brainstorm ideas together, conduct and share research, and provide feedback to each other.

4. **Specific product goals:** Make students aware of the goal of a writing task, including the purpose of the task (for example, to inform or explain) and the structure and characteristics of the final writing product. Additionally, set specific goals throughout the writing process, such as to add transitions or expand on an idea.

5. **Word processing:** Have students independently or with peers use electronic devices (for example, tablets, laptops, or desktop computers) for a written task. "Compared with composing by hand, the effect of word-processing instruction in most of the studies reviewed was positive, suggesting that word processing has a consistently positive impact on writing quality" (Graham & Perin, 2007, p. 17).

6. **Sentence combining:** Provide instruction on different ways to combine sentences, such as compound and complex sentences, to construct more fluid and sophisticated prose.

7. **Prewriting:** Introduce ways students can generate and organize ideas as part of the writing process, prior to composing a first draft.

8. **Inquiry activities:** Facilitate engaging experiences that help students develop ideas and content for a writing task by analyzing data based on a specific goal. For example, students compare and contrast characters for a

characterization writing assignment, study objects blindfolded to make a list of sensory words and phrases for a descriptive paragraph, or conduct a survey and analyze data of classmates' preferences for an opinion paper.

9. **Process writing approach:** Design various differentiated activities that emphasize writing for uninterrupted and extended periods of time, writing for authentic audiences, student interaction, self-reflection and self-evaluation, and conferencing.

10. **Study of models:** Within instruction, use mentor texts that afford students opportunities to see exemplary writing models they can read, analyze, and emulate for express purposes. For example, examine sensory details, dialogue exchange, or transitional word and phrase usage.

11. **Writing for content learning:** To increase content-area knowledge, have students use writing as a vehicle to demonstrate understanding of material. In social studies, for example, students write journal entries about a miner's experience in the California Gold Rush. In science, students write observational notes during a field trip to a nature reserve.

The research-based recommendations in both *Writing to Read* (Graham & Hebert, 2010) and *Writing Next* (Graham & Perin, 2007) affords teachers valuable suggestions to help increase students' literacy proficiencies. As a team, teachers can share successful results of improving student achievement that they experienced by incorporating any of the strategies. This way they can capitalize on learning from each other to benefit all students they serve.

Feedback

Succinctly stated, "The purpose of feedback is to reduce the gap between current and desired states of knowing" (Hattie & Yates, 2014, p. 67). When students receive effective input on how they attempted or accomplished a task and how they can improve on their work to advance in their learning, feedback ranks high as an influencing factor in their achievement.

For it to be valuable, the input needs to occur after teachers lead instruction, which then provides students an opportunity to practice and apply the taught skill. Feedback is "but part of the teaching process and is that which happens second—after a student has responded to initial instruction—when information is provided regarding some aspect(s) of the student's task and performance" (Hattie & Timperley, 2007, p. 82). To be successful in moving students forward in their learning, both students and teachers must learn to offer salient and usable input.

In chapter 4 (page 93), we discuss the importance of rubrics in clearly communicating success criteria to students so they understand the expectations in place for them. Rubrics ensure that there are no surprises and students know what to aim for in their work. Teachers conduct lessons around specific line items on the rubric, which set the purpose for learning. This way, when providing feedback on students' work, teachers can easily connect that feedback back to particular scoring criteria of which students should already be fully aware.

For writing-focused tasks, teachers conduct conferences where they meet with students individually, and perhaps as a small group as well, to discuss students' writing projects. Although the purpose is to provide feedback so students know what changes or additions they need to make next to improve their writing piece, conferencing has other benefits as well. During this dialogue, students who might be intimidated to share with peers in earshot can feel comfortable talking alone with the teacher. Plus, even though this discussion centers on instruction, it concurrently builds a relationship between the student and the teacher.

Grant Wiggins (2012) suggests key elements of feedback that teachers can incorporate into their instructional program to issue effective feedback and generate successful results. Based on these key elements, feedback should be the following.

▸ **Goal referenced:** Be clear about how the feedback connects to the goals of the task students need to accomplish. Point to criteria on the rubric to help articulate the goal so students are forever mindful of what's expected. This way, teachers use the rubric as an instructional tool, and the feedback connects to it.

▸ **Tangible and transparent:** Feedback to students must draw their attention to the goal, as well as be tangible enough that they know what to do with it. The feedback teachers provide must serve as a learning opportunity.

▸ **Actionable:** If students cannot act on the comments to make the necessary revisions to improve, the feedback is ineffective. Therefore, general, ambiguous comments like "Excellent job!" or "Give it another try!" or even grades leave students wondering what they need to do next. Actionable feedback is specific and gives students clear direction to make necessary improvements.

▸ **User friendly:** Feedback should be comprehensible to students; otherwise, it is useless. So teachers must use language that is accessible based on their students' ages and even characteristics. Also, teachers should be careful to offer the right amount of feedback; if it is too

much, students might feel overwhelmed and shut down or ignore
the comments.

▶ **Timely:** Once students complete an assignment, teachers should strive
to assess and return it with valuable feedback as soon as possible so
students can apply the input. Also, teachers are not the only individuals
who can provide feedback. Train others to give effective input and to do
so in a timely fashion—peers in the classroom, remote peers, parents,
or guardians.

▶ **Ongoing:** Ongoing, continuous feedback should be formative so that
students can use it. Teachers can offer it in myriad ways—oral, written,
and electronic—and give students opportunities to make adjustments
that matter now, rather than waiting until it is too late to make
any changes.

▶ **Consistent:** Teams participate in collaborative-scoring sessions so that
together they interpret the rubric, agree on what constitutes quality,
and collect anchor papers that provide examples of student work at each
performance level on the rubric. In doing so, they come to a consensus
about high-quality work and assess student products consistently and
uniformly (see chapter 4, page 93). Additionally, teachers train students
how to use and interpret the rubric so that they can deliver consistent
and useful feedback to one another.

A host of individuals can offer feedback to benefit students for improving their
products. Peers can do so when they learn how to capably and effectively collect
and communicate it. Teachers can model how to provide feedback using student
samples along with rubrics and target different writing skills as the basis for the
lesson. Figure 7.1 shows an example of a print or electronic tool teachers can give
to students to direct discussion based on the example dialogue unit we have used
throughout this book. Rather than addressing all line items during one feedback
session, teachers or peers focus on one or a few aligned rows at a time.

In addition to the feedback between teachers and students and among peers, the
school-home connection can be powerful and useful in serving students' needs. To
ensure that parents, guardians, or older siblings do not unknowingly detract from a
student's success by doing more of his or her work than they ought, consider send-
ing home a copy of figure 7.2 (page 171). This letter allows someone at home to
offer important feedback without overstepping to rewrite any of a student's paper.
The figure is generic, so consider customizing it to align with a specific writing task.

Feedback Sheet			
Questions to Guide Revision	**Check one column.**		**Comments**
	Yes	Kind of	No	
Is the dialogue important? How so?				
Could the writer include more dialogue to make the story better? How so?				
Is there dialogue that could be deleted? Why?				
Is the dialogue tag appropriate for what the character says or does?				
Does the writer use proper dialogue mechanics?				

Figure 7.1: Feedback sheet.

Visit **go.SolutionTree.com/literacy** *for a free reproducible version of this figure.*

Dear Parent or Guardian,

I am invested in assisting students to improve their writing skills. I invite you to partner with me to help in this endeavor by following these suggestions. If you choose to use any of them, please attach a note to your child's paper briefly describing how you served as a coach. Refrain from writing on his or her paper and rather offer feedback using these pointers as a guide. In doing so, you empower your child to make necessary revisions. This will strengthen his or her writing and allow me to understand each student's writing ability so I can build strengths and address weaknesses.

1. **Assignment guidelines:** Ask to see the writing task, checklist, or rubric. Review it with your child to be clear about the particular assignment's expectations. Work together to see that the paper addresses all parts of the writing assignment.

2. **Oral reading:** Ask your child to read the paper aloud, and do the following.

   - *Listen for clarity*—If a sentence is hard to read, it could reflect a grammar error. Ask him or her to find and correct any grammatical errors.

   - *Listen for natural stops*—When there is a natural stop, ask if there is proper end punctuation (a period, exclamation mark, or question mark). This will help not only with using proper end punctuation but also with avoiding run-ons or fragments. If there is a pause, consider recommending a comma or an end punctuation mark if a rule applies.

3. **Organization:** Ask for evidence of proper organization of the whole paper and within paragraphs. Here are some examples.

   - Plot structure for fictional stories

   - Whole-paper structure for expository writing (introduction, body, and conclusion)

   - Paragraph structure for expository writing (topic sentence, support, and ending sentence)

   - Certain text structures (problem–solution or cause–effect)

   - Text features (chart, graph, table of contents, subheadings, glossary, index, and so on)

4. **Word choice:** Ask your child to review the paper and circle words that he or she feels reflect the best choice. Ask him or her to review the paper again and underline any weak words. Suggest using a print or digital resource (www.vocabulary.com, www.collinsdictionary.com, or www.thesaurus.com) to replace the underlined words with more appropriate and sophisticated ones.

5. **Details:** Work with your child to critique the paper's use of details. Does a reader feel compelled to keep reading? Does a reader find the paper interesting or informative? Are the details appropriate for the writing assignment? For example, short stories need details about setting, character, and plot. Argument and opinion papers need logical reasons and supporting evidence.

6. **Development:** Is the paper well developed? If it's a story, is the plotline fully executed with a central conflict, rising action, a climax, falling action, and a resolution? Are narrative techniques (like dialogue and description) included to enhance it? If it is an opinion or argument paper, is there a clearly stated position with logical reasons and sufficient evidence and elaboration to support it?

7. **Sentence beginnings:** Ask your child to read the first three words of each sentence in the paper. Ask these questions: "What do you notice about the beginnings of sentences? Are the words and parts of speech different? Do they sound the same or repeated?" Ask him or her to revise sentence beginnings, as appropriate, so there is variety.

8. **Title:** Ask your child if he or she included a title. Is it original, and does it reflect the gist of the paper? Are proper words capitalized? For titles, the first and last word of the title are always capitalized. All other words except small prepositions (like *in* and *of*), articles (*the*, *a*, and *an*), and coordinating conjunctions (*for*, *and*, *but*, and *so*) are capitalized.

9. **Spelling:** Ask your child to circle any words that he or she is not sure are spelled correctly. Together, use a resource to verify and correct spelling.

Source: Adapted from Glass, 2017, p. 26.

Figure 7.2: Student feedback suggestions for the school-home connection.

*Visit **go.SolutionTree.com/literacy** for a free reproducible version of this figure.*

Mentor Texts

Teachers use mentor texts as a teaching tool in both reading and writing. Irene Fountas and Gay Su Pinnell (2012) define *mentor texts* as "a book or other text that serves as an example of excellent writing. Mentor texts provide models of specific genres for literature discussion and student writing" (p. 478). Exemplary published works or even student writing samples of different text types (such as opinion, informational, or narrative) can qualify as mentor texts if they reflect tenets of strong writing. Across content areas, teachers share mentor texts with students as models of what they can produce. In reading, teachers also use them by showing students examples of different genres.

Teachers choose specific mentor texts that align with learning targets for a particular unit. During instruction, students examine them to detect and emulate specific skills that exceptional authors include so they can improve their own work. For example, teachers use a narrative text for students to examine the way an author weaves together story elements, uses figurative language to paint an intricate description of a setting, or uses dialogue to reveal characters' thoughts and beliefs. Throughout the unit, however, teachers do not only feature mentor texts. They will also show examples of less-accomplished pieces of student (and even published) work for students to detect, discuss, and perhaps correct deficiencies and weaknesses.

A mentor text can be the complex text teachers use throughout a unit of instruction to address both reading and writing learning standards and direct students' attention to the text multiple times for various purposes. For example, consider that students initially use the exemplary published work of fiction to address reading standards that focus on identifying a narrator's point of view and describing how it impacts plot development. Discussion, activities, and assessments revolve around these types of questions: *From whose point of view is this story written? How does it shape the plot? If the story were written from another point of view, in what ways would it be different? Does the point of view make you sympathetic to certain characters? In what way?* Students then return to the same text to concentrate on writing standards. They evaluate how the author uses point of view to assist them in making decisions about the narrator for their own stories. This prepares them for addressing learning targets, such as *introduce a narrator, determine from whose point of view the story is told, maintain a consistent point of view* (unless students extend the standard to write from multiple viewpoints), and *use point of view to shape and develop the plot.* During the dialogue unit, teachers expose students to complex text that serves as a mentor text so they can emulate published authors' treatment of meaningful and purposeful dialogue for their own stories.

EXERCISE

Consider Literacy Best Practices

Consider the provided recommendations for both reading and writing instruction, suggestions for feedback on students' writing, and ideas for mentor texts. Use this exercise as a springboard for team discussion and action.

Use the following questions to guide this exercise.

★ What reading and writing recommendations featured in this chapter have we used? What student achievement results did we notice as a result of any recommendation? How can our team share these cases with each other and use them as a learning exercise? How might we use these recommendations within our lessons?

★ How can our team implement any of the feedback suggestions? What do we currently do within teacher conferences that proves successful?

★ Have we effectively taught students to offer feedback to each other? If not, how can we design a gradual release of responsibility lesson for this purpose?

★ What digital tools do we use for feedback and writing in general?

★ What mentor texts do we each use? Which texts align with our learning targets?

Spelling Instruction

Steve Graham and Tanya Santangelo (2014) published a meta-analysis that includes fifty-three studies conducted with 6,037 students in grades K–12. In his blog post "Should We Teach Spelling?" Timothy Shanahan (2015b) succinctly relays the findings of this study, which concludes that "explicit instruction improves spelling. . . . Such teaching helps students to read and write better, and the gains that they make in spelling from such instruction is [*sic*] maintained over time."

Responding to a fifth-grade teacher's query, Shanahan (2015b) expresses reasons for teachers to infuse instruction with spelling. He asserts that communities want students to be able to spell, which is why it appears in most educational standards. Additionally, spelling instruction improves reading since it requires understanding of the relationship between letters and sounds, as well as word parts (affixes, base words). It also enhances written discourse because those who are adept at spelling words correctly aren't hampered by word construction. Therefore, they can more easily write to convey their ideas and even express themselves using a wide vocabulary. Another reason teachers ought to teach spelling is to help students avoid the potentially negative stigma that poor spellers experience, including scoring bias. Lastly, although spelling and grammar tools—like those built into Microsoft Word or available online (such as Grammarly; www.grammarly.com)—can help mitigate spelling and grammar problems, they sometimes fail to ameliorate writing errors. If students' spelling skills are deficient, these imperfect tools will often offer incorrect solutions. Students who don't spell well won't recognize when this happens.

To drive home the imperative of explicitly teaching spelling, Shanahan (2015b) offers salient advice applicable to upper elementary students: connect spelling with vocabulary instruction, tie spelling to word interpretation (such as structural analysis, Greek and Latin roots, affixes, and so on), devote no more than fifteen minutes of spelling to the literacy block but do so two to three times a week, and consider assigning spelling homework. He also advocates assigning memorization tasks, although not the kind that ask students to write a word repeatedly as practice. Instead, for example, use rhyme, mnemonic devices, or jingles as retention techniques (think *i* before *e* except after *c*). The next section relates to the first suggestion regarding vocabulary, a valuable mainstay of a literacy program.

Vocabulary Instruction

Vocabulary plays a prominent role in the development of adeptly literate students across the content areas. In fact, increased vocabulary equates to increased meaning making from text: "There is much evidence—strong correlations, several causal studies, as well as rich theoretical orientations—that shows that vocabulary is tightly related to reading comprehension across the age span" (Beck, McKeown, & Kucan, 2013, p. 1). For this reason, we spend more effort in this section on how teams can design and deliver effective vocabulary instruction for their students.

To comprehend complex texts brimming with rich themes, scientific explanations, or detailed historical accounts, students need word knowledge. With the ability to understand the nuances of language, such as figures of speech, word parts, and connotative language, students can comprehend a range of texts on various topics, as well as artfully tell a story or compose a strongly supported opinion. To communicate clearly and accurately with others, students must be equipped with vocabularies that allow for the effortless exchange of thoughts and ideas. For all these reasons, teachers continuously strengthen and refine students' vocabulary skills throughout instruction within dedicated literacy time, as well as in other subject areas.

Vocabulary instruction must extend beyond the surface level of teachers providing students with haphazard introductions to new words that appear in various texts. Rather, teachers emphasize expanding word aptitude through direct instruction to bolster students' academic background knowledge. Although reading widely contributes to word acquisition, it does not play as large a role as one might think. Experts in this area admit that reading's impact as a resource for mastering new vocabulary is overestimated.

Beck and colleagues (2013) state that to use a text to learn new words, the reader must be adept at decoding, realize the actual presence of the unknown word, and have the wherewithal to use the context to figure out what the word means. Students who struggle to decipher text in general are ill-equipped to successfully use context clues. Plus, to effectively learn the word, students require repeated exposure to it. Therefore, direct instruction proves more efficacious when teaching new words to students:

> The case for direct instruction is strong. From a number of perspectives, the research indicates that wide reading probably is not sufficient in itself to ensure that students will develop the necessary vocabulary and conse-quently the necessary academic background knowledge to do well in school. In contrast, direct instruction has an impressive track record of improving stu-dents' background knowledge and the comprehension of academic content. (Marzano, 2004, p. 69)

Furthermore, Marzano (2004) explains that a student's ability and grade level, plus the complexity of the text, dictate the chances of learning a word in context: "A high-ability student has a 19 percent chance of learning a new word in context, whereas a low-ability student has an 8 percent chance" (pp. 67–68).

To educate teams on the finer points of vocabulary instruction that enable wise planning, the following sections focus on the three tiers of word categories and ways to select appropriate words, a suggested amount of words to teach and when to introduce them, and the characteristics of and a detailed process for explicit vocabulary instruction, all suitable for grades 4–5. Additionally, teachers will find a variety of activity options, including ideas for using them within a narrative unit.

Tiers and Selection of Words

Not all unknown words need to be taught through direct instruction. Teachers need to carefully select vocabulary words based on various criteria—which words are necessary for students to fully comprehend a text, fundamental to the study of new concepts across disciplines, or enduring in that they are likely to emerge in social or academic settings. To determine how to best choose words for instruc-tional purposes, teachers should be familiar with the three-tier system of catego-rizing words that Beck et al. (2013) devised.

▸ **Tier one:** This tier includes basic words used frequently in conversation. Students acquire these words in everyday life; therefore, explicit instruction is usually unnecessary for native English speakers. Examples include sight words and other common words like *boy, chair, pretty, red,* and *hand.*

▸ **Tier two:** This tier includes words that mature language users commonly use. They are words that often appear in texts but not as frequently in conversation. Examples include *investigate, determine, claim,* and *infer.* These words change meaning based on the context in which they are used. For instance, *parallel,* in mathematics, conjures up a geometric shape; in physical education, it refers to parallel bars; and in language arts, it refers to a grammatical construction—parallelism or parallel structure. Since tier two words mean something different according to context, they can confuse students.

▸ **Tier three:** Often called *domain-specific words,* this tier refers to words that appear most often in a specific content area and are associated with a particular topic. Examples include *nucleus, genes, treaty,* and *electoral.* Sometimes, these words are so esoteric that people rarely experience them, such as *panjandrum* or *antidisestablishmentarianism.*

Teams plan direct instruction lessons to teach both tier two and tier three. However, Beck et al. (2013) and the Common Core designers (NGA & CCSSO, n.d.) suggest teachers expend more effort to teach tier two words. For one, most content-area texts assist teachers in their quest to present tier three words since many textbooks or other nonfiction materials use text features to point out their importance—through print features (bold, italicized, or highlighted typeface; sub-headings; bullets; and so forth), graphic aids (such as diagrams, graphs, or time-lines), organizational support (such as tables of contents, indexes, or glossaries), and illustrations. Plus, tier three words are used repeatedly in the text and explic-itly defined, and teachers in content areas focus squarely on these words during instruction. On the other hand, tier two words are more challenging for students to decipher on their own within a text, are used in many contexts, and help provide the pathway to learning tier three words. To help teams select appropriate tier two words, review the following four guidelines. These guidelines originate in Beck et al. (2013), but the text is adapted from Kathy Glass (2015). Answering *yes* to most of the listed questions indicates the word is worth teaching.

1. **The word is useful and appears across texts:** Is the word tier two, and is it useful enough to warrant attention and teach students? Will students encounter the word in many texts in other domains, and is it indicative of words mature language users use?

2. **It increases sophisticated word choices:** Are there words familiar to students that are similar to the target word? In this case, it is beneficial for students to learn the new word because it extends their inventory of vocabulary to include more expressive and specific words. This does not include adding synonyms to words already in their lexicon; rather, provide students with new words that are more precise and complex versions of the familiar words they already use.

3. **It aids in comprehension:** Does knowing the word enhance comprehension, and does it serve an important function within the context of the text? Does the word contribute to the student's meaning making? If a student doesn't know the word, will he or she not understand important concepts or find the text confusing?

4. **It connects to other learning:** Does the word relate to other concepts that students are studying? This might include concepts in other subject-matter texts or in other content areas. Does the word have the potential for students to build representations of it and connect to other words and concepts?

When to Teach Words and How Many

To import words into their personal working vocabularies and use them fluently in writing and speaking, students require repeated exposure to the new words and multiple opportunities to observe, write, and use them within meaningful contexts. Teachers can expose students to new words before they read a complex text, while students read it, and sometimes even after they read it. If students are reading on their own, teachers should preteach words that contribute to meaning prior to beginning the text. However, if teachers conduct a whole-class reading experience or students read together in a group, teachers should introduce the words and their meaning as they appear in the text. Stopping to briefly explain a word in the moment contributes to comprehension; later, teachers can engage in a more thorough explanation for vocabulary acquisition.

It is a fine balance to determine when to teach words and how many words to teach. If teachers frontload too many, students will forget what they mean when authors use them later within the text. However, if teachers pause too many times during the text to define words, it interrupts the flow and potentially interferes with comprehension. Beck et al. (2013) suggest teaching six to ten words through direct instruction over five to nine days. They admit that when they conducted one study, in which they taught fourth graders ten words in a given week but introduced them all on day one, it was too much.

Lastly, consider teaching some words after reading the text if they are not essential to understanding but worthwhile to learn. In sum, choose words carefully, and plan in advance when and how they will be taught.

Characteristics of Effective Instruction and a Process for Building Vocabulary

Marzano (2004) states that the following eight research-based characteristics steer the development of effective instruction:

- Effective vocabulary instruction does not rely on definitions.
- Students must represent their knowledge of words in linguistic and nonlinguistic ways.
- Effective vocabulary instruction involves the gradual shaping of word meanings through multiple exposures.
- Teaching word parts enhances students' understanding of terms.
- Different types of words require different types of instruction.
- Students should discuss the terms they are learning.
- Students should play with words.
- Instruction should focus on terms that have a high probability of enhancing academic success. (Kindle locations 1219–1512)

Using the aforementioned research, Marzano and Pickering (2005) and Marzano (2020) suggest a six-step process for students to build a strong vocabulary across content areas, including ELA. Marzano and Pickering (2015) recommend that teachers use direct instruction for the initial three phases—which are taught in succession—as teachers introduce each new vocabulary word. They use their discretion in terms of when and how often to address the balance of the steps, which teachers can implement over several successive days as students engage in multiple activities to discuss, use, and apply word meanings.

1. Teachers preassess and provide a description, explanation, or example.

2. Students restate the meaning of the word.

3. Students create a picture, symbol, or graphic (nonlinguistic representation).

4. Students engage in speaking and writing activities periodically.

5. Students discuss the word with each other periodically.

6. Students participate in vocabulary games periodically.

The following explanations and examples of each step in the process were inspired by Marzano and Pickering (2005) and Marzano (2020). Teams can expand on the forthcoming information to incorporate it into their own instruction.

As part of these steps, consider having students keep a journal or academic notebook in which they record by hand or electronically what they learn so they amass a growing inventory of words and their meanings. They use this resource throughout the year to embellish existing entries (for example, with synonyms, examples, and sentences) and continue to insert new words. Teachers might provide students with graphic organizers for this purpose. Teachers can conduct an internet search to find myriad graphic organizers (see page 203), including those used expressly for vocabulary development, which students can download and insert in their resource binders. Or, teams can access this resource as an inspiration to design organizers. Whichever ones teams select, teachers should ensure the organizers leave space for students to include a nonlinguistic representation.

Teachers Preassess and Provide a Description, Explanation, or Example

In this first step, teachers initiate the direct instruction of new words by preassessing students. Through preassessment, they can determine what the students already know about terms and put to rest any misconceptions. Informally, teachers can merely discuss terms with students to determine their levels of understanding. More formally, teachers can use a tool like the one in figure 7.3 (page 180). This example uses four levels of word knowledge (Dale, O'Rourke, & Barbe, 1986) to highlight students' understanding of vocabulary words. Teachers can preassess words, like *speaker tags*, *theme*, and *protagonist*, as well as those from the text they use during instruction.

After preassessing, teachers introduce the targeted words. Refrain from sharing sterile dictionary definitions, which can be weak and artificial. Plus, these definitions are oftentimes confusing since words have multiple meanings. Rather, share accessible descriptions, explanations, or examples of each word both in linguistic

Word	Place an X in this column if you've never seen the word before.	Place an X in this column if you recognize the word but don't know what it means.	Complete the sentence: *This word has something to do with . . .*	Complete these three columns if you know the word.		
				Provide a definition and examples.	Write a sentence that shows you know the word.	Write different forms of the word.
Disturb				Disrupt or interfere with the peace of something; bother or annoy	The baby seemed to disturb all the passengers on the plane by screaming and crying loudly.	Disturbing Disturbed Disturbs Disturbance
Intrusion				Entry by force or without permission Examples: • Burglary • Reading someone else's diary	The cat made an unwelcome intrusion into the dog's territory, causing him to growl in anger.	Intrude Intruded Intruding Intrudes Intrusive Intrusively Intruder

Source: Adapted from Glass, 2015.

Figure 7.3: Vocabulary preassessment.

(written or oral) and in nonlinguistic ways (for example, photograph, picture, computer image, symbol, or a representation that is not oral or written). Engage students by telling a personal story, connecting the word to students' interests, or sharing a current event that applies to the word—or in another way that introduces the word in an interesting fashion. As a resource to prepare for introducing these words to students (and for them to use later as their own resource), access www .vocabulary.com or www.collinsdictionary.com, each of which includes explanations, examples, parts of speech, and so forth.

Students Restate the Meaning of the Word

Next, students restate a description, explanation, or example in their own words and avoid regurgitating what the teacher has said. Teachers can employ strategies such as a turn-and-talk or a give-one-get-one to accomplish this. They can execute the latter strategy by giving students the following verbal directions.

1. "Think of your own example and explanation of the new word I just introduced to you. You may write down your ideas."

2. "Turn to your elbow or shoulder partner. Decide who is partner A and partner B."

3. "When I say *give*, partner A has thirty (or more) seconds to share an example and explanation of the word with partner B."

4. "When I say *get*, partner B has thirty (or more) seconds to share an example and explanation of the word with partner A."

As students share with one another, teachers formatively and unobtrusively assess by walking around the room to ensure that students share accurate information with each other. If necessary, teachers stop to redirect and adjust students' conversations in which words are portrayed incorrectly. After the activity, students record the word and its meaning in their journals or notebooks.

Students Create a Nonlinguistic Representation

For this step, students create nonlinguistic representations of the word, which means using pictures, graphics, symbols, images, or physical sensations. Specifically, students can, by hand or electronically, design a picture, symbol, graphic, chart, map, or outline. Or, they might dramatize the word through a comic strip. Students add these representations to their journals or notebooks next to the words they've been learning. If they create an electronic product, they can print it out to place in their journals or notebooks, or have an electronic folder that houses vocabulary materials.

To prepare students for this activity, teachers provide suggestions; for example, they can share a visualization associated with the word ("When I think of this word, I can imagine in my mind's eye . . ."), act out the word, have students experience the word through touch or smell, or show a picture that helps explain the word. Additionally, make sure to feature student samples of nonlinguistic representations using other words to equip students with plenty of ideas before they begin this activity.

Students Engage in Speaking and Writing Activities Periodically

To help students learn the words introduced in the previous three steps, teachers provide explicit practice and review opportunities. This gives students a chance to revisit their understanding of the vocabulary and make revisions or additions to words they've recorded in their journals or notebooks. Such engagement activities—which all yield assessments teachers review to check for understanding—can include sentence frames (see figure 7.4), examples and nonexamples (see figure 7.5 for two completed examples), and a diamante poem (see figure 7.6 for directions and a completed example). Each of these activities involves writing; however, teachers can include speaking as a component. For example, students independently write, then explain their work to peers. Or, they can work collaboratively on the activity in pairs or trios as they discuss options for what they can each include in their product, which they ultimately generate individually.

_____ makes me think of a time when . . .

_____ makes me think of the color _____ because . . .

_____ reminds me of _____ because . . .

_____ is used to describe _____ because . . .

If I were to paint a picture of _____ , I'd paint . . .

Source: Glass, 2015, p. 90.

Figure 7.4: Vocabulary sentence frames.

Although vocabulary is the focus, teachers can adapt these activities for other topics as well. For example, in a narrative unit, students can use the name of a character or setting from a novel or short story they are reading in the sentence frames. (Teachers can narrow down the list and offer students two or three choices from figure 7.4.) They can write examples and nonexamples of imagery or what a character says (example) or does not say (nonexample). For a diamante poem—which

Verb

+ a word that shows action

+ the words *scream*, *plead*, *reply*, and *whisper*

− a noun, adverb, adjective, or pronoun

− the words *house*, *quietly*, *beautiful*, and *you*

Illumination

+ the brightness of the sun at noon

+ a night-light in a bedroom

− a dark movie theater

− nimbus clouds (gray rain clouds that indicate an approaching storm)

Figure 7.5: Examples and nonexamples.

Diamante Poem
Directions

Line 1: Write one topic; skip to line 7, and write down an opposite topic.

Line 2: Write two adjectives related to line 1.

Line 3: Write three participles (verb forms ending with *-ed* or *-ing*) related to line 1.

Line 4: Write two nouns related to line 1 and two nouns related to line 7.

Line 5: Write three participles related to line 7.

Line 6: Write two adjectives related to line 7.

Line 7: Write the opposite topic of line 1.

Essential

Necessary   *Crucial*

Breathing   *Loving*   *Sleeping*

Air   *Water*   *Chocolate*   *Perfume*

Speeding   *Swearing*   *Whining*

Unimportant   *Meaningless*

Unnecessary

Figure 7.6: Vocabulary diamante poem.

focuses on two opposite topics, such as two characters, individuals, ideas, concepts, or words—students can write about the physical characteristics or viewpoints of the protagonist and the antagonist, two different settings, or two groups' perspectives of war.

Teachers can assign a sentence frame or example and nonexample task as a bell ringer or exit slip. The diamante poem, which takes more time to complete, is better suited for an in-class activity or homework assignment. A *bell ringer* (also referred to as a *sponge activity*) is a three- to five-minute warm-up activity that teachers plan in advance to maximize class time. They post the bell-ringer prompt (in this case, one involving vocabulary) on a whiteboard or interactive board to launch the class or transition a period to a new subject, and they incorporate it into the daily classroom routine. While students work on the bell ringer, teachers can take attendance, collect homework assignments, or tend to logistics that need attention. The prompt serves to connect learning from yesterday's lesson to the upcoming lesson; prepare students for what they will learn next; or reinforce content, a concept, word, or topic.

Teachers can also allot three to five minutes near the end of class or just before moving into a new content area for students to complete an exit slip (also called an *exit card* or *ticket-to-leave card*). They need not issue one every day, but it provides a quick check for understanding of something students learned. See an explanation of exit slips in step 5 of the dialogue learning progression (figure 3.1, page 61), which describes how teachers can use this strategy to formatively assess in a fourth-grade unit.

In addition to the suggestions shown in this section, teachers can plan and conduct other activities around the skill of identifying the similarities and differences between words (or any topics), which deepens understanding. Robert J. Marzano, Debra J. Pickering, and Jane E. Pollock (2001) offer these ways to identify what is similar and different: (1) *comparing* (identify what is alike and different among or between ideas, concepts, subjects, and so on), (2) *classifying* (group items into categories based on their similar characteristics), (3) *creating metaphors* (connect two unlike ideas, concepts, objects, and so on without using the words *like* and *as*), and (4) *creating analogies* (identify a relationship between two ideas, concepts, or objects; the typical construct is *A is to B as C is to D*).

Students Discuss the Word With Each Other Periodically

So that students can experience new words used naturally, teachers intentionally infuse targeted vocabulary while speaking to the class and with students individually. Additionally, they can devise oral communication activities using the following or other ideas.

▸ Teachers create situations where students converse with one another about word entries they have recorded in their journals or notebooks. For example, students select words they would like to discuss because they are new favorite words, or the teacher might ask students to self-select a couple they feel they have yet to master. With these words, students exchange information based on what they have entered and add information they learn from each other.

▸ Teachers write selected words onto cards and distribute one card to each small group of students. During a group activity, students are asked to weave these words into a discussion to accomplish whatever task is at hand. For example, when they talk about characters, the word list can include tier two words associated with personality traits—*mysterious, adventurous, stubborn,* or *reluctant.*

▸ After school, teachers instruct students to share specific words with a parent, guardian, older sibling, relative, or school employee and ask one (or more) of them how he or she has used the words. Or, students teach one of these people these words. In class, students share what they learned or what experience they had while discussing the words.

▸ Teachers conduct an activity in which they distribute a "Find Someone Who . . ." sheet to each student (see figure 7.7, page 186). Students walk around the classroom and approach a peer, who selects and responds to a prompt on the student's sheet orally, in writing, or both. When the owner of the paper agrees that the peer has responded correctly, he or she asks for a signature on the line provided. If the owner deems the response incorrect, the line remains empty. The two switch roles and repeat the process. Students then find another partner and repeat this process until all their sheets' cells include a signature.

In the case of this last item, teachers can make different versions of "Find Someone Who . . ." to avoid each student having the same one. This activity is easily adapted; in any unit, teachers can design text-dependent prompts. For example, students might find someone who can identify the protagonist's or historical figure's personality trait and a supporting detail, make a prediction based on textual evidence, or explain how events impact characters or individuals. Prompts can also revolve around grammar or conventions—for example, *find someone who can define* speaker tags, *find someone who can tell you how beginning dialogue tags should be punctuated,* or *find someone who can explain the purpose of dialogue.* Students can also have the complex text in hand while responding so they can point to clear-cut evidence referenced in the prompt.

Find someone who . . .		
Can spell the word that means "highly unusual or exceptional" _____	Can define *precept* _____	Can find an antonym for *forewarn* _____
Can teach you a word you don't know _____	Can give an example of *sarcasm* _____	Can use the word *deed* in a sentence that shows the word's meaning _____
Can create one sentence using the words *accommodate* and *catastrophe* that shows these words' meanings _____	Can draw a symbol or picture for *contagious* _____	Can create a metaphor for *mortality* _____

Figure 7.7: Find someone who . . . activity.

Students Participate in Vocabulary Games Periodically

Teachers might create vocabulary games for their students to engage in, as well as invite students to invent their own to play with peers. Teachers can use academic games within instruction to teach other skills; however, the examples shown in this section relate to acquiring new words.

Concentration

Concentration is a game in which players—typically two to four—match pairs of cards. To play concentration, students place the cards facedown in rows so they are in a square or rectangular shape. When it is a player's turn, he or she turns over two cards to seek a matched pair. If successful, the player removes and collects the pair, then gets a second turn. If unsuccessful, he or she returns the cards facedown to their original spots, and the next player takes a turn. The winner is the player who amasses the most pairs. As a modification, students can place the cards faceup to play a matching game that doesn't involve guessing and memory. The challenging element of memory in concentration might not be appropriate for struggling learners.

Figure 7.8 shows cards students can use for a concentration game to practice vocabulary. Teachers or students can adapt concentration for other purposes; they

your best try; an attempt	absolutely horrible; the worst possible situation	examples: wearing a biking helmet; looking both ways when crossing a street	a place where clothes are kept	the opposite of outgoing and talkative
peaceful; tranquil; quiet	move by getting on your hands and knees	courteous	bashful	polite
effort	dreadful	caution	cornered	feeling trapped
quickly	rapidly	bureau	serene	crawl

Figure 7.8: Vocabulary concentration game.

could, for example, create a concentration game centered on the key details of a complex narrative text. The matching pairs could include a character and an action, a character and a line of dialogue, a setting and a brief phrase describing it, or a line of figurative language and the type (simile, personification, and so forth). If students write the cards, teachers collect and review them as a formative assessment and then return them to students so they can play the game with classmates.

Board Game

Figure 7.9 (page 188) features a generic board game for any question cards that teachers or students design. Figure 7.10 (page 189) includes example cards for a vocabulary game to use with the board.

To prepare to play, each student finds a token to place in the Start cell, such as a penny, paper clip, ring, or bean. Students stack the student- or teacher-generated game cards and star cards facedown in the designated places shown on the board. Star cards, which teachers or students must also create, function similarly to chance cards in Monopoly in that players will move up or back based on the card they pull. For example, the cards might state, "You helped make dinner and cleared your plate without being asked. Move forward two spaces," or "You offered to

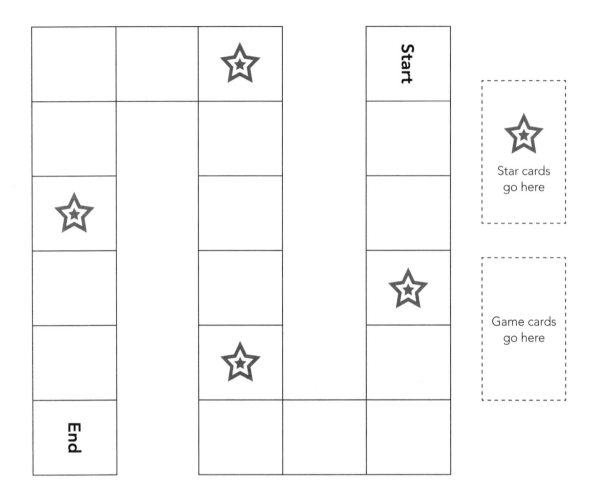

Source: Glass, 2018, p. 117.

Figure 7.9: Generic game board.

help a classmate who had trouble understanding a new word. Move forward three spaces," or "You dropped a drink on the floor and walked away without cleaning it up. Go back two spaces."

Taking turns, each player chooses a game card and provides an answer. If an answer is incorrect, the player moves back the number of spaces indicated on the card had he or she gotten it correct (except if a player is on the Start spot). It then becomes the next player's turn. If correct, the player moves his or her token up based on the card's worth, which appears alongside the answer on the reverse side of the card. When the player lands on a star, he or she takes a star card and moves accordingly. The player's turn then ends. The game continues until someone reaches the End cell.

Front of Card	Back of Card
What are two synonyms for the word *dissolved* in this sentence? "On the other side of the wood, the sense of easiness dissolved."	Answer: disappeared, left Worth two spaces
What is not a definition of the word *intrude*? a. To go to a party without being invited b. To break into someone's house c. To go through a fence that has a No Trespassing sign d. To walk away from a place	Answer: d Worth one space
Identify and define words from the sentence that show this setting is depressing and rough. "All at once the sun was uncomfortably hot, the dust oppressive, and the meager grass along its edges somewhat ragged and forlorn."	Answer: *Uncomfortably:* miserably *Oppressive:* depressing *Forlorn:* sad Worth one space for each correct word and its definition
Why does the author Natalie Babbitt use the word *melancholy* in this sentence from *Tuck Everlasting*? "He was still asleep, and the melancholy creases that folded his daytime face were smoothed and slack."	Answer: When Mae's husband is asleep, he is happy dreaming about being in heaven and not in Treegap, where he is immortal and sad about his situation. Worth three spaces

Source for quotes: Babbitt, 1975.

Figure 7.10: Vocabulary game cards.

Which One Is False?

In this game, the teacher reads aloud four options—one of which is unrelated to the others—and students' job is to determine which one does not belong. After the teacher reads the options, he or she says, "Wait," and then says, "Show." When cued to wait, students determine which option they believe is false. When cued to show, each student reveals the item that is false by holding up the number of fingers at chest level that corresponds to the listed option—one, two, three, or four—while the teacher scans the room to informally assess. If students are not sure which is false, they show a fist. Signaling at chest level helps students not be influenced by each other's answers, which might occur if students hold their fingers up in the air for everyone to see. Once all students have signaled, the teacher merely states, "The correct answer is _____," and holds up the correct number of fingers. As with most activities, teachers model how to respond before starting the game. The example options in figure 7.11 focus on literacy-related terms. However, teachers and students can adapt this strategy to focus on, for example, explicit information from a text to check comprehension, tier two vocabulary words, or writing conventions (such as sentence fragments or subject–verb agreement).

Sensory Details—Which One Is False?

1. Words and phrases that use the five senses to create descriptions—for example, *greasy, sticky, slither,* and *thunderclap*

2. "The child was very loud."

3. Words and phrases that help readers or listeners create visuals in their mind's eye

4. "The toddler's ear-shattering screams were louder than the crash of symbols."

Dialogue Tags—Which One Is False?

1. Dialogue tags are words and phrases that let readers know who is speaking.

2. Dialogue tags are written before, after, or in between lines of dialogue.

3. Dialogue tags all use the same punctuation and capitalization rules.

4. Dialogue tags include verbs such as *remarked, questioned,* and *said.*

Figure 7.11: Which one doesn't belong?

Whatever instructional approach your team implements, the endorsement to use direct instruction for teaching vocabulary is undeniably strong. Educators would benefit from reading the original works of the many authors and researchers we referenced in this section, in addition to others in this resource-rich field.

EXERCISE

Address Spelling and Vocabulary Instruction

Teacher teams often approach spelling and vocabulary in similar ways, but individual teachers undoubtedly bring their own ideas to teaching these skills. Use what you've learned in this chapter to facilitate a team conversation of sharing what you and your team members each do so you can collectively improve your practices.

Use the following questions to guide this exercise.

★ What resources do we each use to teach spelling and vocabulary?

★ How has the research and direct instruction for teaching vocabulary presented in this section changed our thinking?

★ Which strategies from this section have we used with success?

★ How will we implement any of the strategies? What assessments can we collect when conducting these strategies?

Summary

Though reading and writing should transpire throughout a student's school day, schools must safeguard a dedicated period of time for literacy instruction and learning. This affords students ample time to improve their literacy skills and become word wizards as they broaden their vocabulary inventory, acquire knowledge about spelling patterns, learn and apply various strategies to aid with comprehension, read abundantly, engage in rich discussion around texts to broaden their perspectives and think more critically, and write frequently and enthusiastically.

To develop truly literate students with the capacity to engage in higher-order independent thinking requires strategically planned and implemented instruction devoted to literacy that honors reading and writing as well as speaking and listening. Though specified times will be set aside for the explicit teaching of these domains of literacy and all that they each entail, skillful teacher teams continuously intertwine and embed all of them within instruction. They guide students in making natural connections between these domains and work to develop well-rounded, independent readers and writers with the knowledge and skills to reach new heights in their learning.

In addition to the topics and concrete examples in this chapter focusing on the tenets of a dedicated literacy block, the next chapter provides teams with detailed instruction for using three specific and highly adaptable strategies that result in positive student performance when instructing on literacy.

CHAPTER 8

Select Appropriate Instructional Strategies

Chapter 7 provides suggestions for managing time dedicated to literacy instruction. Within this component of the school day, teachers conduct well-orchestrated, effective lessons to assist students in acquiring a new skill, strategy, or procedure using a sound instructional model like gradual release of responsibility (see chapter 6, page 137). The learning progression directs a pathway for instruction and compels teams to ask, "If the assessment expects students to produce _____ to show evidence of learning, what does the instruction actually look like?" Therefore, this chapter provides information about using a learning progression as a guide to select and implement appropriate strategies during instruction that yield an assessment.

When delivering lessons, teachers pair instructional strategies with learning activities since the two go hand in hand. *Instructional strategies* (also called *teaching strategies* or *teaching methods*) are the techniques teachers use throughout instruction—whether it be a structure, procedure, or process—to make learning attainable for all students. *Learning activities* are the tasks students engage in to practice and demonstrate their learning, which results in some form of assessment.

Sometimes a tool teachers employ for an instructional strategy also functions as the activity and even the assessment. For example, a teacher uses a graphic organizer as an instructional strategy to model how to organize research information, to prewrite for an essay, or to demonstrate understanding of a text passage. After modeling for students how to fill it in, the teacher hands students a clean copy of the graphic organizer to complete as a learning activity. Afterward, he or she collects the students' graphic organizers to check for understanding. Sometimes instructional strategies that teachers conduct, learning activities that students participate in, and formative assessment all coalesce to facilitate learning (Glass, 2012).

This chapter features three specific teaching strategies that are effective not only for grades 4–5 literacy instruction within ELA, but also across subject areas: (1) annotation, (2) graphic organizers, and (3) concept attainment. We include a thorough explanation and detailed steps for conducting an activity that relies on the strategy, plus differentiation suggestions to further students' learning goals and contribute to their competency. Although this chapter's examples remain focused on dialogue, the strategies are transferable, and teachers can alter and employ them to teach other skills in a variety of contexts. Therefore, we provide ideas for teachers to tailor any strategy to assist students in meeting different learning targets throughout the school year.

Annotation

Complex text is precisely as the term denotes—complex. Annotation, a widespread strategy readers typically employ, involves interacting with the text to glean more information from it so that what seems challenging becomes less so. Sometimes, teachers instruct students to return to the text repeatedly to annotate, each time with a new focus. In doing so, they uncover layers of meaning and have the opportunity to appreciate various aspects of a complex text.

To conduct this strategy, teachers ask students to annotate a passage or whole text by posing a question or prompt that is based on a learning target. Students annotate the text by taking two actions that are interrelated: (1) mark pertinent words and phrases (such as by underlining, highlighting, circling) in response to the purpose of the task, then (2) comment about the marked parts—which serve as textual evidence—by explaining, elaborating, analyzing, or drawing an inference. Merely doing one action without the other might render the annotation incomplete. Students can also annotate electronically. If they cannot write in the text, they can draw arrows on a sticky note to point to text they would mark and use another sticky note to explain its meaning.

Typically students write commentary in the margin (or on a sticky note) adjacent to marked text. However, in lieu of writing, sometimes teachers ask students to draw a symbol, picture, or emoji, which can work well for grades 4 and 5 when students first encounter a text. To conduct this activity using symbols, teachers explain the purpose of the annotation task and give specific directions. For example, a teacher might say the following as well as write what each symbol means so students have a visual reference:

Today we will begin a new novel titled _____, which is written by _____. I'll read the first part of chapter 1 aloud. Then, I'm going to ask you to reread it silently. When you do, annotate by using symbols. If you feel some words and phrases are important to remember, underline them, and in the margin, draw an asterisk to indicate this information is important. If you are confused about something, underline words and phrases that show where you need clarification, and in the margin, draw a question mark. You can use more than one asterisk and question mark since you might find many spots in the text that are important or confusing. Later, you will discuss with others what you marked.

Depending on the purpose for reading and the text type, the symbols can stand for something different. In the preceding example, the asterisk is for parts students find important; however, an asterisk can indicate the main idea of a text or an example of a skill that is the focus for instruction (such as transitions or descriptive words). The question mark in this example signifies confusion; students could also use it for areas they think are unclear or perhaps untrue or unrealistic. Teachers might include another symbol, like a plus sign, to show ideas that agree with a student's thinking, new information or ideas, an opportunity to make a prediction, or strong evidence to support reasoning in an opinion paper. Of course, there are other symbols, like checkmarks, arrows, or exclamation marks. Use caution to avoid too many directives; sticking to three symbols will likely work well for grades 4–5 students.

Pictures or emojis can also communicate a student's takeaway or interpretation. After reading the following passage from the book *From the Mixed-Up Files of Mrs. Basil E. Frankweiler* (Konigsburg, 1967/1995), students might underline the text indicated and draw a sad face emoji or teardrops in the margin:

> After the big blobs of tears stopped, [Jamie] said, "At least they treated us like grown-ups. That letter is full of big words and all."
>
> "Big deal," Claudia sobbed. "For all they know, we *are* grown-ups." She was trying to find a corner of her shredded Kleenex that she could use. (p. 117)

Teachers model and use think-aloud to show how to use symbols or pictures to annotate from a previously read text excerpt. Students then annotate on their own using the new text to apply this strategy. Afterward, students engage in discussions to share their thinking about what symbols or pictures they used and the corresponding textual evidence they flagged. (See Conducting the Activity, page 199, for more on this topic.)

Teachers can assign various annotation exercises for express purposes. After the first exposure to the text, teachers ask students to return to the same passage or a different one in that text to annotate with writing. For instance, students underline or highlight examples of similes, and explain what they mean; mark parts of the text that lead them to make a prediction, and write what they predict will occur; or mark repetitive phrases or words the author uses, and write about the impression the repeated text leaves. For a partial list of other kinds of standards-based annotation tasks that teachers might assign, review figure 8.1.

When asking students to annotate, teachers judiciously target one or two aligned skills at a time and assess student mastery before moving forward to tackle others, especially if the skills are challenging. Older and more proficient students can perhaps handle simultaneously annotating for multiple purposes; however, some students might feel overwhelmed and not master to the fullest extent any one purpose. In such cases, teachers' eagerness to employ this strategy may backfire by asking too much of students at once.

Providing excessive reading tasks concurrently might interfere with students' enjoyment and meaning making. Plus, it may result in students hastily skimming the text for cursory observations rather than doing the deep introspection teachers aim for them to achieve. Therefore, use professional judgment and knowledge of students' characteristics when determining the purpose or purposes for annotation and the orchestrated way to use this strategy. Furthermore, the purpose of the task must align with each text, so distributing a prepared list of annotation exercises that students use repeatedly throughout the year will not necessarily be prudent. Rather, tailor each exercise to the purpose and the specific complex text.

In the dialogue unit for our fourth-grade team, step 2 of the learning progression (figure 3.1, page 61) involves an annotation exercise fifth-grade teams can also emulate. (It is featured in the first row of figure 8.1, as well.) As a result of students' annotation and ensuing discussion, they come to realize that skilled authors purposefully write dialogue to facilitate exchanges between characters. Students specifically focus on excerpts familiar to them and consider the function of dialogue within the context of the story. Teams working with a different learning progression will need to consider how or if annotation might apply to the knowledge or skill items students are to learn. In any case, teams can use the following sections to understand how to prepare for an annotation activity, conduct it, and explore other ideas for implementing and differentiating it.

Sample Annotation Tasks

Skill	What Students Underline, Circle, or Highlight	What Students Write in the Margin or on Sticky Notes	Annotation Task	Next-Step Ideas for Teachers (Partial List)
Determine the purpose of a text.	Parts of the dialogue that are meaningful	Why this part of the dialogue is important	Underline words and phrases in dialogue passages that you think are important. In the margin, respond to these questions: Why do you think what you underlined is important? What does it reveal to the reader?	Students share their annotations as the teacher makes a list of the purposes of the dialogue using student input. The teacher guides students in grouping common purposes. The goal is to see that authors create meaningful dialogue to develop a plot or show characters' responses to situations.
Make inferences using details and examples in a text.	Words and phrases in the text that give clues about the personality of a character or individual (The individual can be a historical figure, leader, or prominent figure.)	A personality trait	Underline any words and phrases that help you understand the personality of a character or individual. In the margin, write the personality trait that corresponds to the textual evidence you underlined.	Students write a paragraph that describes the character or individual in detailed terms without actually mentioning the trait so that peers can infer it. Students can focus on different characters or individuals, then trade papers to reveal the personality traits based on the evidence.

continued →

Figure 8.1: Sample annotation tasks.

Use context clues to determine the meaning of unknown words.	Vocabulary words or terms they do not know	Definition, example, and symbol	Circle unknown words. Underline any clues surrounding each word that helps you learn what it means. In the margin, write a definition, example, and symbol (or one of these options) based on the context of the passage.	The teacher conducts direct instruction activities that help students learn the new words. Students use the new words in various writing exercises and tasks.
Refer to details in the text to explain what it states explicitly or inferentially.	Words or phrases that indicate a historical era in a historical fiction piece or a setting in realistic fiction	The historical period or setting	Highlight any part of the text that indicates a historical period (or setting in realistic fiction), such as a date, location, time of year, or even climate. In the margin, write your impression of the setting.	Students share their annotations as the teacher makes a class-generated list of specific setting indicators from the complex text. Using this list as inspiration, students augment or revise the settings in their stories to be more robust.
Use details in the text to identify a theme.	Textual evidence that gives clues to the theme	Theme	Underline any words or phrases that help you understand the story's theme. In the margin, write the theme using a complete sentence.	Students share their themes with a small group, which then reports them to the class along with supporting textual evidence. The teacher discusses similarities and differences in students' contributions to point out that the same work can have several different themes.
Describe the impact of a character's or an author's point of view on a text.	Textual evidence that shows a character's or an author's point of view	Brief explanation of what the character or author thinks or believes	Underline any part of the text that helps you understand a character's or an author's point of view. In the margin, explain what this character or author thinks, feels, or believes. Later, you will use what you annotate to figure out how this character's or author's viewpoint influences the text.	After students annotate to determine a character's or an author's viewpoint, they discuss with peers how this attitude impacts the work. Then, they respond in writing to the prompt, How does the character's or author's point of view impact the story?

Preparing for the Activity

In preparation for this annotation exercise, teachers can use the following three suggestions to help ensure that it runs smoothly.

1. **Identify the text that will be used for annotation:** Use one short text, such as a paragraph or brief article, or multiple shorter excerpts from a novel, as in the example for annotating dialogue in figure 8.2 (page 200). Alternatively, select a whole chapter if that is most appropriate for students.

2. **Plan annotation tasks:** Based on the learning targets, write one or more annotation tasks for different encounters with the text, as appropriate. Decide in what order to assign the tasks and which ones might couple together in a manageable way.

3. **Determine logistics:** After selecting the text, determine how students will actually annotate, and decide where to write the directions for students to see. Consider fashioning a table with the task directions embedded in it, one that allows students to mark parts of the text and write accompanying explanations (as in figure 8.2). Or, identify the selected text's page numbers and paragraphs and obtain sticky notes for students to use. If students have electronic devices, consider formatting the text and table electronically or indicating the page numbers of the digital text. Additionally, teachers decide the logistics of how they will model and use think aloud. They might elect to input a prepared example on the first row, as shown in the figure. Alternatively, they plan in advance what they will write on this row or compose authentically on the spot.

After teachers identify and prepare the text, decide how they will focus instruction (model and think aloud), and write the annotation task, they plan for execution of the activity.

Conducting the Activity

When teachers model annotation to show what words and phrases to mark based on the task, they prevent students from needlessly flagging too much text. Aloud, teachers share their thought process for marking judiciously, admit the natural tendency to excessively underline, and explain how to resist this temptation and focus on what matters most based on the prompt. After marking the text, teachers also use the think-aloud strategy while writing a response. As mentioned, teachers can write an example as shown on the first row of figure 8.2 or

Underline or highlight words and phrases that you feel are important.	Explain what is important or purposeful about the parts of the text that you marked.
Mama looked at Esperanza with eyes that said, "forgive me." Then she dropped her head and stared at the ground. "I will consider your proposal," said Mama. Tío Luis smiled. "I am delighted! I have no doubt that you will make the right decision. I will be back in a few days for your answer."	*Mama's actions show her sadness about feeling trapped to consider marrying Tío.*
"Ramona," said Tío Marco, remaining on his horse. "Another sadness in so short a time. We are deeply sorry." "I have come to give you another chance," said Tío Luis. "If you reconsider my proposal, I will build a bigger, more beautiful house and I will replant everything. Of course, if you prefer, you can live here with the servants, as long as another tragedy does not happen to their homes as well. There is no main house or fields where they can work, so you see that many people's lives and jobs depend upon you. And I am sure you want the best for Esperanza, do you not?"	
"Mama, no!" said Esperanza. She turned to Tío Luis and said, "I hate you!" Tío Luis ignored her. "And Ramona, if Esperanza is to be my daughter, she must have better manners. In fact, today I will look into boarding schools where they can teach her to act like a lady." Then he turned his horse, dug his spurs into the animal, and rode away.	

Source for quotes: Ryan, 2000, pp. 44–46.

Figure 8.2: Dialogue annotation—Exercise 1.

prepare in advance what they write down and discuss in front of students in real time. Sometimes teachers purposefully do not prepare what they will write so that students witness them productively struggling to generate ideas and cross out and replace text as a natural process of writing.

Then, teachers orchestrate a think-pair-share strategy in which students first annotate independently (think), discuss their responses with another student (pair), and finally report their impressions to the whole class (share). During sharing, teachers record an abbreviated collection of students' input. In the dialogue example, they point out that both the dialogue and the dialogue tags surrounding what characters say might be important. Next, the class reviews the entries, which could include, for example, the dialogue or dialogue tags that show how a character thinks, feels, or acts; indicate a historical setting; provide a hint about something to come; uncover interactions between characters; or reveal emotions. Since this annotation exercise occurs on the learning progression after students discuss the purpose of dialogue, they know that dialogue either advances the plot or shows characters' reactions. Teachers ask students to categorize the class-generated list into one of these two categories (or even both) and a justification for their responses.

Considering Other Annotation Tasks

After students initially annotate to consider the importance of the excerpts, teachers can pose a subsequent annotation task that calls on them to delve deeper. Figure 8.3 shows such a task, which can serve as a precursor to making inferences, a forthcoming learning target in the dialogue unit.

Circle a character. Underline or highlight words and phrases that show this character's response to a situation.	Identify the character and how he or she responds to the situation. Explain what this response might mean.
(Mama) looked at Esperanza with eyes that said, "forgive me." Then she dropped her head and stared at the ground. "I will consider your proposal," said Mama. Tío Luis smiled. "I am delighted! I have no doubt that you will make the right decision. I will be back in a few days for your answer."	Mama: She looks sadly and apologetically at her daughter because she seems ashamed of her decision. When she drops her head and stares at the ground, it seems she doesn't want to marry Tío but feels forced to pretend that she might.

Source for quotes: Ryan, 2000, p. 45.

Figure 8.3: Dialogue annotation—Exercise 2.

Teachers can also conduct exercises to address learning targets for the craft of writing; for example, annotate an author's use of sensory details (imagery) to convey experiences or use transitional words and phrases to show a time sequence. After students use the annotation strategy to examine authentic ways authors employ these skills in mentor texts, they practice what they learn. For example, teachers distribute anonymous student samples that exhibit weakness in using transitions and pose this task: *Underline any transitional words and phrases in the student sample that are effective, circle any that are weak or repetitive, and draw a caret mark (proofreader's symbol) to indicate missing transitions. In the margin, write a replacement for those that you circled, and write to add any transitions that are missing.* Students discuss their revisions with peers and, together, agree on these changes or arrive at new revisions.

Graphic Organizers

Graphic organizers—visual representations of ideas—are a staple in teachers' repertoire of instructional strategies across content areas. Teachers often collect the completed organizers and use them as a formative assessment to determine levels of competency aligned to learning targets. In literacy, an organizer can serve as an effective reading and writing tool. In reading, it facilitates comprehension, plus helps students remember content. In writing, students can use one for prewriting and planning. There are a host of other ways graphic organizers aid in literacy across content areas, including the following.

▸ Identify and explain the structure of a text—compare–contrast, problem–solution, cause–effect, sequence, or description.

▸ Brainstorm and collect ideas for a writing task.

▸ Organize information in a reading selection to deepen understanding.

▸ Demonstrate comprehension and communicate ideas.

▸ Record and categorize research notes.

▸ Learn new words and terms.

Teachers can find blank organizers online by accessing the following links or design their own to align the organizers to a particular text structure and the purpose of using them.

▸ edHelper.com (www.edhelper.com/teachers/graphic_organizers.htm)

- ▸ Education Oasis (www.educationoasis.com/curriculum/graphic _organizers.htm)

- ▸ Freeology (http://freeology.com/graphicorgs)

- ▸ Houghton Mifflin Harcourt Education Place (https://www.eduplace .com/graphicorganizer/)

- ▸ Teacher Files (www.teacherfiles.com/resources_organizers.htm)

- ▸ TeacherVision (www.teachervision.com/lesson-planning /graphic-organizer)

To differentiate graphic organizers, teachers design or offer choices for students within an overarching structure based on learning style and readiness levels. For example, a Venn diagram typically requires students to compare and contrast two topics or ideas. That might be sufficiently challenging for some students, whereas others would benefit from an extended Venn diagram with three overlapping circles to examine three different subjects. Further, some students prefer a compare–contrast organizer in a column format rather than the traditional circular one.

Since any strategy teachers implement is done with the learning target in mind, in this section, we highlight how to customize a specific graphic organizer to address using details and examples in the text to draw inferences. The activity we feature is conducted in trios as students revisit three dialogue passages from a familiar classroom text and examine it to make inferences. This collaborative learning exercise compels students to rely on group members' input to crystallize and extend their thinking together. Teams can use the following sections to understand how to prepare for this graphic organizer activity; conduct it; and explore other ideas for implementing, adapting, and differentiating it.

Preparing for the Activity

To prepare, teachers select three passages from their classroom text suitable for their purposes—in this case, for inferencing. Then they create three graphic organizers, each with a different preselected excerpt. The graphic organizer in figure 8.4 (page 204) features an excerpt of a dialogue exchange between two brothers—Sam and Tim—from *My Brother Sam Is Dead* (Collier & Collier, 1974), which would be one example of three teachers would prepare.

Dialogue Passage A:

"Captain Arnold says it's all right to be scared; the true brave man is always scared. At least that's what the sergeant said he said."

"You seem to be pretty proud of Captain Arnold."

"Oh, he's a marvelous horseman, and brave, and he doesn't take any nonsense from anybody. He'll lead us through the Lobsterbacks like a hot knife through butter."

Round 1: _____	Round 2: _____
Round 3: _____	Collective impression:

Source for quotes: Collier & Collier, 1974, p. 16.

Figure 8.4: Graphic organizer with excerpted dialogue.

Visit **go.SolutionTree.com/literacy** *for a free reproducible version of this figure.*

Conducting the Activity

Teachers organize students into groups of three, distribute a graphic organizer with a different passage to each student in the trio, and conduct this activity by explaining to students what they do in the following four rounds.

1. Each student writes his or her name in the *Round 1* space on his or her organizer; reads the passage of text on the graphic organizer; and writes an inference, using textual evidence, under his or her name. Students may choose to underline or highlight salient words and phrases in the passage as they deem necessary to assist them with making an inference. Tell students they have about seven minutes for this activity, but you may provide extra time, if necessary.

2. Students pass their graphic organizers clockwise. On the graphic organizer they receive, they enter their names in the *Round 2* spot. Then, they each

read their new organizer's passage as well as the *Round 1* entry from the fellow group member and write something in their box in the organizer. They can add to (elaborate on) an inference that this group member made or write their own inference. What they cannot do is circle their group member's entry and draw an arrow from it to their box. They must make a contribution of some kind.

3. Students rotate their papers again and write their names in the *Round 3* spot. They repeat what they did in the second round by reading the author's passage and their group members' entries. Then, they elaborate on an existing entry or make a new inference.

4. Students rotate the graphic organizers one last time, so that *Round 1* students should have their initial organizer back. Taking turns, each student leads a group conversation to discuss the entries the group members each made about the passage. Together, they synthesize the conversation and agree on what each student will write in his or her graphic organizer to represent the group's collective impression of an inference for each passage.

This exercise is designed for students to capitalize on the thinking of their peers. While working together, they delve more deeply into three key passages to arrive at new insights.

Adapting the Activity

Teachers can utilize this four-square graphic organizer strategy for fiction or nonfiction prose and for poetry, where making inferences enhances understanding. In addition to (or in lieu of) making inferences, this strategy can be a tool for identifying the main idea of text passages, paraphrasing, rewriting a passage in students' own words, or using context clues to define unknown words in a passage, making it an ideal exercise for literacy-focused instruction across content areas.

To differentiate, teachers can arrange groups homogeneously and prepare organizers that include appropriately challenging text passages. To scaffold, teachers can supply definitions of challenging words within the passages where there are no context clues or remind students about the background situation of the featured text for groups that struggle. Teachers provide each group with the necessary support to move learning forward during the activity by asking questions or providing clues or hints when students are stuck. For example, these questions can help students draw inferences: *What background knowledge do you have about this passage that leads you to draw a conclusion? What details do you know about the characters, setting, or events that have occurred that can help you make an inference?*

Concept Attainment

Concept attainment, a collaborative strategy that teachers can use across content areas, fosters critical thinking and decision making. It produces a situation in which students productively struggle to process and understand concepts. To accomplish this, teachers orchestrate a well-planned series of actions students take aligned to a learning target.

Specifically, teachers ask students to perform several tasks within the lesson—discern examples from nonexamples, identify categories and attributes, create definitions, and apply the new learning. In literacy, for example, teachers can implement this strategy to teach dialogue mechanics, which is explained in this section, or to teach students how to vary the way sentences begin, identify types of figurative language or sentence structures, determine methods of characterization, investigate types of evidence used in an informational paper, or identify the purpose for writing. In other disciplines, concept attainment can also prove useful, such as for identifying types of ecosystems, characteristics of geographical features, or qualities of a leader.

The following list articulates the concept-attainment steps at a high level (Glass, 2018) and explains what student groups of three or four do when they participate in this strategy. The next section applies these directions for a specific exercise to see this strategy in action.

1. **Examine and group a set of items according to their commonalities:**
   For this first step, teachers prepare a set of items, such as pictures, words, sentences, paragraphs, or even student samples, that students sort based on a learning target. They can design this step in one of two ways—either students group the items into several, specific categories (for example, words grouped according to a part of speech or sentences into a structure), or they group them into two categories in which some items represent examples (they belong together) while a random collection of other items are nonexamples. The following provides instruction to students for each approach.

   - *Option A*—"Study the _____ (pictures, words, sentences, paragraphs, or papers). Categorize items into groups that share common elements. You will need to figure out how many groups you will have based on the items. Be ready to share your reasoning."

   - *Option B*—"Study the _____ (pictures, words, sentences, paragraphs, or papers). Group together those items that share common elements on one side. Put random items that don't share these elements on the other. Be ready to share your reasoning."

2. **Identify the specific attributes of this grouped set, and name the set:**
Instruct students to list the common attributes or distinguishing characteristics of the items in each grouped set and verify them with the class. Students state the name or concept for their groups (for example, *similes*, *narrative elements*, or *subordinating conjunctions*). If they are unfamiliar with the name of the grouped set, provide them with it and tell them that the targeted group with similar attributes becomes the focus going forward. If they grouped all items into separate categories (as in the preceding option A), then identify which category will receive attention first. Later, you can focus on another group of like items. Instruct students to take notes about these attributes in their journals or notebooks.

3. **Provide a definition:** Ask students to define the term or idea that is the focus for this activity. Student groups share their definitions with the class to arrive at a consensus. Ask students to add the definition to their notes.

4. **Find and critique examples:** Guide students to a complex text, such as a textbook passage, print or digital article, website, video, or picture (if applicable), and have them find examples of this skill that published authors, artists, or professionals in the field use. Instruct students to discuss and analyze these examples with group members then share their interpretations or observations with the class.

5. **Create examples:** Students review the items in the grouped set, their list of these items' attributes, the definition, and the published work to help them construct new examples. For instance, if the grouped set has similes, students invent their own similes. If the set includes sentences that begin with dependent clauses, students construct similar sentences. (Teachers can switch this step and step 4, if they prefer.)

6. **Apply the skill:** Students independently practice the skill by applying it, for example, to a piece of writing, a speech, or a drawing.

In the example we use for this section, teachers use the concept-attainment strategy to teach dialogue-writing mechanics—capitalization, quotation marks, commas, and so on—which represent steps 5 and 6 of the learning progression from figure 3.1 (page 61). This skill can be tricky since many rules apply and some appear counterintuitive. In teaching any grammar and conventions target area, teachers refer to the classroom complex text as a resource to show how established authors authentically incorporate these skills. However, when teachers use published work as a mentor text to teach these writing areas, they should focus on content first, then the writer's craft, so that students experience the richness of the text before homing in on conventions.

As a resource to assist teachers in conducting lessons around dialogue mechanics, they might need to review the applicable terms in figure 8.5. When two characters converse back and forth, sometimes authors omit dialogue tags after initially establishing who is engaged in the conversation. In fact, this figure represents knowledge items; therefore, teachers can reference it in their PREP process template associated with the language standards.

Dialogue: Conversation between two or more characters or people; can be words, sentences, or paragraphs

Dialogue (or speaker) tag: Words and phrases that indicate which character or individual is speaking

Types of Dialogue (or Speaker) Tags	Examples
Beginning dialogue (or speaker) tag: A term used to describe dialogue tags that come before the dialogue	He nodded his head at Gloria and cleared his throat and said, "Dear God, thank you for warm summer nights and candlelight and good food."
End dialogue (or speaker) tag: A term used to describe dialogue tags that are found after the dialogue	"How do you do?" said the preacher.
Middle dialogue (or speaker) tag: A term used to describe dialogue tags that interrupt the dialogue	"Daddy," I said, "this is Otis."

Source for quotes: DiCamillo, 2000.

Figure 8.5: Dialogue tag vocabulary terms.

The following sections address preparing for the activity, conducting the activity, and implementing other ideas and differentiated instruction.

Preparing for the Activity

In this concept-attainment example, teachers prepare manipulatives of sentence strips that students will categorize into groups. They find examples of beginning, middle, and end speaker tags from the complex text students have been reading, like the examples from *Because of Winn-Dixie* (DiCamillo, 2000) in figure 8.6.

Beginning Dialogue Tags
The manager screamed, "Somebody grab that dog!"
The manager said, "Don't you know not to bring a dog into a grocery store?"
The preacher said to Winn-Dixie, "I should have guessed you were going to be trouble."
Miss Franny looked down at him and said, "He most certainly is a large dog."

Middle Dialogue Tags
"Winn-Dixie," I hissed, "come back here."
"I'm going to tell my mama you said that," shouted Stevie, "and she'll tell your daddy and he'll shame you in front of the whole church."
"Certain ones," said Miss Franny, "a select few."
"An installment plan," I said, ignoring the parrot, "you know, where I promise to give you my allowance every week and you give me the leash and the collar now."
"Hey," said Dunlap, "that ain't a very nice way for a preacher's daughter to talk."

End Dialogue Tags
"I can hear you," I hollered back at them.
"That witch is going to eat the dog for dinner and you for dessert," Stevie said.
"Get lost, you bald-headed babies," I said.
"We'll tell the preacher what happened to you," Dunlap shouted after me.
"Is she the owner?" I asked.

Source for quotes: DiCamillo, 2000.

Figure 8.6: Dialogue sentence strips—*Because of Winn-Dixie.*

*Visit **go.SolutionTree.com/literacy** for a free reproducible version of this figure.*

Copy the sentence strips on heavy bond paper, laminate them, and cut out the strips. Place a set of sentence strips with a combination of dialogue tags in an envelope; prepare enough envelopes for groups of three students. Also, unless they are using the provided heading strips for Beginning Dialogue Tags, Middle Dialogue Tags, and End Dialogue Tags, give each trio a pack of sticky notes on which to write these categories. (To differentiate the set of strips, see the Adapting the Activity section for this strategy, page 214.) Teachers then determine which students will work together in the groups of three, and they instruct students to sit in their trios.

Conducting the Activity

Set the stage for the upcoming concept-attainment exercise by asking students to take their books out and to find any passage of dialogue. When they do, have them put their fingers on one or two passages, then verify with a partner that they are each pointing to dialogue. Ask them what specifically indicates that the passages contain dialogue. Likely, they will reply that quotation marks show a character is speaking or that the author includes the name of a character to show exactly who is talking. After validating (or correcting) their responses, instruct them to point to the part that reveals who is speaking. Tell them this part of the sentence is called a *dialogue tag* or *speaker tag*. Next, say the following or something similar:

Authors place dialogue tags in different positions when writing dialogue. A tag is placed sometimes before the character speaks, sometimes after the character speaks, and sometimes even in the middle to interrupt a sentence. And sometimes, authors do not even state who is speaking. They might do this when two characters talk back and forth. In this case, authors expect readers to keep track of who is speaking.

There are different mechanics or conventions based on where these tags are located— for example, rules for capitalization, plus rules for commas, periods, and other punctuation marks. The focus for today and tomorrow is to answer these guiding questions: What are the different types of dialogue tags? *and* What are proper dialogue mechanics for each type? *These are our learning targets:* I can name and identify the different types of dialogue tags, *and* I can write dialogue using proper mechanics.

You will use what you learn to properly treat dialogue in your own stories.

At this point, use the concept-attainment steps detailed in the following sections to review an explanation of the process that will help students distinguish between the beginning, middle, and end tags.

Examine and Group a Set of Items According to Their Commonalities

Distribute a set of dialogue sentence strips to each trio with these instructions:

In your trios, I will give you an envelope with sentence strips of dialogue from the story we have been reading in class. Categorize the strips into different groups based on the location of the dialogue tags. To help you, consider these questions: Where are the dialogue tags? Which sentences can be grouped together because the tags are in the same place? *Pay attention to what is capitalized and where the quotation marks, commas, periods, and other punctuation marks are located.*

Write the name of each group on a sticky note if you know what it is. Afterward, you will share your thinking with others in the class to explain how you grouped your sentences.

Identify the Specific Attributes of This Grouped Set, and Name the Set

Ask each trio to share how it grouped the sentences by answering these questions: "What is similar about the items in this group? What heading did you write on the sticky note for each one?"

While students specify the common attributes of each group, feature the sentence strips on a document camera or another projection device. Invite volunteers to come to the front and point to an example from the sentences that supports their explanations. Ask them to provide a name for each group if they can—for example, "These two sentences belong together because they each have a dialogue tag at the beginning of the sentence, so we named this group *Beginning Dialogue Tag. [Points to the tag.]* The author identifies the character who is talking before the actual dialogue, so it is placed at the beginning of the sentence."

Invite students to return to their sentences and ensure that they are properly grouped with the right headings: *Beginning, Middle,* and *End Dialogue (or Speaker) Tags.*

Provide a Definition

Ask students to return to their sentence strips and determine the rules that apply to each grouped set. You might divide this task by asking some trios to focus on beginning tags, others on end tags, and the remaining groups on middle speaker tags. Provide these directions:

In your small groups, you will each be assigned either a beginning, a middle, or an end tag. For your type of tag, discuss and write down all the rules that apply for writing dialogue with this type of tag. You will share these rules; then we will verify them to make sure they are correct.

Focusing on one kind of dialogue tag at a time, groups each share their rules as the teacher records what they say. As a class, verify the entries; delete and add rules as needed. Then distribute figure 8.7 (page 213), which lists a series of rules of dialogue mechanics. Instruct students to focus on the line items in the figure that apply to each type of tag one at a time. They compare the class list of rules with the handout to verify proper mechanics. Students can record these rules in their academic notebooks or journals.

Dialogue Mechanics	
Rules	**Example**
1. **Beginning tags:** After writing the tag, insert a comma, quotation mark, and the dialogue, which begins with a capital letter (see circled examples). At the end of the dialogue, place a question mark, exclamation point, or period followed by the final quotation mark (see what is in the square).	The manager said, "Don't you know not to bring a dog into a grocery store?" The manager screamed, "Somebody grab that dog!" The preacher said to Winn-Dixie, "I should have guessed you were going to be trouble."
2. **Middle tags:** For this type of tag, insert a quotation mark, and start the dialogue. Place commas and quotation marks before and after the middle dialogue tag. Do not capitalize the word after the tag since it is a continuation of a sentence. The only exceptions are the pronoun "I" and proper nouns, which are always capitalized. At the end of the dialogue, place a question mark, exclamation point, or period followed by the final quotation mark.	"Winn-Dixie," I hissed, "come back here." "Well," I said, "I found a Less Fortunate at the grocery store." "Hey," said Dunlap, "that ain't a very nice way for a preacher's daughter to talk."
3. **End tags:** Place a quotation mark at the beginning of the dialogue, and capitalize the first letter of the dialogue (see what is underlined). To indicate the end of the dialogue, place a question mark, exclamation point, or comma—which is used instead of a period—then a quotation mark. Add the speaker tag, but only capitalize a proper noun (see circled examples). Insert a period after the tag.	"What's the theme?" she asked. "Gertrude's a pretty bird!" screamed Gertrude. "You got to think of a theme," she told me.
4. Begin a new paragraph for each new speaker no matter the length of the dialogue.	"Seen what?" I said. "I seen all them animals out of their cages and keeping real still. Is that man magic?" she asked. "Kind of," I told her. She hugged Winn-Dixie around the neck. "Just like this grocery-store dog, right?" "Right," I said. I started walking, and Sweetie Pie took her knuckle out of her mouth and put her hand in mine.

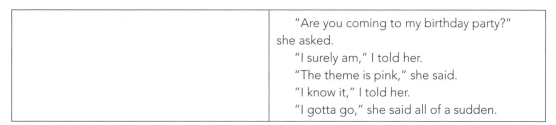

| | "Are you coming to my birthday party?" she asked.
 "I surely am," I told her.
 "The theme is pink," she said.
 "I know it," I told her.
 "I gotta go," she said all of a sudden. |

Source for quotes: DiCamillo, 2000.

Figure 8.7: Dialogue mechanics.

*Visit **go.SolutionTree.com/literacy** for a free reproducible version of this figure.*

Find and Critique Examples

Instruct students to each participate in a scavenger hunt where they find examples of each type of tag (one at a time) in their literature textbook, independent book, or class text. Have them use figure 8.7 as a resource for this exercise. Then, ask students to check with others in their group to be sure that the examples they have found are correct, using specific evidence from the figure as the basis for verification. This step is not present in the learning progression but is representative of the kind of informal assessment teachers might conduct in their classrooms.

Create Examples

Students practice creating their own examples of each type of dialogue tag using any of the resources they accessed from the previous steps to aid them. Then, teachers assess students by asking them to write examples of all three types of dialogue tags on an exit slip to check for understanding, which is included in step 5 of the learning progression.

Apply the Skill

Before teachers ask students to revise their dialogue passages in their drafts—step 6 on the learning progression—teachers might assign a practice activity for pairs of students to compose dialogue with proper mechanics. In this exercise, students assume the roles of different characters or personified objects. Pairs must first determine the topic or situation that forms the basis for the conversation; then, they pass a paper or electronic device back and forth to continuously contribute lines of dialogue. Ask students to use all types of tags—beginning, middle, and end. Although each student will write his or her respective dialogue, tell students to check each other's work and make changes as needed to ensure proper conventions. Teachers assist students to stimulate the dialogue exchange in one of two ways.

1. **Brainstorm a list:** Allow students to choose the two subjects engaged in a conversation. Provide these kinds of ideas to help them brainstorm their characters—two toddlers in a playground or at the beach, a stuffed animal and a child, two animals in a zoo or in the wild, a bat and a ball, a lost cell phone and the person who finds it, autumn leaves and a rake, a swimmer and a lifeguard, and so on.

2. **Use pictures:** Teachers can conduct an internet search to find pictures of people or inanimate objects (like empty chairs) to share with the class. Students select a picture and assume the roles of two subjects in their chosen visual. Access the following or other sites to locate pictures for this activity.

   - *National Geographic (www.nationalgeographic.com/photography /photo-of-the-day/archive)*—An archive of all the "Photo of the Day" pictures

   - *Archive (www.artchive.com/ftp_site.htm)*—A collection of innumerable pictures of works of art categorized by artist (Cassatt, Picasso, Bruegel, Bernini, and so on) and by genre (impressionism, cubism, and so on)

   - *Google Arts & Culture (https://artsandculture.google.com)*—A rich resource of artwork; art movements; historic events; virtual tours of famous landmarks, sites, and museums; and more

By using the concept attainment strategy, teachers can engage students in productive struggle to ensure they use proper writing conventions to embed meaningful dialogue into their stories.

Adapting the Activity

As stated earlier, teachers can incorporate the concept-attainment strategy not only in lessons on writing mechanics but also across disciplines. This strategy can stretch students' learning and facilitate self-discovery of concepts or ideas in myriad ways.

For the first part of this dialogue lesson, when students examine and group items, teachers can scaffold instruction for some trios who need extra support by having them sort rather than categorize. When sorting, teachers supply the headings for each dialogue tag group from figure 8.6 (page 209). This gives learners who struggle the advantage of knowing how many groups they will ultimately form, plus the name for each. Categorizing, the method shown in the exercise, requires more cognitive challenge since it asks students to determine how many groups they will fashion and the name for each. Both sorting and categorizing ask students to determine the number of items in each group; however, sorting—which is beneficial and still necessitates mental acuity—relies on an easier construct. Across content areas, teachers can differentiate activities where some students sort and others categorize items for an express purpose.

For this strategy, students can group pictures (ecosystems), words (types of prepositions or geographical terms), sentences (structures), paragraphs (hooks used in introductions), and even longer texts (purpose of writing). When teachers prepare what students will sort or categorize, they can prepare items of varying degrees of challenge. Students who struggle receive a limited number of items to sort, perhaps ones that have more accessible content. To extend their learning, higher achievers can categorize additional and more sophisticated items. All students profit from teachers circulating around the room to check on progress and provide questions or clues to move them forward in their learning.

EXERCISE
Design a Complete Lesson

Chapter 6 (page 137) provides a research-based model for building well-orchestrated lessons (gradual release of responsibility), and chapter 7 (page 153) explores the tenets of high-quality literacy instruction. Use the information in these previous chapters, the instructional strategies presented in this one, and those you and your team have acquired through your work and collaboration to create or enhance a lesson from a team learning progression that utilizes gradual release of responsibility and at least one of the strategies from this chapter.

Use the following questions to guide this exercise.

★ How can our team use line items on the learning progression to design effective lessons? To maximize our time, can we divide the line items, draft lessons, and share with each other?

★ What strategies presented in this chapter meet the needs of our students and align to our team's learning progression?

★ What other strategies can we collectively share as a team to support student learning and embed in lessons?

★ How will we assess student learning in the lessons?

★ How will we differentiate instruction to account for learners who do not master skills and for those who show they are ready for more?

Summary

Within instruction, it is incumbent on teachers to select appropriate strategies that meet the needs of students so their learning moves forward and they master standards based on a learning progression. As Robert J. Marzano (2017) purports in *The New Art and Science of Teaching*, the focus of instruction should rest on student outcomes as opposed to teacher outcomes: "Instructional strategies generate certain mental states and processes in learners' minds which, in turn, enhance students' learning. . . . Without these mental states and processes, a given strategy will have little or no effect on students" (p. 5).

Teachers should also aim to infuse lessons with strategies that pique students' interest and engage them in the task at hand. They should deliberately select strategies expressly designed for students to accomplish a skill and check for understanding to ensure the strategy is producing the desired results. If a particular strategy misses the mark and students are unfortunately still grappling with proficiency, teachers need a different one so students have an alternative avenue to master intended skills.

The next chapter, which focuses on equity, includes information that teachers can use to further engage students in learning. Through literacy education, teachers can endeavor to create a more cohesive and inclusive learning environment.

CHAPTER 9

Consider Equity in Literacy

In thinking about literacy in general, consider for a moment the daily activities that require even the most basic form of reading and writing skills. What percentage of your day or week might you spend reading any kind of text? What literacy skills did you need to get yourself to work today? Did you read signs along the road while driving or consult maps when accessing public transportation? What else in your week required a form of literacy? Did you sign a contract or consent form? Read a list or determine a budget to grocery shop? Peruse a restaurant menu? Fill out a voting ballot? Can you think of a job that does not, in some way, involve written communication?

Now, consider every form of communication you rely on to connect with the people in your life, from the internet and email to social media and text messages. To fully participate in society in the Information Age, teachers must provide *all* students a literacy level that positions them to function effectively in society. They cannot afford to allow even one student to leave their care without guaranteeing he or she can read and write at grade level, as well as engage in fruitful discussions. For example, in fourth and fifth grade, students must be adept at locating information from print or digital sources to find answers to a question or solve a problem, or they assert a viewpoint and back it up with reasons supported by facts and details. These, and other grade-level skills, can serve them well to fully participate in and navigate life.

What does this have to do with equity in learning? Well, if society strives to truly honor the fundamental tenet that all humans are created equal, it must ensure equal access to the necessary skills for all members in that society to aim for success. Literacy is an essential prerequisite for this endeavor and for full engagement in the world. It equips students with the essential building blocks that form the gateway to all learning. Through reading, writing, speaking, and listening, teachers grant their students access to the skills and resources necessary to appreciate a richly diverse society.

Teachers are living and educating students during important times filled with defining movements. From racial- and gender-equality movements to simply understanding and accepting the formation of one's identity, committed people passionately work to generate a society where everyone recognizes and accepts one another for each of our unique qualities. Schools and, more specifically, classrooms provide a venue for students to learn about building toward a more equitable, diverse, and welcoming society. Within the classroom's walls, teachers strive to create a cohesive and inclusive learning environment as a microcosm of a broader, accepting society. In this regard, educators model and teach how to be inclusive of others despite differences—or, rather, *because of* differences.

This approach also helps to create environments in which all students are able and willing to take risks to learn. Teachers aim for this goal but often feel ill equipped to establish it. Therefore, this chapter supports them in this regard and addresses how teachers and administrators can answer the following compelling and difficult questions concerning equitable school practices. These queries require teachers and administrators to be vulnerable and face what could be brutal facts about the current state of equitable practices in their classrooms and schools. Since movements abound, and the richness of a diverse world has expanded, teams should also generate additional questions while reading to examine other issues that affect their students and school.

▶ "How can our team and school identify and eliminate invisible biases that might influence our instructional approach to students and affect their trust in us?"

▶ "How can our team and school avoid excluding any student from rigorous learning opportunities in curricula and promote high expectations for all students?"

▶ "How can our team ensure the resources we select or are asked to use authentically reflect the demographics of our students, diverse perspectives, and the experiences of others?"

The following sections address equity of access to three fundamental aspects of teaching that align to the previously posed questions: (1) instruction, (2) expectations, and (3) resources. These sections act as our final road map to ensuring all fourth- and fifth-grade students leave your team's care with a strong foundation in literacy skills that will serve them well in future grades and in life. Educators working together as part of a strong PLC culture have the potential to make a positive impact for students, schools, and society but only if they are willing to step up to do the hard, reflective work on an ongoing basis. It is an educator's obligation, as someone in a position to positively influence students, to ensure each student—regardless of gender, race, ethnicity, language, or disabilities—feels included in his or her classroom's culture. Your team's approach to literacy instruction can be a critical part of making that happen. Focusing on the material in this chapter can facilitate open conversations and perhaps necessary change for the betterment of your students.

Access to Instruction

Before considering equity in curriculum and resources, your team should begin by examining privately or publicly any internal, personal biases that might be present in how you each approach students. This is not about blame or judgment. It's simply important and valuable to look critically at the intended and unintended messages you each might send to students through your words and actions. This critical introspection might prove challenging, but at the same time might prove rewarding because it fosters growth and perhaps can uncover or lead to areas in instruction that require revision.

Start by inviting team members to share and acknowledge examples of inclusivity within each classroom that most likely occur. Then, ask yourselves how your instructional approaches might foster or inhibit equitable practices in the classroom, particularly as they pertain to literacy. Articulate what existing or new practices do or would lead to more equitable outcomes. While engaging in this discussion, you might discover a sense of vulnerability or the need to confront some uncomfortable issues. Open, honest dialogue is healthy and likely results in identifying one area as a team focus to promote the kind of change that benefits all your students.

To practice, this section offers an examination of factors teams should consider in how their approach to gender might influence their instruction. Although gender represents one defining difference among people, it is not binary—someone identifies as either a boy or a girl. Rather, researchers state that gender is multidimensional residing somewhere along a continuum or spectrum (Bockting, 2008; Connell, 2009; Harrison, Grant, & Herman, 2012). Some students may not explicitly identify solely with one gender, and gender does not always characterize one's inclinations and tastes. For example, women and girls can enjoy sports and play video games, which are often thought of as traditionally masculine preferences. Additionally, men and boys might choose to dress in pink or play with dolls, traits conventionally regarded as feminine.

Transgender individuals might possess a sense that their gender identity misaligns to their physical anatomy even before they enter fourth or fifth grade:

> Research indicates that there is a significant gap between a child's understanding that their gender doesn't conform to expectations and when they communicate with others (namely parents) about it. In one study, the average age of self-realization for the child that they were transgender or non-binary was 7.9 years, but the average age when they disclosed their understanding of their gender was 15.5. (Gender Spectrum, n.d.)

According to Gender Spectrum's Charles Margulis (n.d.), "gender non-conforming behavior in preadolescents is particularly visible . . . most of them are already aware that they do not fit expected gender norms." Furthermore, this source states that while some youth assert transgender or non-binary identity with relative ease or confidence, others feel uncomfortable, experience bullying, and become withdrawn. A teacher's support and understanding can go a long way to mitigate these effects. Consider how you group students currently. Do you separate them by gender? You or other team members may do this with the best of intentions, as this is a seemingly efficient grouping strategy, and it's one you may have experienced as a student or even early in your career if you are a veteran teacher. However, this strategy sends the message that students are defined based on their gender. Avoid singling out gender as a defining characteristic, which signals to students that they ought to identify with all the associated aspects that a particular culture deems as the norm. In fact, grouping by gender, which implies a clear-cut identification of male or female, can be confusing to students grappling with their gender identity. Rather, use themes, colors, or shapes to arrange students into groups; randomly assign them by drawing sticks; or, leave it up to students to formulate their own.

Research shows that "Stereotyping in childhood has wide-ranging and significant negative consequences for both women and men, with more than half (51%) of people affected saying it constrained their career choices and 44% saying it harmed their personal relationships" (Fawcett Society, 2019). In the case of grouping, any students with a nonbinary identification who question their gender may feel forced to select one group or the other. When confronted with such a choice, no safe space exists for these students. Research affirms the damage this causes. Gender stereotyping "is harmful when it limits women's and men's capacity to develop their personal abilities, pursue their professional careers and make choices about their lives" (Office of the High Commissioner for Human Rights, n.d.). This effect often occurs in literacy-based instruction when teachers suggest girls read books with princess or dancer characters while recommending their male counterparts read adventure or sports stories. In this scenario, educators rely on cultural norms to make decisions for students about their interests as well as expectations for them.

Diversity education expert Dana Stachowiak (2018f) asserts in the article "The Power to Include" that "literacy classrooms are spaces with unique opportunities to do the work of creating an environment that is gender inclusive" (p. 29). To support teachers in this endeavor, Stachowiak (2018f) provides the following six suggestions that teachers of literacy can implement:

1. Learn and understand terms and definitions.

2. Work through your own biases and beliefs.

3. Be proactive, not reactive.

4. Plan to support gender-noncomforming students.

5. Integrate, don't separate, curricula.

6. Commit to growing. (pp. 29–30)

To become more educated about this area so you can strive to create a gender-inclusive classroom environment, consider reading Dana Stachowiak's (2018f) full article as well as numerous print and online resources about this expansive topic.

Gender is just one example of many that teams must consider when making instructional choices involving students. Race, culture, and religion are all areas we implore teams to explore when reflecting on how instruction might reflect invisible biases or suppositions that could send overt and covert, unintentional messages to students whose identities are still forming. The following sections examine some of these through the lens of curriculum and resources.

Promote High Expectations

It may seem unnecessary to ask, "Should any student be excluded from challenging learning opportunities?" Obviously, the answer is no. Sadly, some educators quickly jump to unfounded conclusions about student capabilities and determine that maybe some students are not ready for or able to participate in rigorous learning experiences. Or, an educator may apply arbitrary reasoning to determine that certain students are not competent enough to learn all the standards that others typically address in their grade level. Both are fallacies. With the exception of those who have a significant cognitive impairment, all students are entitled to and obligated to master all standards.

Learning opportunities are often withheld, to various degrees, from three different subgroups of students who are able to learn grade-level standards.

1. Students who are evaluated and qualify for an individualized education plan or who are entitled to specific learning goals as a result of having a disability

2. Students who are culturally and linguistically diverse but not yet English proficient and are therefore labeled as English learners

3. Students who begin school disadvantaged in some way, such as economically, or who lacked access to early learning and therefore are unfairly labeled as *low performers*

The students who fit into these groups possess thinking and learning assets. However, some teachers possess limiting beliefs about them, which results in lowered expectations for these students. This dynamic of unfairly setting inappropriate expectations can inadvertently sabotage students' success:

[Unfounded] judgments about [students'] capability often apply stereotypes about social groups such as about race and gender, reflect myths about development and behavior, confuse what is with what could be, and put too much weight on test scores rather than daily performance as evidence of ability. The actions taken in response to these judgments often determine very different learning opportunities and convey strong messages about capability. (Weinstein, 2002, p. 4)

Consider this common mistake teachers unintentionally make that leads to inherent inequities in access to education: Educators often think a student identified as an English learner lacks skills and cannot achieve the standards. They spend a significant amount of time focusing on those prerequisite language skills and fail to provide instruction in the actual grade-level standards prior to the end of the academic school year. This propels a vicious cycle in which the student cannot catch up, resulting in lost learning opportunities. When this occurs, the teachers miss the importance of having a learning progression to achieve a standard (chapter 3, page 59), and they do not use individual student data to drive instruction (chapter 5, page 117). Further, the teachers neglect to design optimal literacy instruction (chapter 7, page 153). Making inaccurate assumptions that lead to lower expectations may lead teachers to use less-rigorous strategies, groupings, and materials, producing less growth or no growth for students in this population.

Therefore, teachers must realize their influence on students and present possibilities for them. To determine how you and your colleagues can promote high expectations or commit to do so, review these actions together and formulate concrete ways that you can apply them in your classrooms:

- Articulate the belief that students can achieve at high levels
- Create warm social-emotional relationships focused on strengths, funds of knowledge, cultural understandings, and interests/aspirations
- Provide informative feedback on performance to scaffold learning
- Teach content and use tasks with high cognitive demand
- Ask frequent, high-level questions
- Encourage a productive struggle (refraining from giving answers, allowing wait time, guiding to answer)
- Maintain close physical proximity
- Interact frequently
- Use positive nonverbal communication (Budge & Parrett, 2018, p. 81)

Another detrimental situation that aligns to limiting expectations is when we assign labels to students. For example, students with disabilities are often named *SPED* (short for *special education*) or *IEP kids*. Students who work to acquire English are often referred to as *limited* in some way, which is shortsighted since they may understand conceptual ideas but lack the language to articulate them. Further, some students are called *low* due to a disadvantage they encountered at some point in their life that might be ill-defined.

In reality, these students are capable of learning grade-level standards; their learning needs just look different than other students' needs do (DuFour et al., 2016). Unfortunately, no positive asset orientation is associated with these students, as unwarranted expectations and labels cloud teachers' vision, misrepresent students, and communicate what students cannot do rather than what they can.

In their book *Disrupting Poverty*, Kathleen M. Budge and William H. Parrett (2018) provide a powerful insight into the negative ramifications of using labels that has merit in this discussion. After reading the following quote, apply the thinking of these authors and discuss with colleagues how to reframe the way educators refer to students in these subgroups since a positive shift in language can correlate to an improved mindset:

> How we think about and refer to our students is an important consider-
> ation. . . . Words are powerful, and they often can perpetuate or challenge
> our beliefs. Have you ever thought about the various ways we describe our
> students who live in poverty—*Title I kids*, *free and reduced-priced meals kids*,
> *low-SES kids*, *high-poverty kids*, or *poverty-kids*? What do we mean when we
> use these labels? What is a "high-poverty kid"? What do the kids and others
> think when they hear these terms? (Budge & Parrett, 2018, p. 22)

Teachers need to ask, "How can our team and school avoid excluding any student from rigorous learning opportunities and promote high expectations for all students?" If there are teaching practices that exclude some students from grade-level learning, teachers must work in collaborative teams to identify how to include all students. For example, can they shift from an English learner pull-out model, in which students are removed from grade-level instruction, to a model that allows these students to work within the classroom? Similarly, teams must address if the needs of students who qualify for an IEP can be met with accommodations or modifications within the classroom.

In our experience, some teachers catalog the obstacles that deter them from supporting these students as a means to justify limiting students' access to the curriculum; for example, they state that programmatic shifts are larger than any one person can consider or implement, that these shifts take time and resources, and that administrators and the board of education generally need to approve them. If discouragement sets in within your team, endeavor to adopt the mindset that change certainly can occur, and begin to educate and engage in supportive, critical conversations as an ally to your most vulnerable students. Remind teachers that they must maintain high expectations for all students within literacy instruction (and across content areas) since the key learning associated with literacy skills supports students in success beyond school. Excluding students risks further marginalizing populations that have been historically treated as peripheral.

Offer Culturally Rich Resources

In addition to providing all students with a quality education that prepares them for their futures, teachers should grant students diverse perspectives through access to a plethora of culturally rich resources. It's not enough to simply select reading materials that align to learning targets; teachers must ask and address the crucial question, "How can I ensure the resources I select or am asked to use authentically reflect the demographics of my students, diverse perspectives, and the experiences of others?" To attend to this question, teachers should aim to share a variety of culturally responsive classroom texts that create both mirrors and windows for students. To elucidate this point, reflect on this quote from Aline O'Donnell's (2019) article in *Literacy Today*: "Curriculum can serve as a mirror when it reflects your own culture and identity, as well as a window when it offers a view into someone else's experience" (p. 19).

Critical to student identity development is a sense of belonging and acceptance (Brendtro, Brokenleg, & Van Bockern, 2019). Teachers can help promote this sense of inclusion by ensuring that students see pieces of their identity positively represented in the texts that they read, discuss, and analyze in the classroom. In this regard, teachers invite students to hold up mirrors. Additionally, resources can create windows by exposing them to a breadth and depth of perspectives and experiences that expand their own view of the world. These windows give students an opportunity to appreciate diverse perspectives from their immediate surroundings, the greater community, and beyond. When students of a dominant culture do not experience "windows into the realities of the multicultural world," they are at risk of "developing a false sense of their own importance in the world" in relation to others (Bishop, 2012, p. 9). So, let's be clear about the meaning of *diversity*.

People often use the term *diversity* in reference to race, class, or gender identity or expression; however, it encompasses so much more. It also includes ethnicity, age, sexual or affectual orientation, geographic background, spirituality or religious beliefs, learning style and abilities, marital or partner status, parental or caregiver status, national origin, language, economic status and background, work experiences, personality, and education. The totality of an individual derives from his or her fixed and fluid traits, characteristics, and experiences. As teachers make decisions about selecting diverse texts, they must commit to learning about each individual student, including his or her preferences and experiences. Additionally, they must exercise caution to avoid making assumptions about people who might outwardly appear to possess similar characteristics when they may perhaps differ completely. It is a teacher's charge to use classroom resources to create learning experiences and environments that further the belief that all humans are created equally and that everyone can appreciate what makes each individual unique.

Part of this challenge is that teachers often do not have experience in the vast array of cultures represented by their students. Therefore, they may find it very difficult to know how to successfully incorporate these cultures when choosing resources to support instruction. As a result, teachers commonly make the mistake of believing they must understand *everything* about their students' backgrounds before they can adopt a culturally responsive pedagogy—that is, instruction that helps students connect their learning to their own cultural experience. In "Partnering With Families and Communities," Katherin Garland and Kisha Bryan (2017) explain why this isn't accurate:

> The most successful implementation happens when teachers partner with families and community members to negotiate classrooms' cultures and curricula that actually reflect the communities where students develop and grow. Family and community members can play a major role in teachers' plans to (1) communicate high expectations to all students, (2) help students learn within the context of their cultures, and (3) value students' cultural backgrounds through content integration. (p. 52)

With this in mind, and at the onset of your team's audit of current resources for diverse representation or selecting new resources, consider the following example from a member of our fourth-grade team. Our team member worked in a suburban school district outside Chicago where Katie Sheridan, director of language and early literacy, asked each administrator from across the district to interview a parent from a background different from their own. Many families in the school community were immigrants, and this exercise was intended to create connections between the school and home environments as part of a district goal to build cultural proficiency and intercultural skills. The experience would allow administrators to gain insight into their students' cultures and share what they learned with colleagues in the school community so they could positively impact students' involvement at school.

Many administrators wished they had a prepared script of questions to pose, as they felt anxious about approaching parents for a candid conversation on potentially sensitive topics. Intentionally, Katie did not provide a script since she conjectured that the administrators might cycle through a list of questions rather than truly concentrate and engage in effortless dialogue. Instead, they were instructed to begin the conversation by asking, "What do you think I need to know about you—for example, your country of origin, background, family, religion, or culture—that will help me better educate your child or children?" Authentically listening to what parents had to share presented a lesson unto itself.

Based on the reason they selected a particular parent, the administrators each steered the conversation and posed questions. Unsurprisingly, responses were diverse and often centered on differences in education systems in other countries. Some parents pointed out the deficit of diverse resources and the lack of images of people who resembled their families on the school or classroom walls. Parents shared stories of their children feeling uncomfortable in school because teachers used resources that included stereotypes of the children's background. As the administrators probed further to learn more, an easy, fluid exchange of conversation emerged and lasted longer than anticipated.

After the discussions, the administrative team members met to share what they each gleaned from parents to educate one another. At times, they discovered conflicting views among the parents. For example, some parents thought their children's homework lacked rigor because their experience of homework had been different as students. Other parents felt strongly that homework intruded on quality family time in the evenings. In this case, the administrative team admitted it was unable to make changes that catered to every perspective on homework. However, through communication with the administrators, the fourth-grade team felt empowered to understand reasons some students did not return to school with homework, and the team members could work to create systems that would allow all students to succeed. Additionally, the team members could educate parents who demanded more homework by sharing the research and reaching a compromise about what made the most sense in terms of students' success.

Another recurring concern the administrators learned from families was that many students did not see themselves represented in the school. They took this feedback to heart. As a result, they guaranteed change since the inadequate display of diversity on the walls was unintentional and lacked presence of mind. For the team, this meaningful experience launched a journey to discover what else they had overlooked by neglecting key cultural implications; thus, the team committed to continuous learning and improvement to inculcate diversity into the fabric of the school and across the district.

The most significant outcome from this experience was to refrain from making assumptions, learn about diverse perspectives, and be forthright and comfortable to ask questions. Educators must engage in and commit to the vulnerable act of learning from others. As educators, we sometimes hold back when we have a curious impulse. We recoil from asking questions for fear of offending someone or saying something wrong. In truth, there are those who may not appreciate educating others about their background. But many willingly share about their identities and recognize that helping others learn about myriad cultures creates a more inclusive society for everyone, their children included.

The point of this example is to stress that, as your team continues to audit and augment existing classroom resources, it must take into consideration the demographics of your community. (This aspect of choosing classroom texts aligns with one of the measures of choosing texts highlighted in chapter 3—Discuss Options for Complex Text, page 80). To expand expertise in this effort, Sharroky Hollie (2019) advises teachers to be cognizant of three types of culturally responsive texts that will assist teachers in wisely choosing core reading material that reflects students culturally and linguistically.

1. **Culturally authentic texts:** This preferred text type refers to fiction or nonfiction that mirrors authentic cultural experiences of a certain group. It might focus on religion, gender, ethnicity, geographic location, or other aspects of culture. (Access www.responsivereads.com to find culturally authentic titles.)

2. **Culturally generic texts:** Although these texts center on characters with racial identities, they include few or superficial cultural details about these characters within the overall storyline.

3. **Culturally neutral texts:** This least-preferred culturally responsive type of text is considered neutral because, although the text focuses on a character of color, the other aspects of the story—its plot, theme, or methods of characterization—are largely traditional or mainstream. Teachers might select these texts for other purposes, such as to focus on the author's strong use of figurative language, vocabulary, or suspense. But in doing so, they should not mistake these texts for culturally responsive texts when their value is predicated on the author's craft.

When selecting texts, keep in mind that one story does not tell the whole narrative of all who identify with a gender or cultural group. It is impossible to know everything about all dimensions of diversity that make us different from one another. Therefore, solicit input from your colleagues, your students, and your students' parents, many of whom are incredible allies and will likely prove willing to educate teacher teams and freely share about their cultures. Be receptive to learning by asking them questions that allow you to gain perspective, as this can ultimately prove useful when selecting texts.

Works from authors of all different cultures and backgrounds artfully bring stories and the world to life that touch on a variety of topics and themes that students might find relevant and interesting. In addition, shine a spotlight on authors since the texts they craft might reflect their personal experiences and provide an additional dimension into a culture. Of chief importance is your team's awareness of the impact the literature it selects will have on every student in its classrooms. By exposing students to a rich repository of resources, teachers allow students to mirror their own cultures and also afford them opportunities to experience lives different from their own and learn to appreciate diverse perspectives. Presenting an array of rich texts that positively contribute to building students' knowledge, cultural awareness, and acceptance ensures students grow not only as readers and writers but as human beings.

EXERCISE
Address Important Questions About Access

An educator's job entails creating an inclusive environment in which students appreciate differences. Literacy can serve as a vehicle for expanding students' thinking and exposing them to the richness of the world. Through culturally responsive texts, they experience people, places, and situations perhaps previously unfamiliar to them. Engage in a discussion with your team to determine how you can all make classrooms more inclusive and literacy materials more diverse and culturally authentic.

Use the following questions to guide this exercise.

★ Do we send unintended messages about student identities through our day-to-day instructional practices? If so, how might we reconsider our actions or words?

★ Does our team exclude students from rigorous learning opportunities? Which students are pulled out and do not participate in grade-level classroom instruction as others do, and why do they not? How can we improve this situation?

★ How can we positively shift our collective mindset and language we use when referring to students who need something different? What language can we adopt that shows an asset-based orientation?

★ Do the resources that we select, or that we are asked to use, authentically reflect the demographics of students in our classrooms? Do the resources show a balanced representation of students in our classrooms?

★ Do the resources reflect diverse perspectives and experiences of others? Or, do the texts predominantly reflect one perspective? If they do, how can we positively adjust our plans to be more inclusive?

★ How do we know our resources support diverse cultural experiences? Have we engaged with an ally of that demographic background? Have we considered the author of the text and to what degree the author's experience is authentic?

Summary

We have the opportunity to substantially improve the education experience and outcomes for our students. Literacy instruction is the place to begin this change. Each and every student of a different gender, race, ethnic background, language ability, disability, or other quality contributes uniqueness to the collective composition of a classroom, school, and community. Educators of literacy, in particular, are privileged to provide students with access to learning experiences and resources that highlight and celebrate what each student brings to the classroom and world. With literacy instruction, students read about, write about, talk about, and listen to issues and discussions surrounding equity. Engaging in diverse texts and thoughtful discussions that spawn a change in perspective engenders appreciation for the lives others live and the way they think, which might be different from our own perspectives and experiences. Through teachers' thoughtful guidance, students can transfer what they learn within the class to their communities and make inclusive contributions. This chapter is but a starting point to a potentially rich conversation and a launching point for action through which teams can use literacy as a powerful tool toward inclusivity.

EPILOGUE

Undeniably, possessing strong literacy skills can benefit all members of society. The International Literacy Association (2019) asserts in its position statement, "The ability to identify, understand, interpret, create, compute, and communicate using visual, audible, and digital materials across disciplines and in any context—and access to excellent and equitable literacy instruction are basic human rights" (p. 1).

Whether teaching students to function as generators or receivers of written, digital, or oral discourse, a teacher's obligation is to advance students' literacy capabilities so they can actively and fully engage in our world. Building competencies around literacy instruction is the strongest catalyst for supporting student growth in every area of school curricula.

As schools commit to exemplary instruction to advance learning, educators must not overlook the power of a PLC. Regardless of the structure of teams in your PLC, this work always begins with teaming teachers who are focused on improving their own capacity to impact student learning. Teams dedicate themselves to working collaboratively to position students for success. Specifically, these teams of professionals engage in the PREP process to unwrap standards and identify learning targets, create a learning progression, design assessment tasks and rubrics, develop differentiated lessons, collect and analyze data to inform instruction, and intervene to provide necessary support, all in an effort to move students' learning forward.

While this book speaks directly to fourth- and fifth-grade teachers who want to hone their teaching of literacy within their classrooms, this is one installment in a series that supports teacher collaboration and strategic literacy-infused teaching in all elementary grades. Each text in this series focuses on building common instructional and assessment practices with a common language that ensures a literacy focus across academic disciplines. Ultimately, the literacy skills and embedded critical thinking required to master them will prepare grades 4–5 students for the rigor of middle school and beyond.

All teachers possess a pressing responsibility to increase students' literacy capacity that opens the doors wide to myriad and boundless opportunities. Teachers working in cohesive, effective, and goal-oriented teams can more capably educate students who will forge ahead with more confidence to meet the next challenge that lies ahead for them. Preparing them amply is our responsibility. Let us embrace this awesome duty.

APPENDIX A

TEMPLATES AND TOOLS

This appendix provides a series of reproducible tools your team can use as it works to build literacy-focused instruction through its curriculum. Here, you will find the complete version of the PREP template (including areas for adding essential understandings and guiding principles), the learning progression and assessments template, and rubrics for measuring text complexity.

PREP Template

Unit: _____ Time Frame: _____

Grade: _____

Unit Standards

Essential Understandings (optional)	Guiding Questions (optional)

Strand (Reading Literature, Reading Informational Text, Writing, Language, and so on):

-

-

-

-

-

Reading and Writing Instruction for Fourth- and Fifth-Grade Classrooms in a PLC at Work © 2020 Solution Tree Press
SolutionTree.com • Visit **go.SolutionTree.com/literacy** to download this free reproducible.

Strand (Reading Literature, Reading Informational Text, Writing, Language, and so on):

-
-
-
-
-

Strand (Reading Literature, Reading Informational Text, Writing, Language, and so on):

-
-
-
-
-

Strand (Reading Literature, Reading Informational Text, Writing, Language, and so on):

-
-
-
-
-

Unwrapped Unit Priority Standards	Knowledge Items	Skills (Learning Targets and DOK Levels)

Reading and Writing Instruction for Fourth- and Fifth-Grade Classrooms in a PLC at Work © 2020 Solution Tree Press
SolutionTree.com • Visit **go.SolutionTree.com/literacy** to download this free reproducible.

Learning Progression and Assessments Template

Priority Standard (or Standards):

	Steps	Learning Progression	Assessments
	Step _____	**Priority Standard (or Standards):**	
	Step _____	**Learning Target (Skill) or Knowledge**	
	Step _____	**Learning Target (Skill) or Knowledge**	
	Step _____	**Learning Target (Skill) or Knowledge**	

page 1 of 2

		Learning Target (Skill) or Knowledge	
	Step ____	Learning Target (Skill) or Knowledge	
	Step ____	Learning Target (Skill) or Knowledge	
	Step ____	Learning Target (Skill) or Knowledge	
	Step ____	Learning Target (Skill) or Knowledge	
	Step ____	Learning Target (Skill) or Knowledge	
	Step ____		

Text Complexity: Qualitative Measures Rubric—Informational Texts

Text Title: _____   Text Author: _____

	Exceedingly Complex	Very Complex	Moderately Complex	Slightly Complex
Purpose	○ **Purpose:** Subtle, implied, difficult to determine; intricate, theoretical elements	○ **Purpose:** Implied, but fairly easy to infer; more theoretical than concrete	○ **Purpose:** Implied, but easy to identify based upon context or source	○ **Purpose:** Explicitly stated; clear, concrete with a narrow focus
Text Structure	○ **Organization of Main Ideas:** Connections between an extensive range of ideas or events are deep, intricate and often implicit or subtle; organization of the text is intricate or specialized for a particular discipline ○ **Text Features:** If used, are essential in understanding content ○ **Use of Graphics:** If used, extensive, intricate, essential integrated graphics, tables, charts, etc., necessary to make meaning of text; also may provide information not otherwise conveyed in the text	○ **Organization of Main Ideas:** Connections between an expanded range [of] ideas, processes or events are deeper and often implicit or subtle; organization may contain multiple pathways and may exhibit traits common to a specific discipline ○ **Text Features:** If used, greatly enhance the reader's understanding of content ○ **Use of Graphics:** If used, essential integrated graphics, tables, charts, etc.; may occasionally be essential to understanding the text	○ **Organization of Main Ideas:** Connections between some ideas or events are implicit or subtle; organization is evident and generally sequential ○ **Text Features:** If used, enhance the reader's understanding of content ○ **Use of Graphics:** If used, graphics [are] mostly supplementary to understanding of the text, such as indexes, glossaries; graphs, pictures, tables, and charts directly support the text	○ **Organization of Main Ideas:** Connections between ideas, processes or events are explicit and clear; organization of text is clear or chronological or easy to predict ○ **Text Features:** If used, help the reader navigate and understand content but are not essential ○ **Use of Graphics:** If used, simple graphics, unnecessary to understanding the text but directly support and assist in interpreting the written text

page 1 of 2

Reading and Writing Instruction for Fourth- and Fifth-Grade Classrooms in a PLC at Work © 2020 Solution Tree Press
SolutionTree.com • Visit **go.SolutionTree.com/literacy** to download this free reproducible.

	Exceedingly Complex	Very Complex	Moderately Complex	Slightly Complex
Language Features	○ **Conventionality:** Dense and complex; contains abstract, ironic, and/or figurative language ○ **Vocabulary:** Generally unfamiliar, archaic, subject-specific, or overly academic language; may be ambiguous or purposefully misleading ○ **Sentence Structure:** Mainly complex sentences often containing multiple concepts	○ **Conventionality:** Complex; contains some abstract, ironic, and/or figurative language ○ **Vocabulary:** Somewhat complex language that is sometimes unfamiliar, archaic, subject-specific, or overly academic ○ **Sentence Structure:** Many complex sentences with several subordinate phrases or clauses and transition words	○ **Conventionality:** Largely explicit and easy to understand with some occasions for more complex meaning o ○ **Vocabulary:** Mostly contemporary, familiar, conversational; rarely unfamiliar or overly academic ○ **Sentence Structure:** Simple and compound sentences, with some more complex constructions	○ **Conventionality:** Explicit, literal, straightforward, easy to understand ○ **Vocabulary:** Contemporary, familiar, conversational language ○ **Sentence Structure:** Mainly simple sentences
Knowledge Demands	○ **Subject Matter Knowledge:** Extensive, perhaps specialized or even theoretical discipline-specific content knowledge; range of challenging abstract and theoretical concepts ○ **Intertextuality:** Many references or allusions to other texts or outside ideas, theories, etc.	○ **Subject Matter Knowledge:** Moderate levels of discipline-specific content knowledge; some theoretical knowledge may enhance understanding; range of recognizable ideas and challenging abstract concepts ○ **Intertextuality:** Some references or allusions to other texts or outside ideas, theories, etc.	○ **Subject Matter Knowledge:** Everyday practical knowledge and some discipline-specific content knowledge; both simple and more complicated, abstract ideas ○ **Intertextuality:** A few references or allusions to other texts or outside ideas, theories, etc.	○ **Subject Matter Knowledge:** Everyday, practical knowledge; simple, concrete ideas ○ **Intertextuality:** No references or allusions to other texts, or outside ideas, theories, etc.

Source: Achieve the Core. (n.d.). Reviewing using the IMET: ELA: Module 101—high-quality texts, evidence-based discussion and writing, and building knowledge. *Accessed at https://achievethecore.org/content /upload/Understanding%20the%20IMET_ELA.LIT_Handout_101.pdf on April 29, 2020.*

page 2 of 2

Text Complexity: Qualitative Measures Rubric—Literature

Text Title: _____   Text Author: _____

	Exceedingly Complex	Very Complex	Moderately Complex	Slightly Complex
Text Structure	○ **Organization:** Is intricate with regard to such elements as point of view, time shifts, multiple characters, storylines and detail ○ **Use of Graphics:** If used, illustrations or graphics are essential for understanding the meaning of the text	○ **Organization:** May include subplots, time shifts and more complex characters ○ **Use of Graphics:** If used, illustrations or graphics support or extend the meaning of the text	○ **Organization:** May have two or more storylines and occasionally be difficult to predict ○ **Use of Graphics:** If used, a range of illustrations or graphics support selected parts of the text	○ **Organization:** Is clear, chronological or easy to predict ○ **Use of Graphics:** If used, either illustrations directly support and assist in interpreting the text or are not necessary to understanding the meaning of the text
Language Features	○ **Conventionality:** Dense and complex; contains abstract, ironic, and/or figurative language ○ **Vocabulary:** Complex, generally unfamiliar, archaic, subject-specific, or overly academic language; may be ambiguous or purposefully misleading ○ **Sentence Structure**: Mainly complex sentences with several subordinate clauses or phrases; sentences often contain multiple concepts	○ **Conventionality:** Fairly complex; contains some abstract, ironic, and/or figurative language ○ **Vocabulary:** Fairly complex language that is sometimes unfamiliar, archaic, subject-specific, or overly academic ○ **Sentence Structure:** Many complex sentences with several subordinate phrases or clauses and transition words	○ **Conventionality:** Largely explicit and easy to understand with some occasions for more complex meaning ○ **Vocabulary:** Mostly contemporary, familiar, conversational; rarely unfamiliar or overly academic ○ **Sentence Structure:** Primarily simple and compound sentences, with some complex constructions	○ **Conventionality:** Explicit, literal, straightforward, easy to understand ○ **Vocabulary:** Contemporary, familiar, conversational language ○ **Sentence Structure:** Mainly simple sentences

page 1 of 2

Reading and Writing Instruction for Fourth- and Fifth-Grade Classrooms in a PLC at Work © 2020 Solution Tree Press

SolutionTree.com • Visit **go.SolutionTree.com/literacy** to download this free reproducible.

	Exceedingly Complex	Very Complex	Moderately Complex	Slightly Complex
Meaning	○ **Meaning:** Multiple competing levels of meaning that are difficult to identify, separate, and interpret; theme is implicit or subtle, often ambiguous and revealed over the entirety of the text	○ **Meaning:** Multiple levels of meaning that may be difficult to identify or separate; theme is implicit or subtle and may be revealed over the entirety of the text	○ **Meaning:** Multiple levels of meaning clearly distinguished from each other; theme is clear but may be conveyed with some subtlety	○ **Meaning:** One level of meaning; theme is obvious and revealed early in the text.
Knowledge Demands	○ **Life Experiences:** Explores complex, sophisticated or abstract themes; experiences portrayed are distinctly different from the common reader ○ **Intertextuality and Cultural Knowledge:** Many references or allusions to other texts or cultural elements	○ **Life Experiences:** Explores themes of varying levels of complexity or abstraction; experiences portrayed are uncommon to most readers ○ **Intertextuality and Cultural Knowledge:** Some references or allusions to other texts or cultural elements	○ **Life Experiences:** Explores several themes; experiences portrayed are common to many readers ○ **Intertextuality and Cultural Knowledge:** Few references or allusions to other texts or cultural elements	○ **Life Experiences:** Explores a single theme; experiences portrayed are everyday and common to most readers ○ **Intertextuality and Cultural Knowledge:** No references or allusions to other texts or cultural elements

Source: Achieve the Core. (n.d.). Reviewing using the IMET: ELA: Module 101—high-quality texts, evidence-based discussion and writing, and building knowledge. *Accessed at https://achievethecore.org/content /upload/Understanding%20the%20IMET_ELA.LIT_Handout_101.pdf on April 29, 2020.*

APPENDIX B

PROCESS FOR PRIORITIZING STANDARDS

Teams focus on ensuring a guaranteed and viable curriculum, which this book repeatedly emphasizes as a major doctrine of PLC culture. Because there is simply not enough time within the school year to adequately and deeply teach all the standards listed in a district curriculum guide or provided in a published literacy series, teacher teams must determine which standards qualify as essential. Refer to chapter 1 (page 9) to review and understand the purpose of setting priority standards.

If teacher teams have not participated in a process to prioritize standards, they determine which standards they deem worthy of the priority-standard designation using the process outlined in this appendix. This suggested process includes four steps. Teams might decide to conduct the fourth step earlier if teachers need to familiarize themselves with standards in surrounding grades or with standardized testing expectations.

1. Teams review the task and criteria for determining priority standards.

2. Individuals review standards and critique them against criteria.

3. Individuals share and the team arrives at an initial list of priority standards.

4. Teams consider vertical alignment and expectations for external exams and finalize priority standards.

Use this appendix in conjunction with the content in chapter 1 to facilitate this process.

Teams Review the Task and Criteria for Determining Priority Standards

Before teacher teams begin to prioritize, they review the preceding four steps to get an overview of the expectations. Then, to begin, they read the following criteria for prioritization and gain clarity about what each point means (Ainsworth, 2017; Reeves, 2007).

▸ **Endurance:** Are the knowledge, skills, and concepts embedded in the standard critical for students to remember in the future beyond this grade level and course? For example, the ability to coherently summarize complex text is a skill that extends beyond a particular unit of instruction and grade level. Therefore, to summarize is an enduring skill worth teaching.

▸ **Leverage:** Are the knowledge, skills, and concepts in the standard applicable across several disciplines? For example, summarizing complex text might be taught in language arts when students experience a literary work, but it is equally valuable when reading content in social studies and science.

▸ **Readiness:** Does the standard include prerequisite knowledge, skills, and concepts necessary to prepare students for the next grade? For example, when students learn the structure and elements of an opinion paper, it equips them with needed skills and knowledge to tackle the more rigorous work of argumentation writing.

▸ **High-stakes exams:** Will students need to know and apply the knowledge, skills, and concepts of the standard on external exams? For example, district, state or provincial, college, or vocational exams might include questions or writing prompts geared to this standard, so teachers need to prepare students.

Once team members are clear on the task and criteria, they are ready to proceed.

Individuals Review Standards and Critique Them Against Criteria

Individuals on the team review each standard and determine to what degree each meets the criteria. Each team member will be applying professional knowledge and judgment to annotate the standards she or he believes meet one or more of the criteria. For example, electronically or by hand, teachers enter *E* for endurance, *L* for leverage, *R* for readiness, and *H* for high-stakes exams next to each standard. For those that do not meet any of these criteria, no mark is needed. This silent exercise enables think time to foster individual accountability. Special educators should be full participants in this process if they teach the content, and they should approach this process with typical grade-level expectations in mind.

While they will naturally consider their students' current gaps, teachers should not base the process of determining priority standards on individual student considerations. Priority should be based on high expectations for all grade-level students. Teams can set a time limit for this initial activity regarding what standards it should prioritize.

Individuals Share and the Team Arrives at an Initial List of Priority Standards

For the team to arrive at an initial list of priority standards, each teacher shares his or her choices using a round-robin structure. One person begins by identifying a standard he or she chooses as a priority standard, using the criteria—endurance, leverage, and so on—as justification and explanation. Be wary of support that includes individual bias or personal feelings about continuing a long-standing trend. Team members should select only those standards that meet the criteria.

As team members share, a discussion will naturally ensue. Encourage this discussion since it will likely uncover misconceptions about standards as well as provide clarity about them. For this step to be productive, teams can abide by the following.

- ▸ Assign a scribe to record the standards that are deemed a priority and those that are supporting.

- ▸ Determine in advance how the team will handle a lack of consensus.

- ▸ Have each team member share his or her annotated standards until everyone is satisfied with an initial list of priority standards.

Teams Consider Vertical Alignment and Expectations of External Exams and Finalize Priority Standards

Teachers who are unaware of or not well versed in surrounding grades' content standards and standardized tests might move this step up sooner in the process. However, if they are familiar with grades 3–6 standards and the testing situation, they double-check to ensure how the proposed priority standards align vertically and take into account expectations for external accountability assessments.

For vertical articulation, teams review previous and subsequent grade-level, subject-area, and course standards. In particular, teachers consider future expectations when determining priority standards so they can make certain to amply prepare their students. For instance, in reviewing sixth-grade writing standards, a fifth-grade team realizes that students are expected to write argumentation essays. Therefore, fifth-grade students must master opinion writing and all that it entails; doing so positions students to achieve the next level of learning required in the subsequent grade when the expectations increase in rigor.

Teams also want to pay attention to district, state or provincial, and national accountability assessments to identify the degree of emphasis they should place on particular standards. States or provinces typically release test blueprints or other documents that identify samples of test items aligned to particular standards, the writing tasks students will produce, and holistic rubrics. Teams also consider other district documents or assessment data that reveal grade-level expectations.

Once teams take these factors into consideration, they finalize their list of priority standards. Conscientious teams then share them in person or electronically with other grade-level teams and collect feedback to ensure proper alignment. If the entire school or district participates in this process, all teams or representatives from each grade-level team can work on the vertical progression.

APPENDIX C

DEPTH OF KNOWLEDGE OVERVIEW

This appendix reviews the thinking levels in Webb's (1997, 1999) Depth of Knowledge. The information is adapted from "Applying Webb's Depth-of-Knowledge (DOK) Levels in Reading" (Hess, n.d.) and "Webb's Depth of Knowledge Guide: Career and Technical Education Definitions" (Mississippi Department of Education, 2009). Briefly, here are the four levels of thinking that comprise DOK.

1. **Recall and reproduction:** Recall a fact, term, principle, or concept; or perform a procedure.

2. **Basic application of skills and concepts:** Use concepts or procedures involving some mental processing.

3. **Strategic thinking:** Show reasoning, developing a plan or sequence of steps to approach a problem; reflect some decision making and justification; and demonstrate abstract and complex thinking.

4. **Extended thinking:** Demonstrate analysis or investigation that requires synthesis, research, and analysis across multiple contexts (such as disciplines, content areas, sources, and so on).

The following tables further elaborate on each of the four levels by establishing high-level traits and verbs associated with the level along with a series of activities that generate thinking at the level. Table C.1 (page 248) begins with recall and reproduction, table C.2 (page 249) shows working with skills and concepts, table C.3 (page 250) aligns to short-term strategic thinking, and table C.4 (page 251) illustrates extended strategic thinking.

Table C.1: Recall and Reproduction

Common Traits	
• Basic tasks require students to recall or reproduce knowledge and skills. • The focus in reading is on initial comprehension rather than analysis or interpretation. • Writing does not include complex synthesis or analysis but does include basic ideas.	• Subject-matter content involves working with facts, terms, and properties. • Students produce a finite answer; the answer doesn't need to be figured out or solved.

Verbs			
Arrange	Find	Memorize	Respond
Calculate	Identify	Name	Restate
Define	Illustrate	Quote	State
Demonstrate	Interpret	Recall	Tabulate
Describe	Label	Recite	Tell
Develop	List	Recognize	Translate
Draw	Match	Repeat	Use
Explain	Measure	Report	

Possible Activities	
• Name and explain each element of literature (setting, character, plot, point of view, theme). • Recite a fact related to an informational report topic. • Make a storyboard showing the sequence of events. • Draw a picture of a character from the author's description. • Describe what a character looks like. • Explain the conflict between the protagonist and antagonist. • Identify examples of methods of characterization. • List adjectives to describe the setting or a character's physical description. • Label the plot elements on a plot diagram. • Brainstorm story ideas. • Outline the main points. • Conduct basic mathematical calculations. • Measure the length and width of an object. • Identify the subject and predicate of a sentence.	• Write a list of key words related to . . . . • Make a chart showing . . . . • Retell the events of . . . . • Develop a concept map showing a process . • List the steps in the writing process. • Recite facts about . . . . • Match vocabulary words with their definitions. • Label locations on a map. • Write a paragraph with varied sentence beginnings. • Label the parts of an opinion or argument paragraph (reason, evidence, elaboration, ending). • Identify misspelled words. • Apply conventional spelling patterns or rules to new situations in writing. • Use resources to correct spelling. • Select or recall appropriate vocabulary to aid meaning.

Table C.2: Working With Skills and Concepts

Common Traits	
<ul><li>This level involves some mental processing and reasoning beyond habitual response.</li><li>In reading, students require both initial comprehension and subsequent processing of text; literal main ideas are stressed.</li></ul>	<ul><li>In writing, students begin to connect ideas using a simple organizational structure and produce short, rough pieces.</li><li>If students describe or explain, they go beyond the description or explanation of recalled information to describe or explain a result or answer how or why.</li></ul>

Verbs			
Calculate	Demonstrate	Illustrate	Predict
Categorize	Determine cause/effect	Infer	Relate
Classify	Distinguish	Interpret	Separate
Collect and display	Estimate	Make observations	Show
Compare	Graph	Modify	Solve
Compile	Identify patterns	Organize	Summarize
Complete		Paraphrase	Use context clues
Construct			

Possible Activities	
<ul><li>Classify a series of steps.</li><li>Explain the points of view of characters or historical figures.</li><li>Distinguish between fact and opinion.</li><li>Write an explanation about a topic.</li><li>Use details from the text to infer how a character might act.</li><li>State the relationship between two characters or concepts.</li><li>Research, record, and organize information.</li><li>Use an outline or take notes to organize ideas.</li><li>Organize, represent, and interpret data.</li><li>Explain how to perform a specific task.</li><li>Identify the major events in a narrative and write a one-paragraph summary.</li><li>Use context clues to identify the meaning of unfamiliar words.</li><li>Solve routine multiple-step problems.</li><li>State the relationships among multiple concepts.</li></ul>	<ul><li>Cite textual evidence to support a theme.</li><li>Describe the causes and effects of an event or individual's or character's actions.</li><li>Identify patterns in events or an individual's or character's behavior.</li><li>Compare and contrast two topics, events, settings, characters, or historical figures.</li><li>Make informed predictions.</li><li>Paraphrase the ideas in a text.</li><li>Create a character sketch.</li><li>Write a well-structured paragraph.</li><li>Write a passage of dialogue between two characters.</li><li>Write a diary, journal, or blog entry.</li><li>Edit final drafts.</li><li>Show basic understanding and appropriate use of reference materials (print or digital).</li><li>Identify use of figurative language (imagery or sensory details, simile, metaphor, personification).</li></ul>

Table C.3: Strategic Thinking

Common Traits	
• Items demand deep knowledge and use of higher-order thinking processes. • Students must state their reasoning and cite references from sources. • Items can involve abstract theme identification, inferences between or across passages, or application of prior knowledge.	• In writing, students develop multiple paragraph compositions using the writing process; pieces may include complex sentence structures or some synthesis and analysis. • Key processes include: *analyze, explain, support with evidence, generalize, create,* and *connect ideas.*

Verbs			
Analyze	Compare	Differentiate	Investigate
Apprise	Connect	Draw conclusions	Judge
Argue	Construct	Evaluate	Justify
Assess	Critique	Examine	Predict
Calculate	Debate	Explain phenomena in terms and concepts	Revise
Cite evidence	Decide		Use concepts to solve non-routine problems
Classify	Develop a logical argument	Formulate	
		Hypothesize	

Possible Activities	
• Use a comparison or contrast graphic organizer to show how two topics are the same and different. • Compare multiple texts and cite textual evidence from them to support a common theme. • Survey classmates to find out their opinions. • Create a graphic organizer to show stages in a process or the sequence of events. • Conduct an investigation to answer a question or address a problem. • Make a brochure about five important rules to convince others of their merit. • Create an advertisement about a new product. • Analyze the various solutions to a problem; choose one and justify your reason. • Create graphs, tables, or charts to display data in an organized way. • Develop a scientific model for a complex situation. • Determine the author's purpose and describe how it affects the interpretation.	• Draw inferences about author's purpose, implied causes and effects, or theme using textual evidence. • Describe how word choice, point of view, or bias affects the interpretation of a reading selection. • Summarize or compare information within and across passages. • Analyze interrelationships among elements of the text (plot, setting, characters). • Develop multiple paragraph compositions (literary analysis, critique) or narrative. • Use appropriate organizational structures (cause and effect, problem–solution). • Use complex and varied sentence construction. • Edit and revise to improve quality of writing. • Summarize information from multiple sources to address a specific topic. • Support ideas with details, examples, quotes, references; include citations.

Table C.4: Extended Strategic Thinking

Common Traits	
• Items demand complex, higher-order thinking processes, such as plan, develop, synthesize, and reflect over an extended period.	• In writing, students produce multiple-paragraph compositions that demonstrate synthesis, analysis, and evaluation of complex ideas or themes and evidence of deep awareness of purpose and audience. • Synthesis and analysis of information from multiple sources can include identifying complexities, discrepancies, or different perspectives.

Verbs			
Analyze	Create	Formulate	Propose
Apply concepts	Critique	Modify	Prove
Connect	Design	Plan	Synthesize

Possible Activities	

• Research to formulate and test hypotheses over time.
 	
• Make multiple strategic and procedural decisions based on new information throughout an event.
 	
• Collaborate to identify the problems a particular organization, society, or business faces; define the perspectives of all stakeholders; and formulate a plan of action
 	
• Create a marketing plan to sell a product or idea.
 	
• Conduct a project that requires specifying a problem, designing and conducting an experiment, analyzing data, and reporting results.
 	
• Design a mathematical model to inform and solve a practical or abstract situation.
 	
• Read two or more works by the same author and compare the writer's craft (style, bias, literary techniques, point of view).
	• Gather, analyze, organize, and interpret information from multiple print and digital sources for the purpose of writing a report or essay. For example:
	
	  • Write a multiple-paragraph research report that requires analysis and synthesis of information from multiple sources.
	
	  • Write a multiple-paragraph argumentation essay based on research that synthesizes information from various sources and that includes a counterargument; draw and justify conclusions.
	
	• Analyze complex and abstract themes across literary works.
	
	• Evaluate the credibility of various sources against criteria.

APPENDIX D

ESSENTIAL UNDERSTANDINGS AND GUIDING QUESTIONS

This appendix provides explanations for and examples of essential understandings and guiding questions. If teams wish to extend the six-step process laid out in chapter 1 (page 9) to include these two additional components, the information here can prove useful. As well, if teams are using a published or existing curriculum that includes these components, this appendix might serve as a vehicle for validating or revising what is in their resources.

Craft Essential Understandings

To craft essential understandings, teams carefully review what they have put into the PREP template (figure 1.1, page 13) to see how the synthesized components weave together to form a unified direction for planning lessons and assessments. In doing so, they focus on formulating deeper conceptual understandings, called *essential* (or *enduring*) *understandings*. These statements enable teams to capture the essence of a unit. Essential understandings are predicated on key concepts that teachers want students to realize, such as the following literacy-focused concepts: figurative language, perspective, patterns, phonemic awareness, and narrative.

Many education icons espouse the value of this aspect of curriculum design. Hattie (2012) states that "conceptual understandings form the 'coat hangers' on which we interpret and assimilate new ideas, and relate and extend them" (p. 115). H. Lynn Erickson (2007) states that the "synergistic interplay between the factual and conceptual levels of thinking" is critical to intellectual development (p. 2). Furthermore, Erickson (2007) writes, "When curriculum and instruction require students to process factual information through the conceptual level of thinking, the students demonstrate greater retention of factual information, deeper levels of understanding, and increased motivation for learning" (p. 2).

Teachers formulate essential understandings by using the unwrapped standards and the foundational information from the knowledge section in the PREP template (figure 1.1, page 13). The following example essential understandings from the fourth-grade narrative unit on dialogue featured in this book help ensure that teachers fulfill the promise of high-level instruction and assessment.

▸ Dialogue can move the plot forward by developing experiences and events, showing characters' responses to situations, and revealing characters' thoughts.

▸ Writers employ proper usage of grammar and conventions to support readers in fluidly experiencing their work so they can clearly decipher it.

Review the following points to assist your team in devising essential understandings.

▸ Teachers write essential understandings in adult language to crystallize and articulate the conceptual thinking used to design curriculum.

▸ To write one essential understanding for each standard would be cumbersome and overwhelming. Therefore, each essential understanding can take into account two or more standards. For example, standards related to several concepts—events (plot), dialogue, and characters—were used to formulate the first essential understanding in the previous list.

▸ Essential understandings need to be transferable. To accomplish this, they should not include proper nouns or past-tense verbs, since that would anchor them in a specific situation, context, or time frame. In fact, teachers in grade clusters can use the same essential understandings if they pertain to the content material since they are written in applicable, general terms. In this way, they are similar to themes that can apply across works of literature.

▸ To craft stronger essential understandings, teachers capitalize on action verbs (such as *determine*, *promote*, *challenge*, and *support*) instead of forms of the verb *to be*. In the examples from the narrative unit for dialogue, these precise verbs connect concepts embedded in the essential understandings: *move*, *develop*, *show*, *reveal*, *employ*, *support*, *experience*, and *decipher*.

▸ On the PREP template, knowledge items are what students come to *know*; they reflect foundational information. These entries can be vocabulary, people, places, dates, examples, and even a fact; for example, *Authors write memoirs about themselves.* Essential understandings are always complete sentences and represent what we want students to *understand.* These statements push their thinking further to wonder, *So what? What about it? Why is this important?* Therefore, read how this complete and pertinent essential understanding more clearly articulates *why* writing memoirs are important: *Authors create memoirs to share personal experiences with others so they can teach a lesson, relieve themselves of a burden, or explain the truth to the world.* By using essential understandings that go beyond facts, teachers can plan deeper and more meaningful instructional experiences and assessments.

Once teams craft essential understandings, they use them to build guiding questions to frame instruction and assessment. Teams might find, however, that it is beneficial to work on building essential understandings and guiding questions concurrently.

Develop Guiding Questions

Guiding questions establish a purpose for learning, provide an overarching focus that promotes higher-level thinking, and emanate from essential understandings. They are written in student-friendly language rather than solely teacher speak. These questions compel students to engage in the work ahead and make them aware of the connection between what they are doing and learning outcomes. Teachers should post these questions in the classroom so students are grounded in their purpose for learning; this way, they are aware of the value in what they are learning and derive meaning from it. Teachers can use their learning targets (*I can* statements) in conjunction with guiding questions. In fact, the guiding question can show an overarching focus for a cluster of related *I can* statements as in the following dialogue example.

How do writers use dialogue to move the plot forward?
- *I can refer to dialogue when talking about what the text says explicitly.*
- *I can refer to dialogue when making inferences about the text.*
- *I can use dialogue to describe story events.*
- *I can use dialogue to describe a character in detail.*
- *I can use dialogue to describe a setting in detail.*

Guiding questions differ from text-dependent questions, which help deepen students' understanding of complex text (for example, *Why doesn't Esperanza want her mother to marry her uncle Tío Luis?*), and from granular questions geared to a specific lesson (for example, *What punctuation marks indicate that a character is speaking?*). Rather, guiding questions focus on overarching concepts. They are broad queries that cannot be answered with a list and typically begin with open-ended words, such as *how, why,* or *is.* Teams can craft guiding questions in third-person point of view or personalize them using first-person pronouns.

In addition, guiding questions are global and transferable—similar to essential understandings that can apply to different units of study across grade levels. For example, in literacy instruction, teachers can design and ask these questions: "How does figurative language enhance writing? How and why do characters change over time? Is a story incomplete without a climax? How does the writing process contribute to optimal products? and Should all stories include dialogue?" Across content areas, teachers might ask, "How can human interaction affect the environment? Is conflict avoidable? How do government systems support citizens?"

Each essential understanding holds the answer to an accompanying guiding question. For example, the answer to *How can personal narratives influence readers?* is expressed in the following essential understanding: *Personal narratives can inspire readers by showing obstacles people overcome that strengthen their character.* For this reason, teachers display the guiding questions to set the stage for learning but refrain from showing the essential understandings since they reveal the answer. Later, teachers can share them or lead a brainstorming session in which students recall the key takeaways from activities and lessons to arrive at the essential understandings based on the learning they acquired.

The guiding questions are purposefully brief. While teaching, the intent is to have students come to realize an enduring truth embedded within each essential understanding. Therefore, teachers plan and conduct a series of lessons around these questions where students discover the deeper meaning embedded in these statements. To illustrate, when our fourth-grade team worked to choose essential understandings and guiding questions for the dialogue unit, the team determined that the guiding question *How do writers use dialogue in a purposeful way?* correlates with the essential understanding *Authors can write meaningful dialogue to move the plot forward, show characters' responses to situations, and reveal characters' thoughts and beliefs.*

As teachers, we must vigilantly search for and identify what we want students to understand, and the succinctly stated guiding question helps frame and set the purpose for learning. For examples, refer to figure D.1, which shows the pairing of essential understandings and guiding questions.

Essential Understandings (Students will understand that . . .)	Guiding Questions
Authors can write meaningful dialogue to move the plot forward, show characters' responses to situations, and reveal characters' thoughts and beliefs.	How do writers use dialogue in a purposeful way?
Writers employ proper usage of grammar and conventions to support readers in fluidly experiencing their work so they can clearly decipher it.	How do writers use proper dialogue mechanics?
Characters can change over time through events, settings, or interactions with other characters, which can, in turn, shape the plot.	How and why do characters change over time?
Readers use details from an author's use of literary elements to determine and support the theme of a text.	How do readers determine a theme?

Figure D.1: Example guiding questions paired with essential understandings.

As you review the figure, notice the following.

▸ Teams can use guiding questions across units or grades, so they are purposefully written for this transferability. For example, *How and why do characters change over time?* can apply to various complex texts within a school year and across grades.

▸ Answers to each guiding question, which teams write using language students can understand, are found in an associated essential understanding.

▸ Questions should require open-ended, higher-order responses; beginning them with *why*, *how*, or even *is* can foster such a response. If other question words achieve this goal, use them.

▸ Teachers can write the questions in first-person point of view, which personalizes them to the students, or in third-person point of view, as they wish.

▸ Like learning targets, teachers should post the guiding questions in the classroom and refer to them to set the purpose for learning.

If teams decide to write and use guiding questions within their instructional program, they should make it a priority to collaborate as a team to develop them, connect the questions to learning targets, and ensure that they transpire from the essential understandings.

APPENDIX E

LIST OF FIGURES AND TABLES

*Reproducible figures are in italics. Visit **go.SolutionTree.com/literacy** to download free reproducible versions of these figures.*

REFERENCES AND RESOURCES

Achieve the Core. (n.d.). *Reviewing using the IMET: ELA: Module 101—high-quality texts, evidence-based discussion and writing, and building knowledge.* Accessed at https://achievethecore.org/content/upload/Understanding%20the%20IMET_ELA .LIT_Handout_101.pdf on April 29, 2020.

Ainsworth, L. (2013). *Prioritizing the Common Core: Identifying specific standards to emphasize the most.* Englewood, CO: Lead + Learn Press.

Ainsworth, L. (2017, April 6). *Priority standards: The power of focus* [Blog post]. Accessed at www.larryainsworth.com/blog/priority-standards-the-power-of-focus on March 30, 2020.

Ainsworth, L., & Viegut, D. (2015). *Common formative assessments 2.0: How teacher teams intentionally align standards, instruction, and assessment.* Thousand Oaks, CA: Corwin Press.

Allington, R. L. (2001). *What really matters for struggling readers: Designing research-based programs.* New York: Longman.

Allington, R. L. (2009). *What really matters in response to intervention: Research-based designs.* Boston: Pearson.

Allington, R. L. (2014). How reading volume affects both reading fluency and reading achievement. *International Electronic Journal of Elementary Education, 7*(1), 13–26.

AllThingsPLC. (n.d.). *About PLCs.* Accessed at www.allthingsplc.info/about on November 19, 2019.

Anderson, L. W., & Krathwohl, D. R. (Eds.). (2001). *A taxonomy for learning, teaching, and assessing: A revision of Bloom's taxonomy of educational objectives.* New York: Longman.

Appelbaum, M. (2009). *The one-stop guide to implementing RTI: Academic and behavioral interventions, K–12.* Thousand Oaks, CA: Corwin Press.

Armbruster, B. B., Lehr, F., & Osborn, J. (2006). *Put reading first: The research building blocks for teaching children to read—Kindergarten through grade 3* (3rd ed.). Washington, DC: National Institute for Literacy.

Atwell, N. (2007). *The reading zone: How to help kids become skilled, passionate, habitual, critical readers.* New York: Scholastic.

Avi. (1995). *Poppy.* New York: HarperCollins.

Babbitt, N. (1975). *Tuck everlasting.* New York: Farrar, Straus and Giroux.

Bailey, K., & Jakicic, C. (2017). *Simplifying common assessment: A guide for Professional Learning Communities at Work.* Bloomington, IN: Solution Tree Press.

Bailey, K., Jakicic, C., & Spiller, J. (2014). *Collaborating for success with the Common Core: A toolkit for Professional Learning Communities at Work.* Bloomington, IN: Solution Tree Press.

Baskin, N. R. (2016). *Nine, ten: A September 11 story.* New York: Atheneum.

Bates, C. C. (2013). Flexible grouping during literacy centers: A model for differentiating instruction. *YC Young Children, 68*(2), 30–33.

Beck, I. L., & Beck, M. E. (2013). *Making sense of phonics: The hows and whys* (2nd ed.). New York: Guilford Press.

Beck, I. L., McKeown, M. G., & Kucan, L. (2013). *Bringing words to life: Robust vocabulary instruction* (2nd ed.). New York: Guilford Press.

Bennett-Armistead, V. S. (n.d.). *What is dramatic play and how does it support literacy development in preschool?* Accessed at www.scholastic.com/teachers/articles/teaching -content/what-dramatic-play-and-how-does-it-support-literacy-development -preschool on November 19, 2019.

Biancarosa, G., & Snow, C. E. (2004). *Reading next: A vision for action and research in middle and high school literacy—A report to Carnegie Corporation of New York* (2nd ed.). Washington, DC: Alliance for Excellent Education.

Billen, M. T., & Allington, R. L. (2013). An evidence-based approach to response to intervention. In D. M. Barone & M. H. Mallette (Eds.), *Best practices in early literacy instruction* (pp. 305–321). New York: Guilford Press.

Bishop, R. S. (2012). Reflections on the development of African American children's literature. *Journal of Children's Literature, 38*(2), 5–13.

Blevins, W. (2017). *A fresh look at phonics: Common causes of failure and seven ingredients for success.* Thousand Oaks, CA: Corwin Press.

Bockting, W. O. (2008, October—December). Psychotherapy and real-life experience: From gender dichotomy to gender diversity. *Sexologies, 17*(4), 211–224.

Bourque, P. (2017). Building stamina for struggling readers and writers. *Educational Leadership, 74*(5). Accessed at www.ascd.org/publications/educational-leadership /feb17/vol74/num05/Building-Stamina-for-Struggling-Readers-and-Writers.aspx on November 19, 2019.

Brendtro, L. K., Brokenleg, M., & Van Bockern, S. (2019). *Reclaiming youth at risk: Futures of promise* (3rd ed.). Bloomington, IN: Solution Tree Press.

Brookhart, S. M. (2013). *How to create and use rubrics for formative assessment and grading.* Alexandria, VA: Association for Supervision and Curriculum Development.

Bruner, J. S., Goodnow, J. J., & Austin, G. A. (1956). *A study of thinking.* New York: Wiley.

Buckley, E. M. (n.d.). *Why personalized learning requires technology and thinking humans.* Accessed at http://hipporeads.com/why-personalized-learning-requires-technology -and-thinking-humans on December 2, 2019.

Budge, K. M., & Parrett, W. H. (2018). *Disrupting poverty: Five powerful classroom practices.* Alexandria, VA: Association for Supervision and Curriculum Development.

Buffum, A., & Mattos, M. (2020). *RTI at Work plan book.* Bloomington, IN: Solution Tree Press.

Buffum, A., Mattos, M., & Malone, J. (2018). *Taking action: A handbook for RTI at Work.* Bloomington, IN: Solution Tree Press.

Buffum, A., Mattos, M., & Weber, C. (2010). The why behind RTI. *Educational Leadership, 68*(2), 10–16.

Buffum, A., Mattos, M., & Weber, C. (2012). *Simplifying response to intervention: Four essential guiding principles.* Bloomington, IN: Solution Tree Press.

Casbergue, R. M., & Strickland, D. S. (2016). *Reading and writing in preschool: Teaching the essentials.* New York: Guilford Press.

Clay, M. M. (1993). *Reading recovery: A guidebook for teachers in training.* Portsmouth, NH: Heinemann.

Coleman, D., & Pimentel, S. (2012). *Revised publishers' criteria for the Common Core State Standards in English language arts and literacy, grades 3–12.* Accessed at www .corestandards.org/assets/Publishers_Criteria_for_3-12.pdf on November 19, 2019.

Connell, R. (2009, February). Accountable conduct: "Doing gender" in transsexual and political retrospect. *Gender & Society, 23*(1), 104–111.

Collier, J. L., & Collier, C. (1974). *My brother Sam is dead.* New York: Scholastic.

Crawford, J. (2011). *Using power standards to build an aligned curriculum: A process manual.* Thousand Oaks, CA: Corwin Press.

Dale, E., O'Rourke, J., & Barbe, W. B. (1986). *Vocabulary building: Process, principles, and application.* Columbus, OH: Zaner-Bloser.

Darling-Hammond, L. (1999). *Teacher quality and student achievement: A review of state policy evidence.* Seattle, WA: Center for the Study of Teaching and Policy.

DiCamillo, K. (2000). *Because of Winn-Dixie.* Cambridge, MA: Candlewick Press.

Donohoo, J., & Katz, S. (2017). When teachers believe, students achieve: Collaborative inquiry builds teacher efficacy for better student outcomes. *The Learning Professional, 38*(6), 20–27.

DuFour, R., DuFour, R., & Eaker, R. (2008). *Revisiting Professional Learning Communities at Work: New insights for improving schools.* Bloomington, IN: Solution Tree Press.

DuFour, R., DuFour, R., Eaker, R., & Many, T. W. (2010). *Learning by doing: A handbook for Professional Learning Communities at Work* (2nd ed.). Bloomington, IN: Solution Tree Press.

DuFour, R., DuFour, R., Eaker, R., Many, T. W., & Mattos, M. (2016). *Learning by doing: A handbook for Professional Learning Communities at Work* (3rd ed.). Bloomington, IN: Solution Tree Press.

DuFour, R., & Marzano, R. J. (2011). *Leaders of learning: How district, school, and classroom leaders improve student achievement.* Bloomington, IN: Solution Tree Press.

Dweck, C. S. (2016). *Mindset: The new psychology of success.* New York: Penguin Random House.

Ehri, L. C., & Roberts, T. (2006). The roots of learning to read and write: Acquisition of letters and phonemic awareness. In D. K. Dickinson & S. B. Neuman (Eds.), *Handbook of early literacy research* (Vol. 2, pp. 113–131). New York: Guilford Press.

Erickson, H. L. (2002). *Concept-based curriculum and instruction: Teaching beyond the facts.* Thousand Oaks, CA: Corwin Press.

Erickson, H. L. (2007). *Concept-based curriculum and instruction for the thinking classroom.* Thousand Oaks, CA: Corwin Press.

Fawcett Society. (2019). *Fawcett research shows exposure to gender stereotypes as a child causes harm in later life.* Accessed at www.fawcettsociety.org.uk/news/fawcett -research-exposure-gender-stereotypes-child-causes-harm-later-life on February 2, 2019.

Fisher, D., & Frey, N. (2012). Close reading in elementary schools. *Reading Teacher, 66*(3), 179–188.

Fisher, D., & Frey, N. (2013). *Engaging the adolescent learner: Gradual release of responsibility instructional framework.* Newark, DE: International Reading Association. Accessed at https://keystoliteracy.com/wp-content/uploads/2017/08 /frey_douglas_and_nancy_frey-_gradual_release_of_responsibility_intructional _framework.pdf on November 19, 2019.

Fisher, D., & Frey, N. (2014a). Closely reading informational texts in the primary grades. *Reading Teacher, 68*(3), 222–227.

Fisher, D., & Frey, N. (2014b). Scaffolded reading instruction of content-area texts. *Reading Teacher, 67*(5), 347–351.

Fisher, D., & Frey, N. (2014c). *Better learning through structured teaching: A framework for the gradual release of responsibility* (2nd ed.). Alexandria, VA: Association for Supervision and Curriculum Development.

Fisher, D., & Frey, N. (2018). Building capable kids. *Principal, 98*(1), 14–17.

Fitzgerald, J., & Shanahan, T. (2000). Reading and writing relations and their development. *Educational Psychologist, 35*(1), 39–50.

Foorman, B., Beyler, N., Borradaile, K., Coyne, M., Denton, C. A., Dimino, J., et al. (2016, July). *Foundational skills to support reading for understanding in kindergarten through 3rd grade*. Washington, DC: National Center for Education Evaluation and Regional Assistance. Accessed at https://ies.ed.gov/ncee/wwc/Docs/PracticeGuide /wwc_foundationalreading_070516.pdf on November 19, 2019.

Fountas, I. C., & Pinnell, G. S. (2001). *Guiding readers and writers, grades 3–6: Teaching comprehension, genre, and content literacy*. Portsmouth, NH: Heinemann.

Fountas, I. C., & Pinnell, G. S. (2006). *Teaching for comprehending and fluency: Thinking, talking, and writing about reading, K–8*. Portsmouth, NH: Heinemann.

Fountas, I. C. & Pinnell, G. S. (2012). *Genre student: Teaching with fiction and nonfiction books*. Portsmouth, NH: Heineman.

Fountas, I. C., & Pinnell, G. S. (2019). *Level books, not children: The role of text levels in literacy instruction*. Accessed at www.fountasandpinnell.com/shared/resources /FPL_LevelBooksNotKids_Whitepaper.pdf on November 19, 2019.

Freeman, D. (1968). *Corduroy*. New York: Viking Press.

Frey, N., & Fisher, D. (2013). *Rigorous reading: Five access points for comprehending complex texts*. Thousand Oaks, CA: Corwin Press.

Fried, M. D. (2013). Activating teaching: Using running records to inform teaching decisions. *Journal of Reading Recovery, 13*(1), 5–16.

Friziellie, H., Schmidt, J. A., & Spiller, J. (2016). *Yes we can! General and special educators collaborating in a professional learning community*. Bloomington, IN: Solution Tree Press.

Gallimore, R., Ermeling, B. A., Saunders, W. M., & Goldenberg, C. (2009). Moving the learning of teaching closer to practice: Teacher education implications of school-based inquiry teams. *Elementary School Journal, 109*(5), 537–553.

Gareis, C. R., & Grant, L. W. (2008). *Teacher-made assessments: How to connect curriculum, instruction, and student learning*. Larchmont, NY: Eye on Education.

Gareis, C. R., & Grant, L. W. (2015). *Teacher-made assessments: How to connect curriculum, instruction, and student learning* (2nd ed.). New York: Routledge.

Garland, K., & Bryan, K. (2017). Partnering with families and communities: Culturally responsive pedagogy at its best. *Voices From the Middle, 24*(3), 52–55.

Garrity, L. K. (1991). *Fabulous fables: Using fables with children*. Glenview, IL: Good Year Books.

Gender Spectrum. (n.d.). *Understanding gender and the experience of gender diverse youth and their families*. Accessed at www.genderspectrum.org/policybrief/#myths on March 2, 2020.

Glass, K. T. (2012). *Mapping comprehensive units to the ELA Common Core standards, K–5*. Thousand Oaks, CA: Corwin Press.

Glass, K. T. (2013). *Mapping comprehensive units to the ELA Common Core standards, 6–12*. Thousand Oaks, CA: Corwin Press.

Glass, K. T. (2015). *Complex text decoded: How to design lessons and use strategies that target authentic texts.* Alexandria, VA: Association for Supervision and Curriculum Development.

Glass, K. T. (2017). *The fundamentals of (re)designing writing units.* Bloomington, IN: Solution Tree Press.

Glass, K. T. (2018). *(Re)designing narrative writing units for grades 5–12.* Bloomington, IN: Solution Tree Press.

Glass, K. T., & Marzano, R. J. (2018). *The new art and science of teaching writing.* Bloomington, IN: Solution Tree Press.

Goldman, S. R., Snow, C. E., & Vaughn, S. (2016). Common themes in teaching reading for understanding: Lessons from three projects. *Journal of Adolescent and Adult Literacy, 60*(3), 255–264.

Graham, S., Bollinger, A., Olson, C. B., D'Aoust, C., MacArthur, C., McCutchen, D., et al. (2018, October). *Teaching elementary school students to be effective writers: A practice guide* (NCEE 2012-4058). Washington, DC: National Center for Education Evaluation and Regional Assistance. Accessed at https://ies.ed.gov/ncee/wwc/Docs /PracticeGuide/WWC_Elem_Writing_PG_Dec182018.pdf on January 23, 2020.

Graham, S., & Hebert, M. (2010). *Writing to read: Evidence for how writing can improve reading—A report to Carnegie Corporation of New York.* Washington, DC: Alliance for Excellent Education.

Graham, S., & Hebert, M. (2011). Writing to read: A meta-analysis of the impact of writing and writing instruction on reading. *Harvard Educational Review, 81*(4), 710–744.

Graham, S., & Perin, D. (2007). *Writing next: Effective strategies to improve writing of adolescents in middle and high schools—A report to Carnegie Corporation of New York.* Washington, DC: Alliance for Excellent Education.

Graham, S., & Santangelo, T. (2014). Does spelling instruction make students better spellers, readers, and writers? A meta-analytic review. *Reading and Writing, 27*(9), 1703–1743.

Guskey, T. R. (2010). Lessons of mastery learning. *Educational Leadership, 68*(2), 52–57.

Harris, K. R., Graham, S., Friedlander, B., & Laud, L. (2013). Bring powerful writing strategies into your classroom! Why and how. *Reading Teacher, 66*(7), 538–542.

Harrison, J., Grant, J., Herman, J. L. (2012). A gender not listed here: Genderqueers, gender rebels, and otherwise in the National Transgender Discrimination Survey. *LGBTQ Public Policy Journal at the Harvard Kennedy School, 2*(1), 13–24.

Hattie, J. (2012). *Visible learning for teachers: Maximizing impact on learning.* New York: Routledge.

Hattie, J., & Timperley, H. (2007). The power of feedback. *Review of Educational Research, 77*(1), 81–112.

Hattie, J., & Yates, G. (2014). *Visible learning and the science of how we learn*. New York: Routledge.

Heritage, M. (2008). *Learning progressions: Supporting instruction and formative assessment*. Washington, DC: Council of Chief State School Officers.

Hernandez, D. J. (2011, April). *Double jeopardy: How third-grade reading skills and poverty influence high school graduation*. Baltimore: Annie E. Casey Foundation.

Hess, K. K. (n.d.). *Applying Webb's depth-of-knowledge (DOK) levels in reading*. Accessed at www.nciea.org/publications/DOKreading_KH08.pdf on April 10, 2020.

Hillsdale County Intermediate School District. (n.d.). *RTI Tier 3 intensive intervention*. Accessed at www.hillsdale-isd.org/cms/lib/MI01001046/Centricity/Domain/15 /RtI_Tier_3_Intensive_Intervention.pdf on November 19, 2019.

Himmele, W., & Himmele, P. (2012). Why read-alouds matter more in the age of the Common Core standards. *ASCD Express, 8*(5). Accessed at www.ascd.org/ascd -express/vol8/805-himmele.aspx on November 19, 2019.

Hollie, S. (2019, May 22). *Steps to authenticity* [Blog post]. Accessed at https:// literacyworldwide.org/blog/literacy-daily/2019/05/22/steps-to-authenticity on November 19, 2019.

Individuals With Disabilities Education Improvement Act of 2004, Pub. L. No. 108-446 § 300.115 (2004).

International Literacy Association. (2019). *Children's rights to excellent literacy instruction*. Accessed at https://literacyworldwide.org/docs/default-source/where-we-stand/ila -childrens-rights-to-excellent-literacy-instruction.pdf on March 21, 2020.

Johnson, D. W., & Johnson, R. T. (n.d.). *An overview of cooperative learning*. Accessed at www.co-operation.org/what-is-cooperative-learning on November 19, 2019.

Jonsson, A., & Svingby, G. (2007). The use of scoring rubrics: Reliability, validity and educational consequences. *Educational Research Review, 2*(2), 130–144.

Kagan, S. (1999). Cooperative learning: Seventeen pros and seventeen cons plus ten tips for success. *Kagan Online Magazine*. Accessed at www.kaganonline.com /free_articles/dr_spencer_kagan/259/Cooperative-Learning-Seventeen-Pros-and -Seventeen-Cons-Plus-Ten-Tips-for-Success on November 19, 2019.

Kagan, S., & Kagan, M. (2009). *Kagan cooperative learning*. San Clemente, CA: Kagan.

Kagan, S., Kagan, M., & Kagan, L. (2016). *59 Kagan structures: Proven engagement strategies*. San Clemente, CA: Kagan.

Killion, J. (2008, February). *Coaches help mine the data*. Accessed at https:// learningforward.org/leading-teacher/february-2008-vol-3-no-5/focus-on-nsdcs -standards-coaches-help-mine-the-data on November 19, 2019.

Konigsburg, E. L. (1967/1995). *From the mixed-up files of Mrs. Basil E. Frankweiler*. New York: Simon & Schuster.

Kuhn, M. R., & Schwanenflugel, P. J. (2019). Prosody, pacing, and situational fluency (or why fluency matters for older readers). *Journal of Adolescent and Adult Literacy, 62*(4), 363–368. Accessed at https://ila.onlinelibrary.wiley.com/doi/10.1002/jaal.867 on November 19, 2019.

Lapp, D., Moss, B., Grant, M., & Johnson, K. (2015). *A close look at close reading: Teaching students to analyze complex texts, grades K–5.* Alexandria, VA: Association for Supervision and Curriculum Development.

Lee, J., Grigg, W. S., & Donahue, P. L. (2007). *The nation's report card: Reading 2007—National Assessment of Educational Progress at grades 4 and 8* (NCES No. 2007-496). Washington, DC: National Center for Education Statistics. Accessed at http://nationsreportcard.gov/reading_2007 on November 19, 2019.

Lester, H. (1999). *Hooway for Wodney Wat.* New York: Walter Lorraine Books.

Liben, M., & Pimentel, S. (2018, November 7). *Placing text at the center of the standards-aligned ELA classroom.* Accessed at https://achievethecore.org/page/3185/placing-text-at-the-center-of-the-standards-aligned-ela-classroom on November 19, 2019.

Lupo, S. M., Strong, J. Z., Lewis, W., Walpole, S., & McKenna, M. C. (2018). Building background knowledge through reading: Rethinking text sets. *Journal of Adolescent and Adult Literacy, 61*(4), 433–444.

Many, T. W. (2009). *Three rules help manage assessment data.* Accessed at https://absenterprisedotcom.files.wordpress.com/2016/06/many_tepsa_datarules90.pdf on November 19, 2019.

Manzo, A. V., & Casale, U. P. (1985). Listen-read-discuss: A content reading heuristic. *Journal of Reading, 28*(8), 732–734.

Margulis, C. (n.d.). *Gender across grades.* Accessed at www.dropbox.com/s/qgq2jwwk3gqmuwi/Gender across the grades.docx?dl=0 on March 3, 2020.

Marzano, R. J. (2003). *What works in schools: Translating research into action.* Alexandria, VA: Association for Supervision and Curriculum Development.

Marzano, R. J. (2004). *Building background knowledge for academic achievement: Research on what works in schools.* Alexandria, VA: Association for Supervision and Curriculum Development.

Marzano, R. J. (2006). *Classroom assessment & grading that work.* Alexandria, VA: Association for Supervision and Curriculum Development.

Marzano, R. J. (2017). *The new art and science of teaching.* Bloomington, IN: Solution Tree Press.

Marzano, R. J. (2019). *The handbook for the new art and science of teaching.* Bloomington, IN: Solution Tree Press.

Marzano, R. J. (2020). *Teaching basic, advanced, and academic vocabulary: A comprehensive framework for elementary instruction.* Bloomington, IN: Marzano Resources.

Marzano, R. J., & Kendall, J. S. (2008). *Designing and assessing educational objectives: Applying the new taxonomy.* Thousand Oaks, CA: Corwin Press.

Marzano, R. J., & Pickering, D. J. (2005). *Building academic vocabulary: Teacher's manual.* Alexandria, VA: Association for Supervision and Curriculum Development.

Marzano, R. J., Pickering, D. J., & Pollock, J. E. (2001). *Classroom instruction that works: Research-based strategies for increasing student achievement.* Alexandria, VA: Association for Supervision and Curriculum Development.

Meisinger, E. B., & Bradley, B. A. (2008). Classroom practices for supporting fluency development. In M. R. Kuhn & P. J. Schwanenflugel (Eds.), *Fluency in the classroom* (pp. 36–54). New York: Guilford Press.

Mindset Works. (n.d.). *Decades of scientific research that started a growth mindset revolution.* Accessed at www.mindsetworks.com/science on November 19, 2019.

Mississippi Department of Education. (2009). *Webb's depth of knowledge guide: Career and technical education definitions.* Accessed at www.aps.edu/sapr/documents /resources/Webbs_DOK_Guide.pdf on April 10, 2020.

Morrow, L. M., & Gambrell, L. B. (Eds.). (2011). *Best practices in literacy instruction* (4th ed.). New York: Guilford Press.

National Assessment of Educational Progress. (2002). *The nation's report card: Writing 2002* (NCES 2003-529). Washington, DC: National Center for Education Statistics. Accessed at https://nces.ed.gov/nationsreportcard/pdf/main2002/2003529.pdf on December 2, 2019.

National Assessment of Educational Progress. (2011). *The nation's report card: Writing 2011—Grade 8 national results.* Accessed at www.nationsreportcard.gov/writing_2011 /g8_national.aspx?tab_id=tab2&subtab_id=Tab_1#chart on December 2, 2019.

National Assessment of Educational Progress. (2019). *NAEP report card: Reading.* Accessed at www.nationsreportcard.gov/reading/nation/achievement/?grade=4 on December 2, 2019.

National Association for the Education of Young Children. (n.d.). *Learning to read and write: What research reveals.* Accessed at www.readingrockets.org/article/learning -read-and-write-what-research-reveals on November 19, 2019.

National Governors Association Center for Best Practices & Council of Chief State School Officers. (n.d.). *Common Core State Standards for English language arts and literacy in history/social studies, science, and technical subjects: Appendix A—Research supporting key elements of the standards.* Washington, DC: Authors. Accessed at www .corestandards.org/assets/Appendix_A.pdf on November 19, 2019.

National Governors Association Center for Best Practices & Council of Chief State School Officers. (2010). *Common Core State Standards for English language arts and literacy in history/social studies, science, and technical subjects.* Washington, DC: Authors. Accessed at www.corestandards.org/assets/CCSSI_ELA%20Standards.pdf on December 3, 2019.

Northern Illinois University. (n.d.). *Instructional scaffolding to improve learning.* Accessed at www.niu.edu/facdev/_pdf/guide/strategies/instructional_scaffolding_to_improve _learning.pdf on November 19, 2019.

O'Donnell, A. (2019). Windows, mirrors, and sliding glass doors: The enduring impact of Rudine Sims Bishop's work. *Literacy Today, 36*(6), 16–19.

Office of the High Commissioner for Human Rights. (n.d.). *Gender stereotyping.* Accessed at www.ohchr.org/en/issues/women/wrgs/pages/genderstereotypes.aspx on February 2, 2019.

Owocki, G., & Goodman, Y. (2002). *Kidwatching: Documenting children's literacy development.* Portsmouth, NH: Heinemann.

Palacio, R. J. (2012). *Wonder.* New York: Random House.

Partnership for Assessment of Readiness for College and Careers. (2011). *PARCC model content frameworks: English language arts/literacy, grades 3–11.* Washington, DC: Author. Accessed at https://eric.ed.gov/?id=ED526347 on January 16, 2020.

Pearson, P. D., & Gallagher, M. C. (1983, October). *The instruction of reading comprehension* (Technical Report No. 297). Champaign, IL: Center for the Study of Reading.

Pikulski, J. J., & Chard, D. J. (2005). Fluency: Bridge between decoding and reading comprehension. *Reading Teacher, 58*(6), 510–519.

Pinnell, G. S., Pikulski, J. J., Wixson, K. K., Campbell, J. R., Gough, P. B., & Beatty, A. S. (1995, January). *Listening to children read aloud: Data from NAEP's integrated reading performance record (IRPR) at grade 4.* Washington, DC: National Center for Education Statistics.

Popham, W. J. (2007). All about accountability/The lowdown on learning progressions. *Educational Leadership, 64*(7). Accessed at www.ascd.org/publications/educational -leadership/apr07/vol64/num07/The-Lowdown-on-Learning-Progressions.aspx on November 19, 2019.

Popham, W. J. (2008). *Transformative assessment.* Alexandria, VA: Association for Supervision and Curriculum Development.

Popham, W. J. (2011). *Transformative assessment in action: An inside look at applying the process.* Alexandria, VA: Association for Supervision and Curriculum Development.

Pressley, M., Allington, R. L., Wharton-McDonald, R., Block, C. C., & Morrow, L. M. (2001). *Learning to read: Lessons from exemplary first-grade classrooms.* New York: Guilford Press.

Rasinski, T. V. (2012). Why reading fluency should be hot! *Reading Teacher, 65*(8), 516–522.

Reeves, D. B. (2002). *The leader's guide to standards: A blueprint for educational equity and excellence.* San Francisco: Jossey-Bass.

Reeves, D. (2007). *Ahead of the curve: The power of assessment to transform teaching and learning.* Bloomington, IN: Solution Tree.

Reutzel, D. R., Jones, C. D., Fawson, P. C., & Smith, J. A. (2008). Scaffolded silent reading: A complement to guided repeated oral reading that works! *Reading Teacher, 62*(3), 194–207.

Riley-Ayers, S. (2013). Supporting language and literacy development in quality preschools. In D. M. Barone & M. H. Mallette (Eds.), *Best practices in early literacy instruction* (pp. 58–77). New York: Guilford Press.

Roskos, K., & Christie, J. (2011). The play-literacy nexus and the importance of evidence-based techniques in the classroom. *American Journal of Play, 4*(2), 204–224. Accessed at https://files.eric.ed.gov/fulltext/EJ985588.pdf on November 19, 2019.

Roth, K., & Dabrowski, J. (2014). Extending interactive writing into grades 2–5. *Reading Teacher, 68*(1), 33–44.

RTI Action Network. (n.d.). *What is RTI?* Accessed at www.rtinetwork.org/learn/what/whatisrti on November 19, 2019.

Ryan, P. M. (2000). *Esperanza rising.* New York: Scholastic.

Sachar, L. (1998). *Holes.* New York: Farrar, Straus and Giroux.

Schimmer, T. (2019, February 19). *Should formative assessments be graded?* [Blog post]. Accessed at www.solutiontree.com/blog/grading-formative-assessments on November 19, 2019.

Searle, M. (2010). *What every school leader needs to know about RTI.* Alexandria, VA: Association for Supervision and Curriculum Development.

Serravallo, J. (2010). *Teaching reading in small groups: Differentiated instruction for building strategic, independent readers.* Portsmouth, NH: Heinemann.

Serravallo, J. (2014). *The literacy teacher's playbook, grades 3–6: Four steps for turning assessment data into goal-directed instruction.* Portsmouth, NH: Heinemann.

Serravallo, J. (2018). *Understanding texts and readers: Responsive comprehension instruction with leveled texts.* Portsmouth, NH: Heinemann.

Shanahan, T. (2006). Relations among oral language, reading, and writing development. In C. MacArthur, S. Graham, & J. Fitzgerald (Eds.), *Handbook of writing research* (pp. 171–183). New York: Guilford Press.

Shanahan, T. (2008). *Teaching students to read complex text* [PowerPoint slides]. Accessed at www.shanahanonliteracy.com/publications/teaching-with-complex-text-1 on November 19, 2019.

Shanahan, T. (2015a). Common Core State Standards: A new role for writing. *Elementary School Journal, 115*(4), 464–479.

Shanahan, T. (2015b, April 30). *Should we teach spelling?* [Blog post]. Accessed at https://shanahanonliteracy.com/blog/should-we-teach-spelling on November 19, 2019.

Shanahan, T. (2016, September 6). *Eight ways to help kids to read complex text* [Blog post]. Accessed at https://shanahanonliteracy.com/blog/eight-ways-to-help-kids-to-read-complex-text on November 19, 2019.

Shanahan, T. (2017, February 23). *How should we combine reading and writing?* [Blog post]. Accessed at https://shanahanonliteracy.com/blog/how-should-we-combine-reading-and-writing on November 19, 2019.

Shanahan, T. (2018, October 27). *Gradual release of responsibility and complex text* [Blog post]. Accessed at https://shanahanonliteracy.com/blog/gradual-release-of-responsibility-and-complex-text on November 19, 2019.

Shanahan, T. (2019). *Teaching students to read complex text.* Accessed at www.shanahanonliteracy.com/publications/teaching-students-to-read-complex-text on March 19, 2020.

Shanahan, T. (2020, February 1). *If students meet a standard with below grade level texts, are they meeting the standard?* [Blog post]. Accessed at https://shanahanonliteracy.com/blog/if-students-meet-a-standard-with-below-grade-level-texts-are-they-meeting-the-standard on March 25, 2020.

Shanahan, T., & Allington, R. L. (2014, February 6). *To special ed or not to special ed: RTI and the early identification of reading disabilities* [Blog post]. Accessed at www.cdl.org/articles/to-special-ed-or-not-to-special-ed-rti-and-the-early-identification-of-reading-disabilities on November 19, 2019.

Shanahan, T., Callison, K., Carriere, C., Duke, N. K., Pearson, P. D., Schatschneider, C., et al. (2010). *Improving reading comprehension in kindergarten through 3rd grade: A practice guide* (NCEE 2010-4038). Washington, DC: National Center for Education Evaluation and Regional Assistance.

Shanahan, T., Fisher, D., & Frey, N. (2012). The challenge of challenging text. *Educational Leadership, 69*(6), 58–62.

Shanahan, T., & Shanahan, C. (2012). What is disciplinary literacy and why does it matter? *Top Lang Disorders, 32*(1), 7–18.

Slavin, R. E. (2014). Making cooperative learning powerful. *Educational Leadership, 72*(2). Accessed at www.ascd.org/publications/educational-leadership/oct14/vol72/num02/Making-Cooperative-Learning-Powerful.aspx on November 19, 2019.

Smarter Balanced Assessment Consortium. (2014). *4-point narrative performance task writing rubric (grades 3–8).* Accessed at https://portal.smarterbalanced.org/library/en/performance-task-writing-rubric-narrative.pdf on March 16, 2020.

Snow, C. E., Burns, M. S., & Griffin, P. (Eds.). (1998). *Preventing reading difficulties in young children.* Washington, DC: National Academies Press.

Soto, G. (1990). *Baseball in April and other stories.* New York: Houghton Mifflin Harcourt.

Spinelli, J. (1990). *Maniac Magee.* New York: HarperCollins.

Stachowiak, D. (2018a, July 2). *Part 1: Terms and definitions for gender-inclusive classrooms* [Blog post]. Accessed at www.literacyworldwide.org/blog/literacy -daily/2018/07/02/part-1-terms-and-definitions-for-gender-inclusive-classrooms on December 12, 2019.

Stachowiak, D. (2018b, July 12). *Part 2: Interrogating bias* [Blog post]. Accessed at www .literacyworldwide.org/blog/literacy-daily/2018/07/12/part-2-interrogating-bias on December 12, 2019.

Stachowiak, D. (2018c, July 26). *Part 3: Classroom inventory* [Blog post]. Accessed at www.literacyworldwide.org/blog/literacy-daily/2018/07/26/part-3-classroom -inventory on December 12, 2019.

Stachowiak, D. (2018d, August 2). *Part 4: Supporting gender noncomforming students* [Blog post]. Accessed at www.literacyworldwide.org/blog/literacy-daily/2018/08/02 /part-4-supporting-gender-nonconforming-students on December 12, 2019.

Stachowiak, D. (2018e, August 9). *Part 5: Creating a gender-inclusive curriculum* [Blog post]. Accessed at www.literacyworldwide.org/blog/literacy-daily/2018/08/09/part -5-creating-a-gender-inclusive-curriculum on December 12, 2019.

Stachowiak, D. (2018f). The power to include: A starting place for creating gender-inclusive literacy classrooms. *Literacy Today, 36*(1), 28–30.

Stahl, K. A. D. (2005). Improving the asphalt of reading instruction: A tribute to the work of Steven A. Stahl. *Reading Teacher, 59*(2), 184–192.

Stahl, K. A. D. (2012). Complex text or frustration-level text: Using shared reading to bridge the difference. *Reading Teacher, 66*(1), 47–51.

Stanford Center for Assessment, Learning, and Equity. (2015). *Designing for deeper learning: How to develop performance tasks (Fall-15)* [Interview transcript]. Accessed at http://online.stanford.edu/courses on September 7, 2015.

Stecker, P. M., & Lembke, E. S. (2005). *Advanced applications of CBM in reading: Instructional decision-making strategies manual.* Washington, DC: National Center on Student Progress Monitoring.

Steinbeck, J. (1937/1993). *Of mice and men.* New York: Penguin.

Steinbeck, J. (1939/1993). *The grapes of wrath.* New York: Viking.

Summit Medical Group. (n.d.). *What is ADHD?* Accessed at www.summitmedicalgroup .com/library/pediatric_health/pa-hhgbeh_attention on November 19, 2019.

TeacherVision. (2007, February 8). *Cooperative learning: Teaching strategies (grades K–12).* Accessed at www.teachervision.com/professional-development/cooperative -learning on November 19, 2019.

Tierney, R. J., & Shanahan, T. (1991). Research on the reading-writing relationship: Interactions, transactions, and outcomes. In R. Barr, M. L. Kamil, P. Mosenthal, & P. D. Pearson (Eds.), *Handbook of reading research* (Vol. 2, pp. 246–280). New York: Routledge.

Tomlinson, C. A. (2000, August). *Differentiation of instruction in the elementary grades*. Champaign, IL: ERIC Clearinghouse on Elementary and Early Childhood Education.

Tomlinson, C. A., & Imbeau, M. B. (2010). *Leading and managing a differentiated classroom*. Alexandria, VA: Association for Supervision and Curriculum Development.

Tomlinson, C. A., & Moon, T. R. (2013). *Assessment and student success in a differentiated classroom*. Alexandria, VA: Association for Supervision and Curriculum Development.

Townsley, M., & Wear, N. L. (2020). *Making grades matter: Standards-based grading in a secondary PLC at Work*. Bloomington, IN: Solution Tree Press.

Trehearne, M., Healy, L. H., Cantalini, M., & Moore, J. L. (2003). *Comprehensive literacy resource for kindergarten teachers*. Vernon Hills, IL: ETA/Cuisenaire.

Vagle, N. D. (2015). *Design in five: Essential phases to create engaging assessment practice*. Bloomington, IN: Solution Tree Press.

Virginia Department of Education. (2017). *K–12 English standards of learning and curriculum framework*. Accessed at www.doe.virginia.gov/testing/sol/standards_docs /english/index.shtml on November 19, 2019.

Webb, N. L. (1997). *Criteria for alignment of expectations and assessments in mathematics and science education* (Research monograph no. 8). Washington, DC: Council of Chief State School Officers.

Webb, N. (1999). *Alignment of science and mathematics standards and assessments in four states* (Research Monograph No. 18). University of Wisconsin-Madison, National Institute for Science Education.

Weinstein, R. S. (2002). *Reaching higher: The power of expectations in schooling*. President and Fellows of Harvard College.

Wiggins, G. (2012). Seven keys to effective feedback. *Educational Leadership, 70*(1), 10–16. Accessed at www.ascd.org/publications/educational-leadership/sept12/vol70 /num01/Seven-Keys-to-Effective-Feedback.aspx on November 19, 2019.

Wiliam, D. (2018). *Embedded formative assessment* (2nd ed.). Bloomington, IN: Solution Tree Press.

Winne, P. H., & Butler, D. L. (1994). Student cognition in learning from teaching. In T. Husen & T. Postlewaite (Eds.), *International encyclopaedia of education* (2nd ed., pp. 5738–5745). Oxford, England: Pergamon.

Yep, L. (1989). *The rainbow people*. New York: HarperCollins Publishers.

INDEX

A

actionable feedback, 167

action-oriented data, 128–131

Ainsworth, L., 19–20, 51

analogies, 184

analytic rubrics, 95–99, 114–115

    developing, 99–102

anchor papers, 109, 112–113

annotation, 194–202

    modeling, 199–200

    other tasks using, 201–202

    preparing for, 199

    of priority standards, 22–23

Assessment and Student Success in a Differentiated Classroom (Tomlinson and Moon), 39–40

assessments, 37–57

    collaborative scoring and, 107–113

    common analytic rubrics for, 96–99

    considerations for literacy, 53–56

    constructed-response, 46, 48

    continuum of, 51–53

    criticism of, 118

    determining for learning progressions, 72–74

    end-of-unit, 53

    fluency checks, 49–50

    formative, 14, 38–39

    high-stakes exams, 18, 244

    identifying and designing common, 74–80

    as instructional tool, 118

    as journey, 50–53

    in learning progressions, 60–63

    learning progressions and designing, 60

    options in for writing, 44–45

    performance, 46, 48–49

    prioritizing standards and, 244–246

    rationale for, 75–77

    reliable, 73

    resources on, 50–51

    as road trip, 40

    rubrics and, 93–104

    running records, 49–50

    scoring, objectivity in, 55

    selected-response, 46–47

    self-, 104

    of skills, 29

    summative, 14, 39–40

    time for, 54–55

    timelines for, 84–87, 89–90

    types and formats, 37–50

    unit standards and, 14

    vocabulary preassessment, 179–181

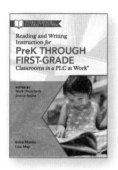

Reading and Writing Instruction for PreK Through First-Grade Classrooms in a PLC at Work®
Erica Martin and Lisa May
Mark Onuscheck and Jeanne Spiller (Editors)

Prepare your collaborative PLC team to fully support and encourage every learner's literacy development. Written specifically for teachers of preK through first grade, this practical resource includes tools and strategies for designing standards-aligned instruction, assessments, interventions, and more.
BKF901

Reading and Writing Instruction for Second- and Third-Grade Classrooms in a PLC at Work®
Sarah Gord and Kathryn E. Sheridan
Mark Onuscheck and Jeanne Spiller (Editors)

Fully prepare students to begin the pivotal transition from learning to read to reading to learn. Written for individual teachers and collaborative teams, this carefully crafted resource outlines a high-quality approach to literacy instruction for second and third grade.
BKF915

(Re)designing Series
Kathy Tuchman Glass

Take the next steps to boost student literacy in your classroom. With support from this collection of resources by Kathy Tuchman Glass, you will learn how to plan and deliver well-integrated units of writing instruction that raise the bar for learners.
BKF711, BKF712, BKF708

The New Art and Science of Teaching Writing
Kathy Tuchman Glass and Robert J. Marzano

Using a clear and well-organized structure, the authors apply the strategies originally laid out in *The New Art and Science of Teaching* to the teaching of writing. In total, the book explores more than one hundred strategies for teaching writing across grade levels and subject areas.
BKF796

"Tremendous, tremendous, tremendous!

The speaker made me do some very deep internal reflection about the **PLC process** and the personal responsibility I have in making the school improvement process work **for ALL kids.**"

—Marc Rodriguez, teacher effectiveness coach,
Denver Public Schools, Colorado

PD Services

Our experts draw from decades of research and their own experiences to bring you practical strategies for building and sustaining a high-performing PLC. You can choose from a range of customizable services, from a one-day overview to a multiyear process.

Book your PLC PD today!
888.763.9045

Solution Tree